The Life of
Paisij Velyčkovs'kyj

HARVARD LIBRARY OF EARLY UKRAINIAN LITERATURE

English Traslations   Volume IV

ГАРВАРДСЬКА БІБЛІОТЕКА ДАВНЬОГО УКРАЇНСЬКОГО ПИСЬМЕНСТВА

Корпус Англійських Перекладів   Том IV

The Life of
Paisij Velyčkovs'kyj

Translated by J. M. E. Featherstone

with an Introduction by Anthony-Emil N. Tachiaos

Millennium Rus'-Ucrainae Sacrum

Distributed by the Harvard University Press
for the
Ukrainian Research Institute of Harvard University

The preparation of this volume was made possible in part by a grant from the National Endowment for the Humanities, an independent federal agency.

The Harvard Ukrainian Research Institute was established in 1973 as an integral part of Harvard University. It supports research associates and visiting scholars who are engaged in projects concerned with all aspects of Ukrainian studies. The Institute also works in close cooperation with the Committee on Ukrainian Studies, which supervises and coordinates the teaching of Ukrainian history, language, and literature at Harvard University.

The publication of this volume was made possible through the generous support of the Trident Federal Savings and Loan Association, in Newark, New Jersey, U.S.A.

Цей том появляється завдяки щедрій підтримці Української Щадниці "Тризуб" в Нюарку, Ню Джерзі, США

Dedicated to the memory of Anne Pennington

Contents

Editorial Statement

The *Harvard Library of Early Ukrainian Literature* is one portion of the Harvard Project in Commemoration of the Millennium of Christianity in Rus'-Ukraine, which is being carried out by the Ukrainian Research Institute of Harvard University with financial support of the Ukrainian community.

The *Library* encompasses literary activity in Rus'-Ukraine from its beginning in the mid-eleventh century through the end of the eighteenth century, and primarily contains original works, although exceptions are made for such seminally important translations as the Ostroh Bible of 1581. Included are ecclesiastical and secular works written in a variety of languages, such as Church Slavonic, Old Rus', Ruthenian (Middle Ukrainian), Polish, and Latin. This linguistic diversity reflects the cultural pluralism of Ukrainian intellectual activity in the medieval and early-modern periods.

The *Library* consists of three parts. The *Texts* series publishes the original works, in facsimile whenever appropriate. Texts from the medieval period are offered either in the best available scholarly edition or in one specially prepared for the *Library*, while those from the later periods are reproduced from manuscripts or early printed editions. In addition, a number of texts of secondary importance are available in microfiche editions from the Editor upon request. Two other series—*English Translations* and *Ukrainian Translations*—contain translations of the original works.

Each volume begins with an introductory essay by a specialist. The two translation series also include a variety of indices. A cumulative index to the entire *Library* will be issued.

Forty volumes are planned for each of the series, although the total may be greater as additional works are accommodated. Volumes within each series are numbered and published in the order in which they are prepared.

The introductions and translations reflect the linguistic and terminological diversity of the original works. Thus, for example, appellations such as the Rus', Rusija, Rossija, Mala Rossija, Malaja Rossija, Malorussija, Ruthenia, Malorussijskaja Ukrajina, Ukrajina, and so on, are presented according to their actual use in the given text. All of these terms have historically been used to designate "Ukraine" and "Ukrainian." In addition, the word Ruthenian is employed to translate early-modern nomenclature for "Ukrainian" and early-modern terminology describing common Ukrainian and Belorussian culture, language, and identity. For much of the period covered by the *Library* Ukrainian and Belorussian cultural figures were active in a shared social, intellectual, and religious milieu. Since the *Library* selects authors and works important to the Ukrainian part of this sphere, their names are rendered in Ukrainian form, even though at times they may also have been of significance in Belorussian territory.

Use of the definite article with "Ukraine" is left to the discretion of the author or translator of each volume.

With the exception of toponyms with already-established English forms, place-names are usually given in accordance with the official language of the state or, in the case of the Soviet Union, of the republic that holds the territory; pre-modern or alternative modern forms are indicated in the indices.

The *Library* uses the International System of transliteration for Church Slavonic, Old Rus', and modern languages using the Cyrillic alphabet; this system has been adapted to transliterate Ruthenian (Middle Ukrainian) texts as well.

INTRODUCTION

The great Ukrainian ascetic and spiritual teacher Paisij Velyčkovs'kyj (1722-1794) was without doubt the creator of a unique spiritual tradition both in the Slavic and in the Romanian Orthodox worlds. His death on the 15th of November 1794 was perceived as a great loss among all those who had known him, but especially among the hundreds of monks of various nationalities who had lived with him and had received direction from him in their spiritual life.[1] As the years passed this sense of loss, intensified by nostalgia, increased the desire for information about him among younger monks who had not had the opportunity of knowing him personally. However, even among the older monks of his circle—those who were with him on Mt. Athos (1746–1763) or during the early years at the monastery of Dragomirna in Moldavia—there were few who were so fortunate as to have lived intimately enough with him to have certain knowledge about many aspects of his life and character, much less to have shared in his spiritual or mystical experiences. Only when gathered together could the reminiscences of these monks provide a complete picture of the personality and life of their teacher. And the need for collecting such reminiscences for the purpose of writing a biography of Paisij became all the more pressing with the realization on the part of the monks that they had been direct or indirect disciples of a great and holy spiritual teacher. Indeed, the growing conviction among wider circles, be it in Moldavia where the elder lived, on Mt. Athos, in the Balkans, as well as in the Ukraine and Russia, that Paisij had been a saint only reinforced a demand for some sort of biographical account of the extraordinary Orthodox elder.

The biographies of Paisij that were produced by the circle of his disciples were conditioned by the fact that the compilers belonged

---

[1]   Near the end of Paisij's life nearly seven hundred monks had gathered about him in the monastery of Neamţ. See S. Četverikov, *Moldavskij starec Paisij Veličkovskij, ego žizn', učenie i vlijanie na pravoslavnoe monašestvo* (1938; reprint, Paris, 1976), 117. In the biography of Pajisij's contemporary, the great Greek ascetic Nicodemus of Mount Athos, it is related that the number of monks under the spiritual direction of the Ukrainian elder surpassed a thousand. Cf. N. Bilalis, ʻΟ Πρωτότυπος Βίος ἁγίου Νικοδήμου Ἁγιορείτου *(1749–1809)* (Athens, 1983), 22.

essentially to two cultural spheres, the Slavic and the Romanian. Both of these groups had a claim to a biography of the elder.[2] Of course, aside from these two, the broader circle around Paisij consisted of a number of other national groups, one of which was certainly Greek.[3] But the languages in general use among the monks most closely associated with the elder were basically two, either East Slavic variants of Slavonic or Romanian, although it appears that already before Paisij's death the Slavonic had to a significant degree been supplanted by Romanian. Yet, whatever the language used in Paisij's monastic circle, he himself embraced the ideals that had prevailed among the hesychasts of the Middle Ages: he was above ethnic prejudices and displayed pan-Orthodox sentiments.[4]

Information concerning the composition of Velyčkovs'kyj's biography is contained in the forewords to the texts published in Slavonic by the Neamţ Monastery in 1836 and by the Optina Monastery in 1847. According to these forewords, some twenty years after Paisij's death the monastic brotherhood of Neamţ, impelled, apparently, by the reasons set out above, conceived a desire for a biography of its spiritual father. This task was assigned to the aged monk Mytrofan, one of the oldest monks of the monastery, who was also a calligrapher and who had a sound grasp of the rules of Slavonic.

---

[2]   From a MS of the Monastery of St. Simon in Moscow, dated 1841–1848, we learn that there lived in Neamţ monks of ten nationalities: Moldavian, Serbian, Bulgarian, Hungarian, Greek, Jewish, Armenian, Turkish, Russian, and Ukrainian. See N. Popov, "Rukopisi Moskovskoj Sinodal'noj (Patriaršej) Biblioteki. Sobranie rukopisej Moskovskogo Simonova monastyrja," *Čtenija v Imperatorskom Obščestve istorii i drevnostej rossijskix pri Moskovskom universitete*, 1910, no. 2:87.

[3]   Article 15 of the typikon which Paisij prepared in 1763 for the monastery of Dragomirna provided that, because the brotherhood was composed of three nationalities, the abbot of the monastery ought to know three languages: Greek, Slavonic, and Romanian. Paisij had only just arrived from Mt. Athos and must have brought with him a sizable number of Greek monks. Although in the beginning in Dragomirna Romanian was only third in importance, in the monastery of Neamţ it gained absolute superiority. For the article referred to from Paisij's typikon, see A. Jacimirskij [Jacymyrs'kyj], *Slavjanskie i russkie rukopisi rumynskix bibliotek* (St. Petersburg, 1905) (=*Sbornik Otdelenija russkogo jazyka i slovesnosti IAN* 79), 538.

[4]   Cf P. A. Syrku, *K istorii ispravlenija knig v Bolgarii v XIV veke*, vol. 1, pt. 1, *Vremja i žizn' Patriarxa Evfimija Ternovskogo* (St Petersburg, 1898), 354–67; and A.-E. N. Tachiaos, ʽΗσυχαστικαὶ ἐπιδράσεις εἰς τὴν ἐκκλησιαστικὴν πολιτικὴν ἐν Ρωσίᾳ. *1328-1406* (Thessalonica, 1962), 91–102

Mytrofan applied himself to the task with zeal and wrote a first draft of a biography of his teacher. However, his impaired vision and advanced age prevented him from producing a definitive text, and he died shortly after completing this first draft.

For some time after Mytrofan's death no further work was done on the composition of the biography. Finally the monk Isaak was entrusted with the task of finishing the text. While he was occupied with this project, the monks urged him to write his own biography of Paisij. He yielded to their request, but since he was Romanian he wrote the biography in his native language. The result was a work that differed considerably from that of Mytrofan, for Isaak was asked to reconcile his own work with the earlier one. But before he managed to finish the final version he, too, died. Nevertheless, the Romanian monks of Neamţ now had at their disposal Isaak's Romanian text, which with certain emendations would be thoroughly acceptable. They applied to the learned deacon Grigorie, later metropolitan of Hungrovlachia (1823–1824),[5] and asked him to prepare a final, abridged edition of what was a rather lengthy text. Grigorie did as the monks desired and produced an abbreviated biography which he entitled *A Partial Narration Concerning the Life of Our Blessed Father Paisij*.[6] He submitted his text for criticism to the metropolitan of Moldavia, Veniamin Costachi, and to Prince Scarlatos Callimachi, who approved it for publication. The edition was prepared by the Neamţ Monastery which printed it on its own press in 1817.[7] It appears, however, that the Romanian text met with displeasure among the Slavophone monks. Since Paisij had been a spiritual father as much to the Slavic as to the Romanian monks, the former felt that his biography should also appear in Slavonic. A general assembly of the Neamţ brotherhood accepted this idea and appointed the monk Platon, who had worked for Velyčkovs'kyj as a copyist, to produce a Slavonic biography based on the information collected earlier by Mytrofan and

---

5   Concerning this famous hierarch, see C. Tomescu, *Mitropolitul Grigorie al Ungrovlahiei* (Kishinev, 1927). Cf. M. Părcurariu, *Istoria Bisericii Ortodoxe Române*, vol. 3 (Bucharest, 1981), 37–47, and p. 48 for a recent bibliography.

6   The Romanian title of the book is *Povestire din parte a vieţii Prea Cuviosului Părintului nostru Paisie*.

7   See I. Bianu, N. Hodoş, D. Simonescu, *Bibliografia românească veche 1508–1830*, vol. 3, *1809–1830* (1936; reprint, Nendeln, 1968), 178–81. Cf. G. Racoveanu, *Gravura în lemn la Mănăstirea Neamţul* (Bucharest, 1940), 14, pl. XIV.

Isaak. Platon's version of the biography of Paisij was printed by the Neamţ Monastery in 1836 in two languages and contained a foreword by the abbot of the monastery, Archimandrite Mardarij.[8]

Platon's Slavonic edition of the biography of Paisij enjoyed great success and was widely circulated. It soon became necessary for the monastery to reprint the text when copies of the first edition ran out. But after some consideration, the project of reprinting the book in the form in which it had appeared was abandoned, both because the Slavonic script and its abbreviations had become alien to the broader community and appeared obsolete, and because the number of Slavonic readers in monastic circles continued to decrease.[9] Thus, eleven years passed before a new edition of the biography appeared, though this time not in Romania but in Russia, and in secular, not ecclesiastical script. The initiative for the edition came from the Russian Slavophile I. V. Kireevskij, who published a text of the biography in his periodical *Moskvitjanin* in 1845. The response to this publication in Russian circles was so favorable that two years later the famous monastery of Optina[10] took the initiative of reprinting it as a separate volume.[11] This edition, too, enjoyed great success, and all of the

---

[8] The title of this edition reads as follows: Во слав8 стыа, єдннос8щныа, жнво-творащїа, й нераздѣлнмыа Трцы, Оца, й Сна, й стагw Дха: Напечатаса, ЖНТІЄ Баженнѣйшагw Оца нашегw Старца Паісіа. Собраное ѿ многнхъ пнсателей, й сочнненно ѿцемъ Платwномъ схнмон: Во днн Бгобѣрнагw Гпдара нашегw МІХАНЛА ГРНГОРІЄВНЧА СТ8РЗЫ ВОЄВОДЫ. Бгословенімъ Преwсщеннагw Мітрополіта Кургꙋ8 Кур ВЄНІАМННА. Прн Архімандрітѣ й Старцѣ стыхъ мн: Намца й Сек8ла, МАРДАРІН. Въ Намецкомъ Вознесенскомъ Монас: Въ Лѣто, Ꙁ wлѕ. Ноем: к.

[9] Concerning the decline of the Slavonic monastic school in Romania, see A. Jacymyrs'kyj, "Vozroždenie vizantijsko-bolgarskogo religioznogo misticizma i slavjanskoj asketičeskoj literatury v XVIII veke," in *Počest'. Sbornik statej posvjaščennyx Prof. M. S. Drinovu* (Xarkiv, 1908), 201–3; and A.-E. N. Tachiaos, 'Ο Παΐσιος Βελιτσκόφσκι *(1722–1794)* καὶ ἡ ἀσχητικοφιλολογικὴ σχολή του, Publications of the Institute for Balkan Studies, 73 (Thessalonica, 1964), 119–30.

[10] About this monastery, see Hieromonk L[eonid], *Istoričeskoe opisanie Kozel'skoj Vvedenskoj Optinoj Pustiny*, 2nd ed. (St. Petersburg, 1862).

[11] See Hieromonk L[eonid], *Skazanie o žizni i podvigax blažennoj pamjati starca Optinoj Pustyni ierosximonaxa Makarija* (Moscow, 1861), 161–63; Archimandrite Nikodim, *Starcy: Otec Paisij Veličkovskij i otec Makarij Optinskij i ix literaturno-asketičeskaja dejatel'nost'* (Moscow, 1909), 32–33, 39–40, 80–81; and S. Četverikov, *Optina Pustyn'. Istoričeskij očerk i ličnye vospominanija* (Paris, 1926), 107–8. The

copies were sold out within the year of its publication (1847). Encouraged by this, the monastery decided to undertake a new edition which now included not only works and letters by Paisij himself, but also writings of his spiritual father, Vasile of Poiana Mărului, and other members of their monastic circle. The biography of Paisij contained in this edition is an elaborated version of the Neamţ text published in 1836, although in order to reach a broader reading public the Optina printers used contemporary Russian script (*graždanskij šrift*).

Until the beginning of the present century the life of Velyčkovs'kyj was known chiefly from the Optina Monastery edition, which in the meantime had been reprinted twice, first in 1892 and again in 1902. In 1906 the Ukrainian Slavist O. Jacymyrs'kyj published his massive work on the Russian and Slavonic manuscripts in Romanian libraries, and here for the first time he revealed that in a manuscript of the Library of the Imperial Academy of Sciences he had discovered an unedited and heretofore unknown autobiography of the great Ukrainian ascetic. While he did not himself edit the text of the *Autobiography*, Jacymyrs'kyj gave a brief description of its contents, citing numerous passages.[12] What Jacymyrs'kyj neglected to note was that Paisij's three biographers, Mytrofan, Isaak, and Grigorie, had in fact known of this autobiography, although none of them had ever mentioned it explicitly. It is indeed difficult to explain how the existence of such an important text was passed over in silence for more than a century.

1. *The* Autobiography *of Paisij Velyčkovs'kyj*

Jacymyrs'kyj's discovery of Velyčkovs'kyj's *Autobiography* brought to light not only a new source for the life and activities of this remarkable man, but also a text of singular literary merit. Comparing the text with the one published by the Neamţ Monastery in 1836, Jacymyrs'kyj observed how Grigorie had "depersonalized the figure of our wonderful elder and gave us not the living and likable man, but

---

book is known by the title *Žitie i pisanija Moldavskogo starca Paisija Veličkovskogo*. The bibliography is on pp. 3–72.

[12] Jacimirskij, *Slavjanskie i russkie rukopisi*, 516–27. The summary of the *Autobiography* as it appears in Jacymyrs'kyj's book was translated into Romanian by Stefan Berechet and published in a small pamphlet with the title *Autobiografia stareţului Paisie Velicikovski* (Iaşi, 1918).

an abstract image of an ascetic possessing all the purely canonical characteristics.''[13] Unlike the text of the printed biography of Paisij, his *Autobiography* reveals fine shades of his personality which, without altering his already familiar portrait, nonetheless greatly enhance it.

According to the information provided by Jacymyrs'kyj, the manuscript containing Velyčkovs'kyj's *Autobiography* originally belonged to the priest Feofil Gepeckij and later came into the possession of Jacymyrs'kyj himself, who donated it to the Imperial Academy of Sciences where it received the call number 13.3.26.[14] The *Autobiography* is contained on fols. 1–113 and was written in a single hand, whereas the remainder of the manuscript (fols. 115–45) contains the traces of at least four hands.[15] The text of the *Autobiography* is certainly not an autograph, as is evident from the running title written at the top of each folio in the same hand: *Povest' blažennago otca našego starca Paisia.* No such title would exist if the text had been written by Paisij himself. One might conjecture that the text in this manuscript is either a copy of an autograph or that Paisij had dictated it to one of the monks of Neamţ when he was old and infirm. It seems more likely, however, that the text is a copy, or perhaps one of several copies, of a protograph. What is, however, beyond doubt is that the

---

[13]   Jacimirskij, *Slavjanskie i russkie rukopisi,* 516.

[14]   Today it is found in Collection No. 58 of the Library of the Academy of Sciences of the Soviet Union. Concerning the collection of Jacymyrs'kyj's MSS, see N. F. Bel'čikov, J. K. Begunov, N. P. Roždestvenskij, *Spravočnik-ukazatel' pečatnyx opisanij slavjanorusskix rukopisej* (Moscow and Leningrad, 1963), 76, 89. A facsimile of the *Autobiography* will be published in the *Harvard Library of Early Ukrainian Literature: Texts.*

[15]   This second part consists of the following texts: a) commentary on the Jesus prayer (fols. 115–20); b) the order of service for the reception of schismatics into the Orthodox faith, copied from a printed book of 1742 (fols. 121–38); c) brief chapters from the *Paterikon* (fols. 139–42); and d) excerpts from a Praise of All the Saints written by Hieromonk Gregorios (fols. 142–45). The matter of the reception of schismatics into the Orthodox faith was of great concern to Velyčkovs'kyj and his school and was evidently closely connected with the problems created by the coexistence of populations of various confessions in Romania and Hungary. These problems are clearly attested in Paisij's Greek correspondence with the eminent Greek theologian of the time, Dorotheos Voulismas. The letters of both on this subject have been published in A.-E. N. Tachiaos, *The Revival of Byzantine Mysticism among Slavs and Romanians in the XVIIIth Century. Texts Relating to the Life and Activity of Paisy Velichkovsky (1722–1794)* (Thessalonica, 1986), 259–89.

Autobiography is the work of Velyčkovs'kyj. No one else would have been in a position to enter with such exactitude into the details of his personal life, or to relate events with such liveliness and leave no doubt that they had befallen the author personally. The sensitivity of the narrative, the articulation of inward experiences and feelings, the pulsating of the soul reflected in the account of events, the knowledge of innermost longings and aspirations, all of this could have come only from the pen of Paisij himself.

Nevertheless, one cannot but wonder how such an important text, by such a great spiritual teacher, was preserved in only one copy. Nor is it any less puzzling that a text such as this should have remained unknown for so long. We shall perhaps be able to clarify both of these issues by looking once again at the manner in which the biographies of Paisij were composed.

When we examine the biography of Paisij written by Mytrofan, we discover that not only was he acquainted with the *Autobiography*, but, as we shall see below, made ample use of it. Clearly only Mytrofan possessed the text of the *Autobiography*, and after his death it passed into the hands of Isaak, who had undertaken to complete the work begun by Mytrofan. The exclusive way in which the biographers utilized the *Autobiography* prevented the text from being copied and transmitted for a considerable period of time. Bearing in mind that Paisij died in 1794 and that his definitive biography was printed in 1836, it follows that the general public had no knowledge of or access to the *Autobiography* for nearly half a century. The copy which survives must have been made in the second decade of the nineteenth century, which is also when Isaak's Romanian version was printed. But it would seem that this copy, too, was made in order to assist in the preparation of a biography of Paisij and not for a wider audience.

Another consideration that helps in clarifying why the *Autobiography* fell into oblivion is of a more theoretical nature. Although the text of Paisij's *Autobiography* is quite extensive, it nonetheless covers only a relatively short period of his life (up to 1746). The monastic brotherhoods of Dragomirna and Neamţ used a short text of Paisij's biography that had a well-balanced distribution of material and was structured like a synaxary. They probably utilized a version that was of a more general nature, one that did not go into personal details, as his *Autobiography* does, and one that was richly adorned with rhetorical expressions and decorative epithets. It could, therefore, serve as edifying and pleasant reading during night vigils held in church or during meal times in the monastic refectory on feast days. The *Autobiography*, on the other hand, was unfinished, yet at the same time lengthy and full of personal details and emotional apostrophe. As such, it did not meet the specifications of a synaxary nor, consequently, the general needs of the brotherhood. Unable to fulfill a clearly defined function within the life of the monastery, Paisij's *Autobiography* thus remained neglected.

Besides its other virtues, that is, its spiritual and literary qualities, the *Autobiography* of Velyčkovs'kyj is unique in eighteenth-century Orthodox Slavic literature. The eighteenth century was a time when autobiography as a genre was generally flourishing.[16] Although in the Orthodox Slavic world autobiography as a literary genre was known long before the eighteenth century,[17] it became especially popular during this period, clearly under the influence of Western models.[18] Two contemporaries of Paisij wrote autobiographies, and both belonged to the Serbian cultural sphere. The first was the bishop Partenij Pavlovič, a Bulgarian who was nevertheless a prelate in the

---

[16]   See, for instance, W. Hubatsch, "Biographie und Autobiographie—Das Problem von Quelle und Darstellung," in *XIII Meždunarodnyj Kongress Istoričeskix Nauk. Do-klady kongressa*, vol. 1, pt. 2 (Moscow, 1970), 248–64.

[17]   The oldest Slavic autobiographical text dates back to the age of Kievan Rus': the *Poučenie* of Volodimer Monomax. See *Povest' vremennyx let*, pt. 1, *Tekst i perevod*, ed. D. S. Lixačev, trans. D. S. Lixačev and B. A. Romanov (Moscow and Leningrad, 1950), 153–67. At the end of the twelfth century the autobiographical form also appears in a Serbian text of the ruler Stefan Nemanja. See R. Marinković, "Vladarske biografije iz vremena Nemanjina," *Prilozi za književnost, jezik, istoriju i folklor* 44, nos. 1–2 (1978):9–11. Another important autobiographical text is the spiritual testament of Photius Monembasiotes, the Greek metropolitan of Kiev and All Rus'. See A.-E. Tachiaos, "The Testament of Photius Monembasiotes, Metropolitan of Russia (1408–1431): Byzantine Ideology in XVth Century Moscovy," *Cyrillomethodianum* 8–9 (1984–1985):77–109. With the appearance in seventeenth-century Russia of the life of Protopop Avvakum, in which the author portrays himself as a profoundly religious and combative zealot, Orthodox Slavic autobiography becomes a purely literary genre. See *Žitie protopopa Avvakuma im samym napisannoe i drugie ego sočinenija*, ed. N. K. Gudzij (Moscow, 1959), 53–122.

[18]   See A.-E. Tachiaos, "L'Autobiographie en tant que genre littéraire de la littérature balkanique slave du XVIIIe siècle," Ἀριστοτέλειον Πανεπιστήμιον Θεσσαλονίκης. Ἐπιστημονικὴ Ἐπετηρὶς τῆς Θεολογικῆς Σχολῆς 19 (1975):429–37; and I. Boeva, *Razvitie žanrov v russkoj i bolgarskoj literaturax XVII i XVIII vv.* (Sofia, 1983), 122–36.

Serbian church. Pavlovič's autobiography is linked to the at that time
fashionable genre of itineraries. It covers just eleven years of the
author's life (1746–1757).[19] Paisij's other contemporary autobiogra-
pher was the famous eighteenth-century Serbian writer Dositej Obradović. The autobiography he composed served a specific purpose,
namely, to buttress his progressive ideas and to justify in the eyes of
his contemporaries his abandonment of the monastic life and turn
towards the principles of the Enlightenment.[20] While the aim of
Pavlovič's autobiography is to describe in a plain manner certain
moments of his own life and to present a picture of the world in which
he lived, Obradović's autobiography, on the contrary, has manifest
ideological tendencies and is a text that aims at social reform.[21] Chro-
nologically, Paisij's *Autobiography* was followed by the autobiography of Sofronij Vračanskij, the Bulgarian bishop of Vratsa.[22] It is
extremely difficult to judge to what extent Paisij was aware of the

[19]   For the most recent edition of Pavlovič's autobiography, see P. Bojadžiev, *Partenij Pavlovič* (Sofia, 1988), 66–81. About Pavlovič and his autobiography, see ibid.,
36–48; B. S. Angelov, *Săvremenici na Paisij,* vol. 2 (Sofia, 1964), 5–59; P. Bojadžiev,
"Chronologie de la vie de l'Autobiographie de Partenij Pavlovič," *Bulletin de
l'Association   internationale   pour   l'étude   du   sud-est   européen*   13–14
(1975–1976):73–92; id., "Partenij Pavlovič," in *Balkanski kulturni vzaimotnošenija*,
Studia balcanica, 15 (Sofia, 1980), 56–80; V. Velčev, "Problemata za obraza na
povestvovatelja v Avtobiografijata na Partenij Pavlovič," *Ezik i literatura* 36, no. 2
(1981):50–60.
[20]   See Tachiaos, "L'Autobiographie," 431, 435.
[21]   The autobiography of Obradović is divided into two parts. The first, which was
published in Leipzig in 1783, covers events up to 1760. The second is written in epis-
tolary form and covers the years 1760–1788. For the text of the autobiography, see
Dositej Obradović, *Sabrana dela*, ed. Dj. Gavela, vol. 1 (Belgrade, 1961), 73–168,
171–284. For a more systematic study of Obradović's life and works, as well as an
analysis of the autobiography, see M. Kostić, *Dositej Obradović u istorijskoj perspek-
tivi XVIII i XIX veka* (Belgrade, 1952) (=Srpska Akademija Nauka, *Posebna izdanja*,
190, *Istoriski Institut*, 2).
[22]   Of the other autobiographies mentioned, that of Sofronij most resembles Paisij's
with respect to its sincere and spontaneous character. For the most recent of the many
editions of Sofronij's autobiography, see N. M. Dylevskij and A. D. Robinson, eds.,
Sofronij Vračanskij, Žizneopisanie (Leningrad, 1976). For a recent French translation, see Sofroni Vrachanski, *Vie et tribulations du pécher Sofroni*, trans. and ed. J.
Feuillet (Sofia, 1981). An analysis of Sofronij's autobiography can be found in I.
Radev, *Sofronij Vračanski, Ličnost i tvorčesko delo* (Sofia, 1983), 108–93. Although
Radev's study is comparative, he ignores Velyčkovs'kyj's *Autobiography*, the most
important work of its kind in the eighteenth century.

earlier Slavic autobiographies and how much he relied on them in making the decision to write one himself. Perhaps he knew the autobiography of Protopop Avvakum, but it is very unlikely that this was the source of his inspiration. The *Autobiography* of Paisij has such an idiosyncratic and independent character that it is difficult to discern common traits between it and the autobiographies that preceded it.[23]

The *Autobiography* of Paisij begins with a long heading in which nothing is said of the writer, but, on the contrary, describes its contents as a history of his monastic circle:

> A narrative concerning the holy community of fathers and brethren, my spiritual children, most beloved in the Lord, who in Christ's name have gathered about me, unworthy that I am, and who by God's providence for the salvation of their souls abide in these monasteries: in the holy and great Monastery of the Ascension of our Lord and God and Savior Jesus Christ called Neamţ, and in the holy Monastery of the worthy and glorious Prophet and Forerunner and Baptist of the Lord, John, called Secu—how and for what reason this holy community was gathered about me, an unworthy sinner.

The personal identity of the writer appears only at the end of the lengthy heading and only in relation to the brotherhood of monks. A little later Velyčkovs'kyj sets forth the reasons that moved him to write his *Autobiography*. When he saw that his life was coming to an end and that death was nigh, he judged that it would not be fitting that the history of the creation of his wondrous monastic brotherhood be relegated to silence: "For everything which is not committed to writing is given over to utter oblivion." Thus, with the intention of making the history of his monastic circle survive in the memory and consciousness of those who should come afterwards, Velyčkovs'kyj decided to compose the biography of the assembly's creator. Although indirectly he betrays the conviction that he himself was the creator and center of his assembly—which, to be sure, fully corresponded to the truth—by focusing on the need for the assembly to know its origins Paisij evades the anticipated accusation that he wrote his *Autobiography* in order to satisfy personal ambition and extol his own virtues. However, no less important for Paisij's decision to write his narrative

---

[23] For a critical comparison of the aforesaid autobiographies, see Tachiaos, "L'Autobiographie."

was a desire to preserve the brotherhood from malicious slander and the misrepresentation of his intentions that his enemies might ostensibly devise.[24]

The length of the *Autobiography* is convincing evidence that Paisij intended to compose an extensive and very detailed account. The extant part, which covers a period of just twenty-four years (1722–1746), that is, from the time of Paisij's birth until his move to Mt. Athos, abounds with details about various persons, occurrences, and places, as well as with the author's personal impressions. Inasmuch as Velyčkovs'kyj told his tale at such a slow pace, he evidently intended to produce a text rich with information both about his own life and the life of the monasteries that he himself founded and led. Unfortunately, either old age and weakness, or death itself, cut short this important undertaking, and the narrative leaves off abruptly at the point where the author is about to depart for Mt. Athos. But even what we do have is astonishing with regard to the limpid clarity of Paisij's mind and the scope of his memory. After the passage of so many years he still remembered persons and events with such accuracy that the reader cannot but be filled with admiration. This only underscores how intensely Paisij experienced his contacts with other persons, and what great importance he attached to changes in his external conditions and circumstances. In a word, from his earliest childhood Paisij appears to have been acutely sensitive to his surroundings and to the significance of what was happening around him.

Velyčkovs'kyj's narrative is completely natural and unaffected. It frequently reveals a childlike naïveté and a spontaneity that make his work not only vivid, but powerful and convincing as well. The *Autobiography* presents an accurate portrait of its author. His sincerity, somewhat confessional in nature, infects the entire text from beginning to end and imbues the portrait of the author with its distinc-

---

[24] It seems that Paisij was especially sensitive to slander and charges made against him. Even when he dwelt on Mt. Athos he was charged with being a heretic by a certain monk named Afanasij and was consequently obliged to make a defense. See *Žitie i pisanija*, 34–35; and below, pp. 104–5. Cf. Četverikov, *Moldavskij starec*, 73–75. But beyond this there were still other reasons for Paisij's fears that his Orthodoxy might be questioned: on his mother's side he had Jewish forebears, and since he was Ukrainian, he might also easily have been suspected of coming from a Uniate family.

tive features.[25] Paisij does not hesitate to declare his weaknesses of character, his childhood fears, his inner conflicts, and, above all, his emotional sensitivity. He freely admits that he is clumsy, impractical, and often lacks spiritual discernment, which is one of the chief monastic virtues. The *Autobiography* gives us the real Paisij, stripped by his own hand of the cosmetics of renown and the aura of glory. This process of self-abasement by the same token reveals the ascetic teacher's spiritual breadth and depth, projecting an image of Paisij that differs quite significantly from the lifeless portrait found in the Optina edition of his biography, an image that is one of spiritual beauty, natural and unembellished.

However, in recording his life Paisij at the same time also provided his monastic disciples with the model of a monk that he urged them to imitate. In this sense, Paisij's *Autobiography* contains a strong didactic element, the essence of which is its confessing author's extreme humility. Indeed, if this element of humility did not exist, the work might be perceived as being the product of spiritual self-gratification. And, while Paisij may in fact have been following the current fashion of the autobiographical genre, there was, nevertheless, a powerful inhibitory factor at work within the ascetic. This factor was the *Autobiography*'s spiritual and other-worldly orientation, and it

---

[25]   Compare the sketch of Paisij by the eighteenth-century Greek chronologer of Romania, Constantine Caragea, who visited the monastery of Neamţ in 1780: "Then for the first time I saw with my own eyes virtue, dispassion, and perfect candor incarnate. His expression was very gracious, his face was extremely white, without the slightest shade of color, his beard was white with a tint of gold due to its cleanliness; his apparel was likewise immaculate, as were the thick woolen blankets covering the seats and couches in his room. He was very gracious in his speech and quite free of dissimulation; he seemed almost to be an ethereal being" (in A. Papadopolous-Kerameus, *Texte greceşti privitoare la istoria românească* [Bucharest, 1909] [=Documente privitoare la istoria Românilor, 13], 109). For other descriptions of Paisij's appearance and of his character, as well as iconographic representations, see Paisij Velyčkovs'kyj, *Autobiografia di uno Starets*, trans. and ed. Fratelli Contemplativi di Gesù (Abbazia di Praglia, 1988), 180–86; E. C. Suttner, "Paisij Veličkovskij im Spiegel des geistlichen Testaments seines Schülers Gheorghe de la Cernica," *Ostkirchliche Studien* 22 (1973):178–83; id., *Beiträge zur Kirchengeschichte der Rumänen* (Vienna and Munich, 1978), 278–83; R. Joantă, *Roumanie: tradition et culture hésychastes* (Abbaye de Bellfontaine, 1987), 207–12; G. Racoveanu, *Gravura,* 25, pl. XIV and XV; and E. Cotescu, "L'Art roumain et l'art bulgare aux XVIIIe et XIXe siècle," *Revue des études sud-est européennes* 8 (1970):61–63.

was precisely for this reason that it was unthinkable that the author might be boasting or extolling himself. Any expression in his text that might be construed as a boast must be viewed as serving some objective, not subjective, purpose, one relating directly to his brotherhood. Given the fact that Paisij was the spiritual father of a monastic assembly, the latter had just cause to know about the details of his life and his impressions, and spiritually to partake of them. The brotherhood should be taught through the example of its teacher's internal and external struggles, struggles that many of the monks themselves had not perhaps experienced. Paisij believed that through his work, that is, the creation of his remarkable assembly, he was accomplishing the will of God and His commandment. Already with his birth he began fulfilling the will of God, which continued to manifest itself through the struggles and vicissitudes of his youth. Thus, just as the monks of Secu, Dragomirna, and Neamţ were intimately bound up with Paisij and his life, so his life was dedicated to them, and it was this relationship that constituted the *raison d'être* of the *Autobiography*. It was only in this context, then, of serving the spiritual needs of his monks that Paisij could write his *Autobiography*. And it is precisely this context that defines the difference between this autobiography and the others of its time.

It is difficult to determine exactly when the *Autobiography* was written. Judging by the expression, "Seeing that I am now near the end of my life," we can conclude that Paisij began writing it when he fell so ill that he thought death was approaching.[26] This condition seems to have begun three or four years before his death and caused him constant aggravation. The very fact that Paisij reached the point where he was unable to continue writing his narrative indicates that he was suffering unbearably. We may, therefore, conclude that he left off work only a few months before his death. The leisurely, unhurried pace of his narration is evidence that when he began his *Autobiography* nothing was forcing him to rush. This explains why Paisij delves

---

[26] The reports on Paisij's illness are confused and contradictory. The aforementioned Constantine Caragea relates that Paisij suffered from gout (Papadopolous-Karameus, *Texte greceşti*, 110). However, from all that is stated in the biographies it seems that he suffered from an ulcerous disease that attacked the right abdominal region; perhaps the disease was herpes. See *Žitie i pisanija*, 63; and Tachiaos, *Revival*, 133–34.

into so many details, drawing on the astounding clarity of his memory. As an old man now, he takes pleasure in submerging himself in the recollections of a youth so full of innocence and dreams, when he was in the midst of spiritual experiences that so strongly impressed themselves on his consciousness. Unfortunately this great Orthodox elder did not succeed in bringing his narrative to the later years of his life, leaving it to his biographers to describe his experiences on Mt. Athos and in Moldavia.

Paisij Velyčkovs'kyj was not so much a writer as he was a spiritual teacher and guide.[27] The texts that he produced relate primarily to the life of monks and are a recapitulation of instructions which anyone may find in the patristic works that he translated from the Greek into Slavonic. His *Autobiography*, however, even in its half-completed state, constitutes not only a source of rare value for the history of monasticism and religious life in the Ukraine and Moldavia during the first half of the eighteenth century, but an original and poetic narrative that to this day manages to captivate its readers.

2. *The* Biography *of Paisij by Mytrofan*

Although the monks of the monastery of Neamţ decided not to publish Mytrofan's *Biography* when it was first composed, the fact that at present it exists in seven manuscripts attests to its considerable popularity among the monks. Two of these manuscripts are in libraries on Mt. Athos, one in the Hermitage of the Prophet Elijah (MS 234/IX/21–105) and the other in the Hilandar Monastery (Slavonic MS 290);[28] one used to belong to the monastery of Secu (no number); one is from the Theological Academy of Petrograd (MS 279);[29] one from the Simonov Monastery in Moscow (MS 56);[30] and, finally, two manuscripts, which contain the original text of Mytrofan's *Biography* of Velyčkovs'kyj, are to be found in the monastery of Neamţ, MSS 153 (207) and 156 (212).[31]

---

[27]   Cf. G. Florovskij, *Puti russkogo bogoslovija* (Paris, 1937), 126–27.
[28]   For a detailed description of the Athonite manuscripts, see Tachiaos, *Revival*, XXVII–XXX.
[29]   Concerning this manuscript, see Četverikov, *Moldavskij starec*, 287– 88.
[30]   For a description, see Popov, "Rukopisi," 86.
[31]   Jacymyrs'kyj discusses these manuscripts briefly in his *Slavjanskie i russkie rukopisi*, 561–62. For a more detailed description, see A.-E. Tachiaos, "Σύμμεικτα

The first of these, MS 153 (207), contains a note indicating that the text of the *Biography* as it appears was reread, corrected, and considerably shortened by its author, the schemamonk Mytrofan.[32] There are, indeed, many alterations in the text, especially on fols. 1–39, but considerably fewer on the remaining folios. If one takes into account that Mytrofan began writing his life of Paisij some twenty years after his subject's death (1794), the text of the *Biography* in MS 153 (207) could not have been copied any earlier than 1814. The second of the Neamţ manuscripts, MS 156 (212), must have been copied even later, since it incorporates the corrections and alterations introduced by Mytrofan into the text of MS 153 (207).

The *Biography* of Paisij in Neamţ MS 153 (207) appears to preserve Mytrofan's text more faithfully than MS 156 (212). And, although in all likelihood it is not in Mytrofan's own hand, there is no reason not to suppose that it is a copy made from the rough version written by Paisij's already aging biographer. When completed, this copy would have been handed back to Mytrofan for correction. It is at this point that the author probably shortened the text by removing the folios missing today and rewrote the narrative in order to preserve its continuity. At the same time, it is by no means out of the question that the scribe or some other scholarly monk of the Neamţ Monastery made further corrections of his own.

Although the text of MS 156 (212) incorporates these emendations, it also contains independent additions and changes that were probably introduced after Mytrofan's death. It is reasonable to assume that these changes belong to the period when an effort was being made in Neamţ to compile a single text of the *Biography* that would be

---

περὶ τῆς σχολῆς τοῦ Παϊσίου Βελιτσκόφσκι,'' 'Αριστοτέλειον Πανεπιστήμιον Θεσσαλονίκης. 'Επιστημονικὴ 'Επετηρὶς τῆς Θεολογικῆς Σχολῆς 10 (1965):673–83; and id., *Revival*, XXX–XXXII. In the monastery's old handwritten catalogue the manuscripts are numbered 153 and 156. They were subsequently renumbered 207 and 212 respectively, without, however, taking Jacymyrs'kyj's catalogue into account.

32   The manuscript comprises 163 numbered folios and three unnumbered ones. The text of the biography appears on the numbered ones. At a point where the sequence of folio numbers is interrupted, without, however, any noticeable break in the narrative, one finds the following note: "Here the person who both composed this Life and reread and corrected this copy removed twenty-eight folios; the schemamonk Mytrofan" (fol. 39).

acceptable to all. In any case, MS 156 (212) is a typical example of the kind of mutilation inflicted upon Mytrofan's original *Biography* of Velyčkov'skyj and which would later be reflected in the dry, unpoetic text of the printed editions. The note on fol. 39 of MS 153 (207) thus only confirms that the text found in the latter is closer to what Mytrofan had originally written. This fact alone would seem to dictate that any further study of Paisij's biography must be based exclusively on the text preserved in MS 153 (207).[33]

Stating, then, his reason for writing a biography of Paisij, Mytrofan says, "I desire to compose an account for my brethren who have entered our community of late, who have not seen his face, and for the benefit of all others who will read it" (fol. 3)[34] At the outset of his narration Mytrofan cites the sources he employed for the *Biography*: his personal recollections, the writings of Paisij, Paisij's *Autobiography*—from which, he says, he took "a little"—and finally what he had heard about Paisij from the older monks. Then, observing the usual order employed by sacred writers, Mytrofan proceeds to a parenthetical display of humility, deprecating his literary and other abilities, and averring that he only dared to write the *Biography* because it was his duty to do so.

Mytrofan clearly felt that he was writing the Life of a saint; for this reason he entitled his work in the manner used in the synaxaria (collections of the Lives of the saints): "On the 15th day of the month of November: the life and ascetic labors of our blessed father the elder Paisij: his flight from the world, his wanderings, the gathering of the brethren about him, and his life with them." Inasmuch as Mytrofan wrote in the style of the synaxaria, he was obliged to observe all the formal rules that apply to such compositions. He was certainly well acquainted with these rules because he had spent many years studying and copying manuscripts.[35] Mytrofan therefore thought that he should begin the *Biography* with a laudatory prologue resembling those of

---

[33]   The textual deviations in the copies of the biography preserved in the remaining manuscripts are so insignificant from a philological and historical point of view that it is unnecessary to establish an *apparatus criticus*.

[34]   See Tachiaos, *Revival*, 96.

[35]   It is not unlikely that Mytrofan translated into Slavonic the Lives of SS. Sabbas and Symeon which are preserved in the Slavonic MS 787 of the Monastery of Hilandar, dated 1788. See D. Bogdanović, *Katalog ćirilskih rukopisa Manastira Hilandara* (Belgrade, 1978), 266, no.787.

the hagiographical texts of the fourteenth century and employing the intricate phraseology known to the Slavonic world as *pletenie sloves*.[36] As Mytrofan was quite lacking in rhetorical skill, it would have been extremely difficult for him to compose a prologue that would meet the standards set by Byzantine hagiographical texts. He resolved this difficulty by resorting to a means not uncommon in the medieval period when the concept of public domain was rather broader than it is today. He simply borrowed the prologue of a well-known medieval hagiographical text which matched well the esteem in which he held his teacher, whose biography he was about to write. The prologue in question is that of the Slavonic translation of the Life of Gregory of Sinai.[37] This choice was certainly not fortuitous, for the Life of Gregory, the great teacher of hesychast prayer, was written by his beloved disciple Callistus, later patriarch of Constantinople. There was a clear analogy here, for Paisij too had been an eminent teacher of the prayer of the heart. Furthermore, Gregory's biography appears to have been a popular text in Velyčkovs'kyj's circle. Mytrofan's prologue translates Callistus' prologue word for word.

The Slavonic translation of the Life of Gregory of Sinai which Mytrofan used was not the one made in the fourteenth century,[38] but one from the eighteenth century produced by Velyčkovs'kyj's school.[39] Besides the laudatory and rhetorical character of the prologue of the Life of Gregory of Sinai, Mytrofan was struck by

---

[36]   See the studies by M. Mulić, "Srpsko 'pletenie sloves do 14 stuljeća,'" *Radovi Zavoda za slavensku filologiju* 5'(1965):117–29; id., "Pletenie sloves i hesihazam," ibid., 7 (1965):141–56; and H. Goldblatt, *Orthography and Orthodoxy: Constantine Kostenečki's Treatise on the Letters*, Studia Historica et Philologica, 16 (Florence, 1987). Cf. Dj. Trifunović, *Azbučnik srpskih srednjovekovnih književnih pojmova* (Belgrade, 1974), 224–37, where the most recent bibliography can be found.

[37]   See Tachiaos, "Σύμμεικτα," 673–82; and id., *Revival*, XXXIV–XXXV.

[38]   The Slavonic translation of the Life of Gregory of Sinai, which was done immediately after his death in 1346, was published by P.A. Syrku, *Žitie Gregorija Sinaita sostavlennoe Konstantinopol'skim patriarxom Kallistom. Tekst slavjanskogo perevoda žitija XIV-go veka i istoriko-arxeologičeskoe vvedenie*, Pamjatniki drevnej pis'mennosti i isskustva, 172 (St. Petersburg, 1909). Cf. I. Pomjalovskij, *Žitie iže vo svjatyx otca našego Gregorija Sinaita* (St. Petersburg, 1894) (=*Zapiski Istoriko-filologičeskogo fakul'teta Imperatorskogo Sanktpeterburskogo universiteta* 35).

[39]   See Tachiaos, "Gregory Sinaites' Legacy to the Slavs: Preliminary Remarks," *Cyrillomethodianum* 7 (1983):153–57. Cf. Jacimirskij, *Slavjanskie i ruskie rukopisi*, 560, no.66 (371); and Tachiaos, Ὁ Παΐσιος Βελιτσκόφσκι, 81–82.

similarities between himself and the author of the biography, Patriarch Callistus, similarities, that is, in the manner in which each was devoted to his teacher. But in one small instance where the experience of Callistus did not correspond with his own, Mytrofan changed the text. This occurs when Callistus says that he lived only a short time with Gregory, whereas Mytrofan had lived with Paisij for a very long time. He consequently changed the text to read ``and spent no short span of time with him.'' In everything else Mytrofan follows the text of Callistus faithfully.

Mytrofan entered Velyčkovs`kyj's Moldavo-Slavonic brotherhood in the year 1767, when it was still at the Dragomirna Monastery in Moldavia. Because he lived with Paisij only from the time of the latter's residence in Moldavia, it is natural that he was ignorant of events prior to 1767, and particularly of the details concerning the creation of the Moldavo-Slavonic circle on Athos in the years 1746–1764. For the events of Paisij's life up until 1746, that is, his youth in Kiev and Wallachia, Mytrofan based himself exclusively on Paisij's *Autobiography*, often following it so closely that he merely exchanged the third person for Paisij's first person. In many places, of course, Mytrofan moves rather far from Velyčkovs`kyj's text, but the *Biography*'s dependence on the *Autobiography* remains manifest. Consequently what is contained in fols. 4–71v of Neamţ MS 153 (207) is nothing more than a repetition of Paisij's text. Mytrofan's own narrative really begins at the moment when Paisij leaves Wallachia for Mt. Athos.

Velyčkovs`kyj's Athonite period covers fols. 73v–88 (pp. 96–106 below) of the *Biography*. Although Mytrofan's text is longer and more detailed than the biography printed by the Optina Monastery, the latter text contains the additional information that Paisij's cell at Kapsala on Mt. Athos was known by the name of Kapari,[40] and it also contains Paisij's instruction on the correct comportment of a spiritual guide.[41] We must suppose that this instruction is an excerpt from one of the letters of Paisij still awaiting publication.[42] It would otherwise be difficult to understand how monks who

[40]   *Žitie i pisanija Moldavskogo starca Paisija Veličkovskogo*, 23.
[41]   Ibid., 26–28.
[42]   Perhaps this instruction comes from one of Paisij's unpublished letters to Abbot Feodosij which is contained in Neamţ MS 13, fols. 48–68. See Jacimirskij, *Slavjanskie*

came after Mytrofan could have known details about Paisij's life of which Mytrofan was ignorant. Indeed, at the time he wrote the *Biography*, Mytrofan was Velyčkovs'kyj's oldest surviving disciple. Furthermore, it should not be forgotten that those who undertook to correct Mytrofan's text did so after his death, by which time it was no longer possible to learn from him further details about Paisij's life and work.

Mytrofan recounts in minute detail the period from 1767 to 1794, the year of Paisij's death. He does not hesitate to interrupt his narrative in order to mention facts of which he himself had personal experience. The details about the monks' life in the Dragomirna, Secu, and Neamţ monasteries are of particular historical interest. Although the printed life omits these details, they are essential for a complete picture of the splendid monastic and ascetico-literary movement in Moldavia during the eighteenth century.

Despite his asseverations to the contrary, Mytrofan is not an entirely inept author. His style is simple and emotional, but not very clear in expression. His language is neither well-turned nor elegant, and he evidently lacks academic training in the use of Slavonic. His syntax is loose and frequently chaotic. Nevertheless, all these deficiencies are counterbalanced by the positive attributes of spontaneity and sincerity. The dominant underlying theme of his narrative is the expression of boundless love for his teacher. The monk Mytrofan remains obedient, as it were, to Paisij even after the latter's death, and he sees himself as serving his teacher by writing the *Biography*, just as he so zealously served him in life. He does not hesitate to compare Paisij's wisdom to that of the ancient philosophers of Athens (fol. 152v; p. 148 below) and to draw parallels between events in Paisij's life and events in the life of Antonij of the Caves, the eleventh-century founder of cenobitic monasticism in Rus' (fols. 149, 151, etc.; pp. 145, 147 below). Of course, such parallels are a standard feature of synaxary texts, but in the case of Paisij they exhibit in the author a surpassing veneration that only profound spiritual love can explain.

Mytrofan's *Biography* succeeds perfectly in its objective, namely, to provide an accurate depiction of Paisij's spiritual figure. Consequently, in both form and content Mytrofan's text is essentially a hagiographical work, a literary type rarely encountered among the

---

i russkie rukopisi, 570–71.

monuments of ecclesiastical writing of the beginning of the nineteenth century. Those who subsequently reworked Mytrofan's text not only mutilated it, but also removed its attractive personal tone, its lyricism, and its vitality; in other words, they disfigured one of the last hagiographical texts written in Slavonic.

The first printed edition of Velyčkovs'kyj's biography—the one published at Neamţ in 1836—was no more than the monk Platon's reworking of Mytrofan's text. This is not, of course, stated on the title page of the book, which maintains to the contrary that Platon's work is the result of a compilation of the works "of many writers." Platon's work consisted chiefly in abridging or editing certain passages of Mytrofan's text. Platon used other written sources for quotations from the works of various ecclesiastical writers in order to give his reader greater spiritual edification. The only real contribution made by Platon to the *Biography* is the identification of certain individuals left unnamed in Mytrofan's text (e.g., Archbishop Amvrosij, Metropolitan Gavriil, and others). Platon did not get these names from written sources; he simply knew them himself or had heard them by word of mouth. For the rest, Platon carefully tempered the emotional and subjective tone of Mytrofan's work, thus rendering it a much starker text. Much the same spirit prevails in the Optina Monastery's 1847 edition of Mytrofan's *Biography*. Here Mytrofan's text has been considerably altered, although it must also be said that the editor did make some attempt to refer to the oral tradition about Velyčkovs'kyj's life and work; the new elements are, nonetheless, of secondary importance. Both these editions, albeit historically accurate, fail to convey any breath of the spiritual life of the monasteries of Dragomirna, Secu, and Neamţ. In every respect, therefore, Mytrofan's *Biography* of Velyčkovs'kyj is a fundamental source for the study of the life of this great spiritual teacher of the eighteenth century.

Anthony-Emil N. Tachiaos

University of Thessaloniki

TRANSLATOR'S NOTE

In the preface to his translation of the Sermons of St. Isaac the Syrian, Paisij writes: "In the translation of this book, as in other similar works I have done, I have always made use of the method of translation called word-for-word (*do slova*), by which holy Scripture and all ecclesiastical and other books have been rendered into the Slavonic from the Greek. The great Greek emperor Justinian commanded that only this method of translation, it being more precise than others, should be used. By this method, then, which is dearest to me, I have translated this book, assiduously observing as best I could the particularities of both languages...." Paisij goes on to explain in detail his manner of translating Greek into Slavonic.[1] Of course, the *Autobiography* is not a translation, but Paisij's style here, as in his other original works, betrays a consciousness of Greek syntax, not unlike that of the hesychast writers in fourteenth-century Bulgaria whose works he so loved to read. Long-winded though many of his periods are, however, Paisij's Slavonic is not unbearably precious: rather than unearthing some Old Slavonic word for a modern thing, he is not loathe to use modern, often Ruthenian words, e.g., *drot, horilka, barylo, rohatka, cebuli*. In this respect Mytrofan is rather more tedious, though he makes the occasional slip in his grammar, e.g., *xodu* (genitive).[2] In rendering Paisij's Slavonic into English I have tried to preserve the dignity of the author's periods without stifling the freshness of the text; likewise, I have tried to convey Mytrofan's more formal tone. All citations from the Old Testament are rendered by Charles L. Brenton's 1851 translation of the Septuagint, and those from the New Testament by the King James version.

In accordance with the format of the series in which this book is published, the personal names in the texts have been transliterated in Ukrainian orthography. Though this may seem to be at variance with the Church Slavonic of the texts, we must remember that most of the

---

[1]   *Svjatago otca našego Isaaka Sirina episkopa byvšago ninevijskago, slova duxovno-podvižničeskija perevedennyja s grečeskago starcem Paisiem Veličkovskim,* (Moscow,1854), I.

[2]   For a more detailed discussion of the language of Paisij's and Mytrofan's texts, see Tachiaos, *Revival,* XL–XLI.

Slavic monks in Paisij's circle were, like himself, from either the Hetmanate or the Right-Bank Ukraine, and Ruthenian was the language
they would have spoken.

The text from which the translation of Paisij's *Autobiography*
was made is that established by Dr. Tachiaos from MS 13.3.26 of the
Library of the Soviet Academy of Sciences (Leningrad), Collection
No. 58, fols. 1–113v; while the translation of Mytrofan's *Biography* is
based on the text in Neamț MS 153 (207).[3] I have also included several
passages omitted by Dr. Tachiaos which are indicated in the Italian
translation by the monks of Praglia.[4] The chapter titles (with some
changes) are taken from Dr. Tachiaos's edition.

When Dr. Tachiaos's edition of these texts was first planned, it
was intended that it should include an English translation by the late
Anne Pennington. Had it not been for the latter's tragic death, the
reader would have had a far better translation than that which follows
here. By a happy circumstance, however the translator found a generous and invaluable collaborator in Dr. Pennington's good friend,
Elisabeth Nikolaevna Obolensky, to whom he shall always be grateful. Many thanks also to R. Koropeckyj for his careful editing of the
typescript, to Th. Kearney and A. Hewryk for their technical assistance, to D. Miller, and to Dr. Tachiaos for his encouragement.

J.F.

---

3   See Tachiaos, *Revival*, XX and XXVII–XXXII; text on pp. 3–150.
4   See Veličkovskij, *Autobiografia*, 57–174.

The World of Paisij Velyčkovs'kyj (1722-1794)

The *Autobiography* of
Paisij Velyčkovs'kyj

A NARRATIVE CONCERNING THE HOLY COM-
MUNITY OF FATHERS AND BRETHREN, MY
SPIRITUAL CHILDREN, MOST BELOVED IN
THE LORD, WHO IN CHRIST'S NAME HAVE
GATHERED ABOUT ME, UNWORTHY THAT I
AM, AND WHO BY GOD'S PROVIDENCE FOR
THE SALVATION OF THEIR SOULS ABIDE IN
THESE MONASTERIES: IN THE HOLY AND
GREAT MONASTERY OF THE ASCENSION OF
OUR LORD AND GOD AND SAVIOR JESUS
CHRIST CALLED NEAMŢ, AND IN THE HOLY
MONASTERY OF THE WORTHY AND GLORI-
OUS PROPHET AND FORERUNNER AND BAP-
TIST OF THE LORD, JOHN, CALLED SECU—
HOW AND FOR WHAT REASON THIS HOLY
COMMUNITY WAS GATHERED ABOUT ME, AN
UNWORTHY SINNER.

The reason for writing the Autobiography

Seeing that I am now near the end of my life, and considering
that everything which is not committed to writing is given over to
utter oblivion, I have thought it good to write at least a partial account
concerning this holy community of holy fathers and brethren, my
most-beloved spiritual children, who have gathered about me in
Christ's name for the salvation of their souls, in order that there may
be at least some knowledge of the community's beginnings and the
manner in which it was brought together, not only among these my
spiritual children, but also among my spiritual children's children, if
with God's blessing the community should endure. I have determined
to leave my spiritual children a partial narrative concerning myself
and concerning my life before I took charge of any brethren. I do this,
in the first place, as one who is aware of certain facts that are unknown
to this holy community and especially those which have their origins
in a non-Orthodox land, lest, after my departure from this life and
after the decease of those holy brethren who well know me and where
I was born, the rest of the holy brethren should be put in doubt about
where I was born. In the second place, I do this out of consideration
for the great desire of my spiritual children, who have conceived a

truly godly love for me, to hear even a partial account of my birth and education, my withdrawal from the world, and my life in the monastic state until the time of their coming to me and their reception into holy obedience. I do this not out of a desire to commit my life to writing—may the Lord Christ, my Savior, keep me from falling into such demonic madness! for who am I? I who have not done one good deed in all the days of my life?—but for the reasons stated above, and even more in order to affirm to the brethren, especially in these unfortunate times deserving of lamentation and wailing, how one must follow the correct and true thinking and doctrines of the holy and apostolic Eastern church, in accordance with the purport of divine Scripture and the teaching of our God-bearing fathers.

Childhood. Paisij's family[1]

I, the hieromonk[2] Paisij, unworthy both of monasticism and of the priesthood, was born and raised by Orthodox parents in the glorious Ukrainian[3] city of Poltava. My father was Ivan Velyčkovs'kyj, archpriest of Poltava,[4] and my mother was Iryna who, when she took the monastic veil, was renamed Julija. My paternal great-great-grandfather, Symon, was a well-known and wealthy Cossack; and my great-grandfather was Luka Velyčkovs'kyj, archpriest of Poltava. My maternal great-grandfather was a famous and wealthy merchant of Jewish origins called Mandja, who was baptized in Poltava in the parish of the Transfiguration of the Lord with all his household; my grandfather was Hryhorij Mandenko. In the fourth year after my birth my father exchanged this temporal life for one eternal, and I was left with my mother and my elder brother Ivan Velyčkovs'kyj, who later became the superior of the cathedral church of the Dormition of our

---

[1]   In the right margin of the MS, in the same hand: *I was born at the end of the year 1722, on the 21st of December. In divine baptism I was given the name Petro, in memory of our father among the saints Peter, metropolitan of Kiev and All Rus'* (metropolitan, 1305–1326).

[2]   Priest-monk (=Greek ἱερομόναχος), a monk who has been ordained to the priesthood.

[3]   *malorossiistem''*.

[4]   It is impossible to be certain whether the poet Ivan Velyčkovs'kyj was Paisij's father or grandfather. See V. P. Kolosova and V. Krekoten', eds., *Ivan Velyčkovs'kyj, Tvory* (Kiev, 1972), 18. Archpriest=πρωτοπρεσβύτερος, the highest rank among the married clergy.

most holy Lady the Mother of God and ever-virgin Mary in Poltava, in which my father and grandfather and great-grandfather had held priestly office. My mother then gave me over to be taught, along with my younger brother Fedir, who departed to the Lord in his seventh year. Within a little more than two years, with God's assistance, I learned the Primer,[5] the Book of Hours,[6] and the Psalter, and straightway I began, with God's help, to read other books with great facility; and from my elder brother, mentioned above, I learned to write after a short time of study at home. Between lessons, whenever I found free time, I read assiduously the books of holy Scripture, the Old and the New Testaments, the Lives of the saints, the writings of St. Ephrem and St. Dorotheus, the *Pearl* of St. John Chrysostom,[7] and as many other books as were to be found in the aforementioned holy church; and from the reading of such holy books, especially the Lives of our pious fathers who pleased God in the holy and angelic monastic state, there began to grow in my soul a longing for withdrawal from the world and assumption of the holy monastic habit. This longing was never absent from my soul so long as I remained in the secular state.

Student at the Kiev Mohyla Academy

When I was in my thirteenth year, my elder brother Ivan also departed to the Lord, having held priestly office for only five years. Pressed by necessity, my mother took her brother, my uncle Vasyl' Mandenko, and me and presented herself to the most holy metropolitan of Kiev, Lord Rafajil Zaborovs'kyj,[8] with a written petition from

---

[5]   For examples of such books that may have been found in Poltava at this time, see Ja. Zapasko and Ja. Isajevyč, *Pam''jatky knyžkovoho mystectva i kataloh starodrukiv vydanyx na Ukrajini*, 2 vols. (L'viv, 1981–1984), nos. 261, 415, 444, 466, 672, 724, 725.

[6]   I.e., Greek ‘Ωρολόγιον, containing the daily offices.

[7]   Cf. P. N. Petrov et al., *Slavjanskie knigi kirillovskoj pečati XV–XVIII vv. Opisanie knig, xranjaščixsja v Gosudarstvennoj publičnoj biblioteke SSSR* (Kiev, 1958), nos. 174, 193, 242, 371 (Ephrem), 99 [=Zapasko-Isajevyč, no. 171], 193, 371 (Dorotheus), 33 [=Zapasko-Isajevyč, no. 32], 141, 354 (*Pearl*).

[8]   Metropolitan, 1731–1747, a great benefactor of the Kiev Mohyla Academy. See V. Askočenskij, *Kiev s ego drevnejšim učiliščem Akademieju* (Kiev, 1856), 1:77–101; P. Molčanov, ''Rafajil Zaborovskij,'' *Kievskije eparxial'nye vedomosti*, 1876, nos. 5:162–72, 7:228–36; K. Xarlampovič [Xarlampovyč], *Malorossijskoe vlijanie na velikorusskuju cerkovnuju žizn'* (1914; reprint, the Hague, 1968), 501–2. See

my god-father Vasyl' Vasylevyč Kočubej, the colonel of Poltava,[9] as
well as from those in authority and all the honored citizens of Poltava,
requesting my confirmation as successor in my father's priestly office
in the aforementioned cathedral church of Poltava through a letter
from His Holiness. And after I had kissed his holy right hand, I
recited before this holy personage, in a loud voice with all manner of
boldness and the appropriate enunciation, several verses composed by
a learned man which I had earlier been unable to recite before my
mother and uncle despite great prodding on their part; and His Holiness was so pleased that he blessed me and pronounced in a loud
voice, "You are the successor." He granted my mother a letter
confirming my succession to the office in the aforementioned church
and dismissed us with a blessing, instructing my mother to enroll me
in the schools in Kiev[10] for the acquisition of secular learning. She
then returned to her house in Poltava and after a short time sent me to
school in Kiev, where for three years I studied grammar with diligence, returning home to my mother every year in July, in accordance
with the school custom, and remaining there for two months. During
this time I enjoyed complete freedom, and I occupied myself with
naught so much as the reading of holy books, by which I was more
and more confirmed in my unswerving intention toward monasticism.
I had already come to understand completely that without good deeds,
that is, without the diligent observance of Christ's commandments, it
is in no wise possible to be saved by orthodox faith alone; and I had
made a covenant in my soul before God, His grace strengthening me,
that I should not judge my neighbor, even if I had seen him sin with
my own eyes, knowing that Christ, our true God, is the only righteous
and true judge of the living and the dead, who will reward each man

---

Zaborovs'kyj's *Instruction* to the professors and students of the Academy in S.
Četverikov, *Moldavskij starec Paisij Veličkovskij, ego žizn', učenie i vlijanie na pravoslavnoe monašestvo* (1938; reprint, Paris, 1976), 292–96.

[9]   Colonel, 1739–1743. Poltava was at the time the center of a regiment (*polk*), an
administrative division of the Hetmanate under the control of the regiment's colonel.
See G. Gajecky, *The Cossack Administration of the Hetmanate* (Cambridge, Mass.,
1978), 2:511–20.

[10]   I.e., the Kiev Mohyla Academy. About the Academy in the time of Paisij, see
M. Bulgakov, *Istorija Kievskoj akademii* (St. Petersburg, 1843), 103–63; Askočenskij,
Kiev, vol. 2; D. Višenskij, *Kievskaja akademija v pervoj polovine XVIII stoletija*
(Kiev, 1903); and Četverikov, *Moldavskij starec*, 15–33.

according to his deeds.[11] For he who judges his neighbor arrogates to himself the dignity of God, making himself judge of the living and the dead—and what is more frightful than this? Further, I made a covenant not to bear hatred against my neighbor, which, by the testimony of holy Scripture, is a sin greater than all others; further, to forgive the trespasses of my neighbor with all my heart and soul, in the hope of forgiveness of my sins from God. For he who does not forgive his neighbor his transgressions shall in no wise receive forgiveness of his own sins from the heavenly Father.[12] This, then, was the covenant concerning the keeping of these commandments which I made before God; and if, on account of my negligence, I have not been deemed worthy to keep these commandments in actual fact, nevertheless, with God's assistance, I have followed and do follow these divine commandments to the extent that I am able by correct thinking, in accordance with holy Scripture, which teaches that this is the easiest and most convenient path to salvation; for there is no more convenient path to salvation.

As I have said above, while at home in the summertime, I occupied myself with the reading of holy books, thus instructing myself in the keeping of God's commandments and in the correct thinking and doctrines of the holy Orthodox church. Then, at the appropriate time, I went off to Kiev and pursued my studies in school with diligence. During these three years I felt no small longing and love for the monastic life, the more so when I befriended several others who had a similar longing and intention toward monasticism, and especially after I had been deemed worthy to find as an instructor and guide in this the most pious hieromonk, Father Paxomij, who lived in the holy Brotherhood Monastery of the Epiphany[13] and had spent some time abroad, in the wilderness, and who kept several books of the fathers. Sometimes through his own invaluable words, sometimes by instructing me to read, this man with his books kindled in my soul a longing for monasticism. But, nevertheless, I still continued my studies at school with diligence.

---

[11] Cf. Matt. 7:1 and Acts 10:42.
[12] Cf. Matt. 6:14–15 and John 13:34.
[13] The boys' school of the Academy was run by this monastery, located beside the Academy, in the Podil district, see above, n. 10.

Visit to the hermitage of Kytajiv

In the fourth year, throughout the winter until the school vacation, which begins on the 15th of July, persist as I did in my studies at school, it was not with such diligence as before, for the desire for monasticism overwhelmed my soul and no longer allowed me to continue in my studies, requiring that I renounce the world as soon as possible and become a monk. And something which happened just then prompted me in this even more. Two of the students in the school went off somewhere secretly in the wintertime, and after some time I learned that they had gone off in order to become monks and were to be found in the hermitage of the Kievan Caves Monastery called Kytajiv.[14] How ineffable was the joy which filled me, and how ardently did I desire to go thither to see them! Finding free time from my studies, I went thither with no little fear on the way; and with God's protection I arrived without incident at that holy abode and received the blessing of the then superior, the all-venerable hieromonk Father Feodosij. With his blessing I conversed also with those blessed servants of God, the students, who welcomed me and restored me from my journey with food. After complin and the completion of their assigned obedience,[15] when night had fallen, they gathered in the refectory with the other novices and read for a considerable time from St. Ephrem with great attention and fear of God; and after the reading they prostrated themselves to one another with great humility and went their separate ways, leaving me in the refectory to rest until matins. After matins and the completion of the divine liturgy, which was finished none too early there, the table was laid, and the superior sat down with the brethren, bidding me, as a guest, to sit at table with the brethren; and while one read from a book of the fathers, all listened in utter silence with the fear of God and great attention. The novices stood by with the fear of God and performed their service in

---

[14]   A dependency of the Caves Monastery to the south of Kiev, below the confluence of the Lybed' and Dnieper, see E. Bolxovitinov, *Opisanie Kievo-pečerskoj Lavry* (Kiev, 1847), 282–83; N. Sementovskij, *Kiev, ego svjatynja, drevnosti, dostopamjatnosti i svedenija neobxodimye dlja ego počitatelej i putešestvennikov* (Kiev, 1846), 240–41; and A. Murav'ev, *Putešestvie po svjatym mestam russkim. Kiev.* (St. Petersburg, 1844), 153–60.

[15]   послѣшаніе is the monastic technical term for a task assigned to a monk by his superior in a monastery.

the refectory with piety. After the meal the novices on whose account I had gone thither, when they had eaten and completed all their assigned tasks, found free time and, their minds illuminated by God, they imparted to me many things profitable to my soul, urging me to leave the world and worldly things and to live with them in obedience in that hermitage, in the expectation of eventually receiving the monastic habit. Even without their urging I desired with all my heart to remain there, but I knew that I should in no wise be able to hide there from my mother, and this I durst not do.

I remained there that day, and early on the third day I asked the blessing of the superior and, taking tearful leave of the brethren, who commiserated with me over my departure thence, I returned to my dwelling, unable to tarry in the hermitage any longer, since it would have been impossible to conceal my secret journey thither if I had delayed further. I returned, then, and continued my studies in school, but with no diligence, only the habit of study, until the end of the school year. After school let out, I did not go home to my mother this fourth summer as I was wont to do previously, in order that I might have complete freedom to seek a way whereby I might be deemed worthy of the monastic habit. I remained in Kiev, in Podil, near the church of Christ's hierarch Nicholas, called The Good,[16] with an old widow who, like a second mother, cared for me in her house with all manner of love and attention. I enjoyed, as I have said, complete freedom, and I went round to the holy and venerable monasteries of Kiev, sometimes to St. Sophia, in order to venerate the relics of Christ's hierarch Makarij, metropolitan of Kiev,[17] sometimes—and rather more often—to the monastery of the archangel of the Lord, Michael,[18] in order to venerate the relics of the holy Great Martyr Barbara, and sometimes to other venerable and holy monasteries. As I went round and beheld the churchly beauty and piety, I profited greatly in my soul, gazing upon the venerable and holy monks: I thought I saw

---

[16] Located near the Magistracy Building, not far from the Brotherhood Monastery/Academy, this church was named for the hospice it once contained. See Sementovskij, *Kiev*, 218.

[17] Metropolitan, 1495–1497; slain by the Tatars. His relics were kept in St. Sophia in a space opposite the altar to St. Michael. See Sementovskij, *Kiev*, 101; and Murav'ev, *Putešestvie*, 68.

[18] St. Michael's Monastery of the Golden Domes, in the district of Old Kiev. See Sementovskij, *Kiev*, 53–64; and Murav'ev, *Putešestvie*, 84–103.

God's angels, and I prayed to God that by His grace He might deem
me, too, worthy of this holy and angelic habit.

The Kievan Caves Monastery

But whatever shall I say about the holy and great Kievan Caves
Monastery, which I loved with all my soul as a holy place chosen by
God, and where in latter years, after the manner of the god-bearing
fathers of old, those worldly angels and heavenly men, our pious and
god-bearing fathers Antonij and Feodosij and the other pious monks
of the Caves Monastery shone forth through their angelic life in the
flesh and were glorified by God, both during their lives and after their
deaths, with miracles and the incorruptibility of their flesh? For I
would go thither on Sundays and feast days more often than to other
monasteries to hear the early as well as the late service of the divine
liturgy; and sometimes I would go also in the evenings and, having no
acquaintances there, as a stranger, I would spend the night somewhere
in the cave near the church, or else in the great monastery itself, near
the great belfry, until the ringing of the bell for the holy office. And
when they had begun the office, I would enter that church which
resembled heaven and, beholding its excellent beauty and good order,
and the great multitude of pious and reverend monks standing inside
with all good order, I rejoiced and was glad in my soul, thinking I saw
our pious fathers, the monks of the Caves of old, and I glorified God
who had deemed me worthy to visit such a holy place so often. After
the completion of the vigil or matins, I would go into the holy Caves
with the other Christians in order to worship and kiss the holy bones
and myrrh-gushing skulls of our pious fathers of the caves; and sometimes in the nearer of the holy Caves, sometimes in the farther one, I
would hear the divine liturgy in the churches within the Caves.[19]
There I glorified God who is wonderful in His saints,[20] and I counted
those pious blessed fathers who lived before the foundation of either
the new or the old monastery and their thrice-blessed solitude[21] and
quiet in the holy Caves, for it is impossible for those dwelling on earth
to attain greater solitude than in that place. And such a desire was

---

[19]   The nearer of the Caves was known as that of St. Antonij, the farther, of St. Feodosij. About them and the churches in them, see Bolxovitinov, *Opisanie*, 35–38.

[20]   Cf. Ps. 67(68):35.

[21]   Slavonic безмолвіе (Greek ἡσυχία), the hesychastic ideal.

kindled in my soul for an impossible thing, namely that, if it had been possible, I should by no means have wanted to leave those holy Caves, but rather, to have remained and ended my days there. Perceiving this to be impossible, however, I would depart from the holy Caves with great sorrow and sighing. At other times, after venerating the holy relics, I would go to hear the divine liturgy in the holy main church of the monastery, and after the dismissal returned to Podil to the house of the handmaid of God where I lived.

Attracted by the monastic life

Now I had several beloved and like-minded friends who had one and the same intention toward monasticism, and in the evening on Saturdays or before certain feasts in the summertime we would gather in the holy Brotherhood Monastery of the Epiphany, in the monastery's gatehouse, a suitably quiet place, having befriended the monastery's guard, a man of great virtue and filled with the fear of God, and there we engaged in conversations profitable to our souls, until the bell rang for the holy office. Most of all we discussed how we might bring our monastic intentions to fruition, and where we might find a place in which, God willing, we might be tonsured and might live in accordance with monastic vows. After frequent deliberation and assiduous consideration, we made an immutable and absolute covenant in the depths of our souls that we should not receive the tonsure in a monastery where there was any abundance of food or drink or any sort of bodily ease; for in such monasteries we should not be able to follow the example of Christ's poverty in accordance with monastic vows nor lead a life of continence, but, on account of our spiritual weakness, should leave the narrow path which leads to life and should stray upon the wide path which leads to destruction.[22] We judged it better to be married in accordance with Christian law and to live in the world than to renounce the world for the pleasure of the flesh, to live in all manner of ease and abundance, in mockery of the monastic state and to the eternal condemnation of our souls on Judgment Day. For this reason, as I have said, we made a firm resolution in our souls that we should depart even from our homeland, to some deserted place of solitude, in order to find an experienced instructor

---

[22] Cf. Matt. 7:13–14.

for our souls and give ourselves over to him in obedience; and after
the appropriate time, we should receive from him the tonsure and
remain with him and with one another inseparably, in monastic
poverty and want of bodily necessities until our last breath, obtaining
the food and clothing necessary to a monk from the righteous work of
our own hands, in all manner of mortification for the sake of the salvation of our souls. In such and similar conversations, then, we passed
the still and quiet time of night until the beginning of the holy office;
and after dismissal from the latter we parted and went home.

During this period of spiritual love and conversations profitable
to the soul and frequent meetings with my friends, a great desire came
upon me to go again to the aforementioned hermitage of Kytajiv, to
see those servants of God of whom I have already spoken and who
were so dear to me; and in as much as it was then summer, it was
easier for me this time to furfill my desire. When I arrived at the holy
abode I was filled with great joy, both because I saw those novices of
Christ who were beloved to me, and because I was deemed worthy to
see also the saintly grey hair and pale, wan faces, wearied from fasting
and abstinence, of the holy fathers who dwelt there. It was no small
profit that I felt in my soul when I attended the holy office with them,
for they read and sang the whole office with great attention and fear of
God, without any haste. Certain of the brethren had a natural gift
from God for melodic song, and they melodiously sang not only the
verses and other sung parts, but also the responses: "Lord have
mercy"; "Grant this, O Lord"; "To Thee, O Lord"; and "Amen";
and they sang in such soft melody and careful measures that even a
hard heart and one ill-inclined to emotion, as mine was, was easily
inclined to emotion and even tears. The very setting of the place, too,
and the way the church was constructed were as to incline the human
soul to emotion. The church was wooden, built in the shape of a
cross, in the name of our pious and God-bearing father Sergej of
Radonež, the Wonderworker.[23] Various fruit trees planted round about
shaded it with their branches, for it was not of great height. All of the
interior was adorned with a covering of icons, even the outermost
narthex, where there was a very pious depiction of the wonderworking

---

[23]   The wooden church to St. Sergej, which was replaced in 1767 by a stone one to
the Trinity (with an altar dedicated to St. Sergej), is mentioned by Sementovskij,
Kiev, 241.

fathers of Russia;[24] and whosoever might gaze upon that holy depiction of the fathers with great piety would feel joy and profit in his soul. Moreover, as I observed the calm and quiet lives of the holy fathers in that place, their piety and silence, meekness and humility, and also the pious obedience of all the novices in all things, completely cut off from their own will and discernment, with humility and the fear of God in everything, I longed to remain there with those holy fathers and brethren, even though I knew well that I should be unable to hide there from my mother; nevertheless, impelled by an urgent desire for monasticism, I was minded to remain there.

Paisij receives spiritual instruction in the hermitage of Kytajiv

Approaching the aforementioned superior of this monastery as he stood alone beside the church, I fell to his feet and implored him fervently for the love of God to receive me, wretch that I was, in holy monastic obedience in his holy monastery. When he had grasped the purport of my request he went off forthwith to his cell, bidding me to follow him. Upon entering his cell, I did the customary obeisance and stood near the doors. He sat down near a table and bade me sit in a place higher than himself, saying to me, "Sit here, brother," and pointing with his hand to the place where he bade me sit. Hearing this, I was terrified by the unexpectedness of the thing and was filled with shame. I made a low prostration and stood in silence. Then he bade me a second time do the same, but again I made a prostration and stood in silence. He bade me a third time do the same, and this time I was greatly terrified, and making another prostration I stood speechless. Opening his holy mouth he said to me, brother, you entreat me to receive you in our holy monastery in order that you may become a monk, but lo, I cannot see in your soul any trace of the monastic state of mind; *I do not see in you the humility of Christ*; I see in you no obedience and renunciation of your own will and discernment, but rather everything to the contrary: *I see in you the wisdom of this world, I see diabolical pride*;[25] I see in you disobedience and

---

[24] *velikorossiistii.*

[25] The passages in italics are omitted in Tachiaos's transcription of the *Autobiography*. Cf. A.-E. N. Tachiaos, *The Revival of Byzantine Mysticism among Slavs and Romanians in the XVIIIth Century. Texts Relating to the Life and Activity of Paisy Velichkovsky (1722–1794)* (Thessalonica, 1986), 13.

adherence to your own will and discernment. For thrice have I bidden you sit in a higher place than I, but you have in no wise obeyed me. Upon once hearing my command, not in my cell only, but even had I wanted you to sit in a place higher than I in the refectory, before all the brethren, you ought to have renounced your own will and discernment forthwith and to have obeyed me in humility and the fear of God. You, however, thrice bidden to do this only in my cell, followed your own will and discernment, or rather diabolical pride, and with hypocrisy feigned humility and prostrated yourself, disobeying my command. Since, therefore, you will not obey and renounce your own will, the mark of true monasticism, how dare you ask me to receive you as a monk? Those who are disobedient and follow their own will and discernment are unworthy of the monastic habit.'' Having said these and many more things to me, he perceived at last that I was horrified by all this and stood with great fear before him making no answer. He then began to speak to me as an affectionate father with love and gentleness: ''Beloved child, be assured that it is for the love of God, in the desire for the salvation of your soul, that I have brought this trial upon you, in order that you may keep the memory of this indelibly in your soul all the days of your life, and that I may in this wise bring you to reason and teach you that the beginning, the root, and the foundation of monasticism is obedience true to God and the purport of divine Scripture and the teaching of the holy fathers. All who wish to be deemed worthy of the monastic habit, even as they renounce the world and all that is in the world, so must they renounce their own will and discernment and submit themselves to their superiors as to God Himself until their very last breath. Thus, my child, be not faint of heart because of this trial which I have brought upon you; for I am sure that it was not in resistance to me that you durst not obey me, but either because you did not yet understand the power of divine monastic obedience, or because of your reverence for me and the holy and great monastic habit of which God has deemed me worthy, unworthy that I am. Wherefore, be you forgiven by God and by me, a sinner.''

He then began to ask me where I was born and whether there was anyone opposed to me becoming a monk. I told him briefly everything about myself, and he said, ''Beloved child, though you have besought me to receive you in monastic obedience in this holy abode, I dare not do this after what you have told me, lest trouble, both for us and for you, be the result. For your mother, once she has learnt where you are, will be able to take you from here very easily by order of the authorities. Do not grieve, therefore, that I dare not receive you for the aforementioned reason, but keep constantly your desire to become a monk and, putting all your cares for yourself in God, strive with His help to find a place in which there will be no hindrance to you becoming a monk. I assure you that God, who is all-powerful and desires the salvation of all, will lead you to such a place and will bring your desire to fruition." Having heard this, I myself realized that for the aforementioned reason it was impossible for me to remain in that holy abode, and I durst trouble the holy man no more with my request. Falling at his holy feet I asked forgiveness; and when I had received this and his blessing, I left his cell.

Whilst I remained there I was deemed worthy to hear the holy words of profit to the soul which he pronounced to one of the brethren. As he stood in the courtyard of that holy abode in the company of several of the brethren, he called out to one of the novices, a very pious brother, and said to him, "I shall send you, brother, to the main monastery for the collection of foodstuffs and drink for the entire week in accordance with our custom: make the appropriate preparations." This brother, then, having prepared himself appropriately, opened the gates of the hermitage and was about to depart. The superior saw this and called the brother, and he said to him, "How dare you, wretched one, leave without my blessing? If sudden and unexpected death befell you on your way, as it befalls many, what would you be able to say in answer to the righteous Judge on the terrible day of His second coming, had you gone off without a blessing? Do you not know what a great sin it is for a novice to do anything without the blessing of his superior?" The other did obeisance and said to him, "Forgive me, Father, I would have left with your blessing; you, indeed, commanded me to go to the main monastery to perform the obedience which you assigned me." The superior answered him, "O wretched one! Was it not enough that you fell into the abyss of maintaining your own will, intending to set off on your obedience without a blessing? For rather than asking forgiveness, humbly saying, 'Forgive me,' you have fallen into another abyss, worse than the first: that of justification. And, what is yet worse, as if you had no fear of God or shame before men, you have dared confuse light with darkness and humility with pride. For it is humility to say, 'Forgive me,' as our holy fathers teach us; but the addition of justification to the words, 'Forgive me,' is pride, the teaching of the devil, and the confusion of light with darkness. 'What communion hath light with darkness?' as the Apostle says.[26] Therefore, whosoever lives in obedience, in the expectation of being deemed worthy of the monastic habit, must at the outset make this the rule of his life: that if he be reproached or upbraided or admonished, be it by the superior or any other of the fathers, he must fall to the other's feet with humility and say, 'Forgive me,' adding nothing to this, save only, 'Forgive me, holy Father, I have sinned,' but adding no justification as you have done.''

That blessed brother listened to these and many more words, standing silently, until the superior finished speaking, and then he fell at the other's feet and asked forgiveness. The superior, as a loving father, said to him, ''It was my intention, my child, to send you on the aforementioned obedience, and I commanded you to make ready, but not to go off. After your preparations you should have gotten my blessing before setting off, for this is the order to be followed in monastic life. It was out of ignorance, not contempt, that you would have set off without a blessing, and it was also out of ignorance that in asking forgiveness you added justification. Of this you have repented with tears and asked forgiveness: be you forgiven and blessed by God and by me.'' Having admonished him sufficiently concerning the power of divine obedience, he dismissed him on the aforementioned obedience; and the brother went off rejoicing and glorifying God. As I stood not far off listening to all of this, I profited greatly in my soul, and I glorified God who had deemed me worthy to hear words so full of benefit to my soul, and I reckoned these to be words of life everlasting. I then received the blessing of the superior and, bidding the aforementioned novices farewell, quitted the hermitage with great sorrow because, for the aforementioned reasons, I had not been deemed worthy to remain there with the holy fathers and novices.

Impressed by the liturgy in Romanian

After my return to the house where I lived, I occupied myself in my accustomed way, going round to the holy monasteries and meeting with my friends to discuss our monastic intentions. When my studies

[26]   2 Cor. 6:14.

at school began as usual at the beginning of the month of September, I feared lest they should somehow hinder me in my monastic intentions, so I left off attending them and cast about diligently in my mind how I might be able to go off to a suitable place and become a monk. Then it so happened, after the conclusion of peace,[27] whilst the armies were returning to Russia, that there came with them to Kiev the Right Reverend Lord Antonij, metropolitan of Moldavia,[28] who stayed in the palace of the right reverend metropolitan of Kiev which was called Kudrjavec'.[29] One day, when Lord Antonij came to the holy Brotherhood Monastery of the Epiphany, he saw the aforementioned hieromonk Paxomij and, recognizing him as one whom he had ordained in the office of hieromonk, he summoned him to stay with the blessing of His Holiness the metropolitan of Kiev in the Kudrjavec' palace. Now, on my frequent visits there to see my master in the Lord, I was through him deemed worthy to receive the blessing of His Holiness the metropolitan of Moldavia and to kiss his right hand. In His Holiness' company I saw, together with other honorable men of the rank of hieromonk, worthy of all manner of reverence, a number of honorable young hierodeacons, meek and humble, who conceived a godly love for me, and I rejoiced greatly in my soul; the more so when I was deemed worthy to hear the divine liturgy performed in the Moldavian language,[30] at which His Holiness and all his clergy took part. How great was the joy which filled my soul as I heard praise being rendered to God in this blessed language! How marvelous are the decrees of God! From that time there began to grow in my soul no small love for this blessed Moldavian language and nation, and for this God-guarded land; and an even greater desire to travel to foreign parts in order to become a monk was kindled in my soul.

---

[27] The Treaty of Belgrade, concluding the Russo-Turkish War of 1735–1739.

[28] Metropolitan of Moldavia from 1729; left with the Russians in 1739; became metropolitan of Belgorod and Obojan', with his seat in Černihiv, in 1741; died 1748. Cf. N. Iorga, *Istoria Bisericii Românești și a vieții religioase a românilor*, 2nd ed., vol. 2 (Bucharest, 1932), 326; and M. Păcurariu, *Istoria Bisericii Ortodoxe Române* (Bucharest, 1981) 3:524.

[29] Located in the district of Old Kiev, behind the Žytomyr Gate, the palace was built in 1716 and stood until 1788. Cf. Sementovskij, *Kiev*, 111.

[30] I.e., Romanian.

He renounces theological studies

Whilst I was thus occupied during that winter, it happened at the end of January that a small trial befell me. One of the students in the school from my city saw that I was neglecting my studies and, feeling sorry for me, went to the then diréctor of the schools, His Reverence Syl'vestr Kuljabka, who subsequently became the archimandrite of the Brotherhood Monastery of the Epiphany and the monastery's school, and later the bishop of St. Petersburg,[31] and told him about me in detail. "He does not want to study," he said, "and his mother is paying the expenses for his studies in vain." Having heard this he sent two students from the school to bring me before him. When I arrived he began to question me brusquely, saying, "Why have you given up your studies in school?" Being by nature quite reticent, and even more so than usual when in the presence of such persons, I do not know how I made bold to answer him, saying, "My first reason for leaving my secular studies is my unswerving intention to become a monk: fearing the unknown hour of death, I desire, if only I could, to go off as soon as possible to such a place where, God helping, I should be able to fulfill my intention. A second reason is that I feel no benefit to my soul from secular studies: for hearing in these studies the oft-mentioned names of the gods and goddesses of the Greeks and the tales of their poets, I have come to hate such studies from the very bottom of my soul. If teachers used the God-inspired words of the holy Church in their secular teaching, receiving spiritual wisdom from the Holy Ghost, they would then be deemed worthy of the double benefit of spiritual wisdom and secular learning. Since, however, students today learn reasoning not from the Holy Ghost, as printed in the *Spiritual Alphabet*,[32] but from Aristotle, Cicero, Plato, and the other pagan philosophers, for this reason they are utterly blinded by falsehood, and they have strayed from the true path in their understanding of words. They learn only locution: within their souls there is darkness and gloom, though upon their tongues there be all manner of wisdom. Thus, in accordance with this testimony, feeling no benefit in my soul from such learning and, moreover, fearing lest as a result of it

---

[31]   Prefect of the Academy, 1737–1740; rector, 1740–1745; archbishop of St. Petersburg, 1750–1761. Cf. Askočenskij, *Kiev*, 2:63–64.
[32]   Cf. e.g., *Kirillovsk. Peč.*, nos. 414, 431.

I should somehow fall into dissolute reasoning, as befalls many, I have abandoned it. A third reason is that I have considered the fruits of this learning upon the spiritual leaders of monastic rank: how they live in great honor and glory and in all manner of bodily ease like secular dignitaries, dressing themselves in costly garments and riding in state in splendid carriages drawn by choice horses. To this I say, heaven forbid!—not in condemnation, but with fear and trembling lest, if I remained long enough in the schools and, having acquired secular learning, then became a monk, I too should suffer not only this, but, because of the weakness of my soul, something ten thousand times worse, succumbing to all manner of spiritual and bodily passions. These, then, are the reasons why I have abandoned my secular studies." The director, as the wisest of men, expressed a great many words in answer to what I had said, correcting my ignorance and explaining how great the benefit of secular learning was. "And if," he said to me, "you have not hitherto felt its benefit in your soul, as you say, there is nothing strange in this, for you have not yet reached the advanced studies. But when in time you come to these and attain real mastery of them, you will rejoice in their great profit and will praise God for delivering you from such ignorance as that in which you now abide." Expressing these and many other similar words to me, urging me in every way to persist in my studies in school, he saw at last that I was not in the least affected by his admonitions, but abided in my obstinacy; and he was greatly vexed and would have punished me for this with a cruel beating. But I considered my extreme and constant bodily weakness, and fearing lest by the beating I should somehow lose the little health I had, I unwillingly complied with his wish, reckoning that this constraint would be exercised upon me for but a short time; for if I endured, with God's pleasure, until the summer, I would be completely free to act upon my intentions without any hindrance. I continued my studies in school, then, but only for the sake of form, making no progress in them whatsoever.

Back to Poltava. Discussion with his mother.

When summer came, I left school and went home to my mother in Poltava. Upon seeing me she was filled with inexpressible joy and thanked God with tears, for she had waited nearly two years to see me. I, too, rejoiced greatly that with God's help I had been deemed worthy to see her, for second to God I loved her greatly and revered her,

inasmuch as she was my mother. Whilst I remained at home I occupied myself in the reading of holy books, having brought with me
several tracts of great profit to the soul which roused me to godly zeal
and monastic struggle. I had copied these latter from the books of the
fathers that I had borrowed from the aforementioned hieromonk Paxomij while in Kiev; and reading through them often, I felt no small
incitement to the monastic life. I had also a like-minded friend by the
name of Dmytro, from among my aforementioned friends, who had
also come from the schools in Kiev to see his mother in Poltava, and
who had lived in the same house with me in Kiev for a considerable
time. During his frequent visits to my house we conversed and took
counsel together. We talked of naught so much as the means whereby
it would be possible for us not only to leave the world for the sake of
monasticism, but even to leave our homeland for foreign parts and
there be deemed worthy of the holy habit. Whilst occupying my mind
with these matters, I thought it good to inform my mother of my intentions; for even if she already knew of them, her knowledge was only
partial, and she therefore hoped that at the end of my studies in school,
even if I did not complete the entire course, I would abandon my plans
of becoming a monk, marry in accordance with Christian law, and
become a priest as successor to my father; that I would look after her
as it was fitting for me to do, and that she would have me as the support and longed-for consolation of her old age. Most of all, she
greatly desired that our family should not become extinct, for she had
had twelve children, all of whom she had already commended to
Christ except me: I was the only one of them left for the godly consolation and sustenance of her and our house in her old age, and also for
our succession, there being no one else to restore the family
Velyčkovs'kyj.

Such were her hopes when I informed her of my monastic intentions, and it is difficult to express the grief and sorrow which seized
her soul. She wailed and lamented, weeping constantly, exhorting me
not to leave her, not to allow our family to become extinct, as would
inevitably result—as indeed it did result—"if you leave the world,"
said she, "to become a monk." Seeing her great grief I felt forthwith
my great love for her, as she was my mother; but nevertheless, I
remained unshaken in my intention and encouraged her to the extent
that I was able, begging and praying that she should not grieve over
my intention to become a monk, but rather should rejoice in it and be

glad and glorify God who by His grace had given me such a design, and that she should put all her hope in His almighty providence for her sustenance. When I saw, however, that she could by no means be consoled and day by day fell into yet greater sorrow, I told my confessor of my intention and of my mother's sorrow. The latter advised me, in order to console my mother, lest she should give herself over to greater grief, to converse with her in a restrained manner, as if in accordance, albeit superficially, with her wishes. Accepting this advice from my confessor, I heeded it. I durst no more make any mention to my mother of my designs, but said to her only such words as were pleasing to her and of consolation to her soul. I told her that I ought first to finish my studies at school, lest I should be a complete ignoramus, unable to say even one word to the Christian people, but rather might become the successor, to the extent that I could, of my great-grandfather, grandfather, father, and brother, not only in their priestly office but also in learning: for they were learned and took pains over the composition of divine words in sermons. Then, after the completion of my studies, if God so blessed, He would bestow upon me, unworthy that I was, their office as well as the labor of expounding Christ's teachings.

Hearing these and similar words which I had learnt from my confessor, my mother derived from them no small relief from her sorrow, for she hoped that in time her desire would be fulfilled. And when the time came to return to school, I began, together with my aforementioned friend Dmytro, to make the appropriate preparations for our departure for Kiev, our ostensible intention being to continue our studies. When all was ready and we were about to set off, by the unfathomable decrees of God I succumbed to a feverish illness and was in no wise able to depart with my friend, though I wanted to do so with all my soul. We made a covenant, then, with great affirmations, that he would leave before me and, after his arrival in Kiev, would with all diligence seek a way whereby, once I had come, we should be able to make our depature thence without delay. And if it happened that, because of my illness, I should be delayed for some time, he was nevertheless to await my coming with all certainty, doubting nothing on account of my illness, but putting all his hope for my recovery in almighty God as I myself did. In no wise was he to return to Poltava because of any short delay on my part, but to await my arrival with all hope, as I have said, and joy. After we had taken this counsel, my

friend set out for Kiev and I remained at home, trusting without a
doubt that he would indeed abide by our covenant. By God's mercy I
regained my health after a few days and, having made the necessary
preparations, I too set off for Kiev, my mother accompanying me as
far as the town of Rešetylivka, thirty versts from our city of Poltava.
Having passed the night there, I set off on my way, my mother still
accompanying me a little farther, and then we stopped in a certain
place. My mother began speaking to me with many tears, as if she
realized that I was going off from her never to return, and that she
would never see me again in this short life. She begged and entreated
me, imploring me in every way not to leave her, but to persist in my
studies in school until the appropriate time and to come home to her
every summer as I had done, in order that she might have in her soul
the joy of seeing me even for a short time. Seeing her inconsolable
tears and knowing well that I should see her no more in this life, I too
wept and sobbed, out of my natural feelings of love for her, and falling at her feet I asked for her maternal forgiveness and her last blessing, repeatedly kissing her holy right hand with tears, consoling her,
albeit restrainedly, with words pleasing to her, in accordance with the
instructions of my spiritual father. Thus I received her maternal
prayers and blessing, and we parted: she went back home, weeping
and consoling herself, deriving some hope from my words concerning
my obedience to her. As I set off, I felt very sorry for my mother,
considering the unendurable grief and sorrow she would feel because
of my parting from her, never to be seen again. But I also rejoiced
and glorified God, having undoubting hope in Him, that by His grace
He would deem me worthy to bring my monastic intentions to fruition.

Irrevocable decision to become a monk

As I made my way with such rejoicing in my soul, lo, beyond all
expectation I saw my friend returning from Kiev in a carriage with
several others, and I was greatly startled by this unexpected thing. He,
too, when he saw me, was sorely embarrassed. We gave each other
the customary greeting and, when the others had gone off a little way,
I took him aside and began to ask him with great sorrow why he had
done this: why without any cause he had so blithely broken the
covenant we had made with such great affirmation. He began to make
excuses, albeit with no little embarrassment, telling me, "In

accordance with our covenant," he said, "I arrived in Kiev, having left you ailing at home. But after I had been there several days, I did not know what to do: whether to begin doing that which we had agreed upon, or not. I lost heart, imagining that you would be ill for a long time and would not be able to come to me soon, and I determined to return to our city *in order to be certain of the state of your health*, if I found you ill, *I thought*,[33] I might await your recovery and if healthy, we might then set off for Kiev together, and secondly I returned in order that I might see my dearly beloved mother once more. Then I saw these Christ-loving men who were returning to our city, and I asked them to take me back. This, then, is the reason for my return." "But, my dearly beloved friend," I said to him, "you ought to have patiently awaited my coming to you; for behold, I have come after these few days. Now, however, inasmuch as you lost heart and returned mostly on my account and with God's help have found me on my way to you, forget the other reason for your return home, that is, seeing your mother one more time, for this is in no wise necessary. Collect your things from the other carriage and take your place beside me in mine, for it is large and will very easily hold both of us. Thus let us set off on our way with all joy, God assisting us, and we shall fulfill our intention without obstacle." But his reply, contrary to my expectation, was as follows: "Inasmuch as I am already so close to our city, do not forbid me, I beg you, to go to my house in order to see my mother and to be deemed worthy of her final maternal blessing. Once having received this, I shall come to you straightway, with no delay whatsoever; and I should expect to catch up to you still on your way to Kiev." Hearing these things from him so contrary to my expectation, I was stricken in my soul: I considered how great the power of the love for parents and for this world was, that it could in the end extinguish in my dearly beloved friend his long felt zeal and ardent desire for monasticism.

I began to entreat him to heed me diligently and not to go to his mother, but to make his way with me. When I saw that he would in no wise heed me in this, I began to speak to him with pain in the depths of my soul: "O dearly beloved friend, behold, I see that through your inattention godly zeal for the thrice-blessed monastic state has been extinguished from your soul. You have loved your

---

[33] Omitted in Tachiaos (cf. *Revival*, 22).

mother and this world more than Christ, our true God, and therefore this world will hold you with inescapable fetters. Even if you later repent and desire to leave the world, it will not be possible, for of your own will, with no pressure from anyone, you will take a wife and will involve yourself with her and with your children in earthly affairs; you will end your days in the world, and you will not be deemed worthy of the monastic habit.'' In reply to this he said to me, ''Who will be able to keep me in the world as long as I retain my unswerving intention toward monasticism? this world? or my love for it, as you say? or my mother? Heaven forbid! I should more easily suffer death than allow myself to heed those who would forbid me to enter the monastic state, though there is no one, as you know, who forbids me in this. Nor is there any need for me to tarry further in this world, whereby I might be compelled to remain in it. Directly I have received my mother's blessing I shall return to you.'' When I saw that he stood firm and immutable in his resolution and disregard of my counsel no longer hoping that he would heed me and leave with me, I addressed these last words to him: ''O dearly beloved friend, so be it as you have said, that no one will be able to restrain you in the world, and that you will return to me without delay. But as I have told you, so I say again: though there be no one to compel you, this secret love of the world which you cherish unwittingly in your soul will hold you fast in the world, until your very death. Believe me in this: to your very last breath in this life you will not see me again. For my part, I shall in no wise wait for you further. I shall go my way, whither the Lord Christ my Savior leads me.'' Thus we exchanged a final kiss and, taking leave of each other, we parted: he went home, and I on my way, grieving sorely and sorrowing over the loss of the dear friend whom this jealous world had taken from me.

Adventures on the way to Černihiv.

Upon arriving in Kiev, I sent the driver and carriage back to my mother with a letter, telling her that with God's help and by her maternal prayers I had arrived without incident in Kiev. Then I began to consider diligently what I should do and where I should go. The thought occurred to me to go to the God-protected city of Černihiv, to my godly spiritual instructor, the aforementioned hieromonk Father Paxomij (for he then lived there, with the right reverend metropolitan, Lord Antonij), in order that I might receive his spiritually profitable counsel, as to where I should go to carry out my intention most easily. Whilst I considered this diligently, I found a student from the schools in Kiev, the son of a priest in Novhorod-Sivers'kyj, who intended to return to his father in Novhorod-Sivers'kyj by way of Černihiv. We hired an old man to take us by river to Černihiv and, having bought provisions for the journey, we took our places in his boat. Then, invoking God's help, we shoved off from the bank and, crossing the river Dnieper, we went into the river Desna, on which Černihiv stands. We sailed upstream on this river and with great difficulty, after ten days' sailing, arrived at a small town named Oster. Who could express the privations which we, or rather I, suffered? Firstly, there was the cold, for it was then the month of October and it was very cold. The others had sufficient clothing and this was not such a privation for them; but I had left everything in Kiev, taking scarcely any clothes, and therefore I shook the whole time from the cold, especially when it rained and snowed and I was completely drenched. At night they would drag the boat ashore and build a large fire (for there was a great quantity of wood all about), and I warmed myself somewhat, though by no means completely. For as I warmed myself on one side, the other froze from the cold, and thus I spent the whole night turning towards the fire, and I was able to sleep only a very little. My companions, however, had sufficient clothing and slept in peace. Secondly, I suffered from the hard labor, for since we were sailing upstream, there was a constant need to row with oars. My companions, being incomparably stronger than I, were able to bear this labor much more easily, but I, by nature weak of body and never having done any labor in my life, toiled beyond my strength; and as a result of such labor my whole body, especially my arms and legs, ached beyond measure, as if from a severe beating. Thirdly, I suffered from a wholly indescribable infestation of lice, which I alone endured, God protecting my companions from this. Under my clothes I had countless lice all over my body, and every night whilst my companions slept soundly I shook my clothes over the fire and, thus ridding myself of them for a short while, found relief from them. Fourthly, and worst of all, I suffered from fear of drowning, for the boat in which we sailed was so very small that it scarcely held the three of us, sailing only three or four fingerbreadths above the water. Whenever there was a disturbance on the river, a great quantity of water poured in, which we diligently bailed out and thus saved ourselves from drowning.

One day it happened that we came upon a shallows in the middle of the river which very nearly upset our boat completely. We jumped out in our clothes in water up to our knees and, standing on the gravel of the shallows, bailed the water out of the boat. But because of the swift current of the river, the sand gave way under our feet and we sank down into the river. Looking downward into the river we saw beneath us the river's great depth, toward which we were being drawn because of the instability of the sand. Great fear and trembling came upon us, as if the watery deep would swallow us forthwith, and we nearly lost our senses out of fear. But God in His grace looked down upon us, and taking courage we called out to one another to make our way upstream along the shallows. With great difficulty, then, because of the swiftness of the current, we only just managed to escape upstream, away from that abyss, dragging the boat along with us; and bailing the water out of it, we scarcely managed to sit down in it. Thus by God's mercy were we spared from drowning.

When we drew near the aforementioned town, a certain Christ-loving man by the name of Danylo Šatylo, who was standing on the river's bank, looked at us and saw how the boat, with us in it, was greatly weighed down in the water. When we came ashore he began speaking to the hired man with whom we got out of the boat: ''How could you, man, have so little fear of God as to take these youths in such a small boat, on so long a journey, on such a large river as this? You are already old, having lived many years in this world, and are careless of your own death; but would it not be a great sin for you to have caused the death of these young men by drowning in the river? For this reason you are not only undeserving of recompense for your labor, but you justly deserve harsh punishment as a destroyer of human life.'' Having said these and similar words to the other, he took us to his house, which stood near the river, and gave us lodging in all manner of ease for several days. My companion gave the man only half the fare, as if for only half the journey, but I secretly gave him the whole amount, that he might be grieved no further, and we dismissed him in peace. Our Christ-loving host then found several large barges on their way to Černihiv and, giving the bargemen money for us, he asked them to transport us; and these latter accepted us with great pleasure. We thanked that Christ-loving man for his kindness toward us and took our places in the barge, and we sailed to the city of

Černihiv with great ease. Those who conveyed us were lovers of Christ and sought no help from us whatsoever, providing us with food and all manner of comfort. But, nevertheless, we almost met with sudden death on this journey as well. For one day as we sailed beneath a high bank, those who conveyed us sensed that a great piece of earth was about to fall upon our barge, and they made quick to push the barge ahead. Directly we had passed that place the ground gave way into the water, a very small piece of it falling on the stern, and this nearly overturned the barge. Everyone was terrified and glorified God who had saved us from death. Thereafter they durst not travel close to such banks.

Searching for a spiritual guide in Ljubeč

After a few days we arrived at Černihiv and, thanking those Christ-loving men, we went ashore. My companion and I likewise bade each other farewell and parted. He went his way, and I entered the city and went to the holy residence of the bishop. There I found my spiritual instructor, the hieromonk Father Paxomij, and I rejoiced greatly in my soul. I kissed his holy right hand, and he took me to his cell and gave me lodging there for several days. Finding an appropriate time, I diligently besought him to direct me to a place from which I should be able more easily to cross the border[34] into foreign parts, where I might be deemed worthy of the monastic habit. He inclined to my petition and counseled me thus, saying, "If, brother, you desire with all fervor to cross the border from our homeland into foreign parts for the purpose of more easily becoming a monk, then go to the holy monastery of Ljubeč, the homeland of our pious father Antonij of the Caves: there you will find the all-venerable hieromonk Father Joakym who, misunderstanding the purport of the words of the Gospel, 'If thy hand offend thee, cut it off,'[35] with imagined zeal for the safeguarding of purity, cut off four fingers from his left hand. This man will instruct you in what you desire, for he is greatly experienced. Moreover, that monastery is situated above the Dnieper, on the very border, and it will be easy for you to carry out your intention from

---

[34] I.e., the border between the Hetmanate and the Polish-Lithuanian Commonwealth.
[35] Mark 9:43.

there. Wait, therefore, until the day when the market is held, and after you have found a man who will take you to Ljubeč, inform me." In accordance with his command, I went out on market day, but I could find only one man from a certain village which lay halfway on the road to Ljubeč, and I hired him to take me home with him to his village. Then I went to inform the holy man of this. He was sorry for me because I had not been able to find anyone from Ljubeč itself, who would have taken me thither, but he put a good face on it and counseled me, saying, "Despair not, brother, for the Lord has the power to bring you without harm to the monastery." I fell at his feet and, receiving a final blessing from him, I went on my way with the man; and he took me to his home and gave me lodging there. In the morning I besought him diligently to take me to the aforementioned monastery, for I feared to make the journey by myself, but I could in no wise persuade him. Putting my hope, then, in God alone, I set out on the journey with great fear, for the way lay through an immense forest, and I had great fear of the beasts. But with God's protection I made the journey without harm; and coming out into an open field, I saw the city of Ljubeč in the distance and, about three versts from the city, the monastery, and I rejoiced greatly in my soul.

A novice at the monastery of Ljubeč

As I approached the monastery I saw that barriers had been set up from the city to the very banks of the Dnieper, and a sentry post, beyond which lay the monastery.[36] When the sentry caught sight of me, I was at a loss for what to do, for I had no written documents stating who I was or where I was from, and I feared lest I should somehow be detained. I prayed, therefore, with all my soul to God, that by the decrees which He knows He might deliver me from so great a trial. Little by little I drew near the sentry, and lo, by God's providence, beyond all expectation, I saw a venerable monk going from the city to the monastery on the other side of the barrier. He approached the sentry post and stood looking at me. As I approached the sentry post, those on duty asked me, "Where are you from?" But the monk forthwith, before me, answered them, as if surprised, "Why

---

[36] The Monastery of St. Antonij of the Caves, which was closed in 1786. See G. A. Miloradovič [Myloradovyč], *Ljubeč i ego svjatynja* (Černihiv, 1892).

do you ask him where he is from? Do you not know that he is a novice in the monastery and is now returning to the monastery from an obedience?'' Hearing this they allowed me to pass freely. Approaching the venerable monk I did obeisance to him and, realizing that he was a hieromonk, I kissed his holy right hand and thanked him for his great charity; and I glorified God's inscrutable providence which had protected me from such a great trial. This venerable monk, Arkadij by name, took me to that holy monastery, to his own cell, to await the arrival of the abbot, who had gone off somewhere on monastery business. Having brought me into his cell, he imparted to me words of profit for my soul until the arrival of the abbot, and he desired, if such be the wish of the abbot, to keep me in his cell. Seeing that he was a spiritual and prudent man, filled with the fear of God, I likewise desired, if it was possible, to live in his cell for the sake of spiritual instruction.

When the abbot arrived in the monastery, the monk pointed him out to me through the window, saying, ''Behold, our abbot is standing in the midst of the monastery. See here, brother: do your abbots in Kiev go about thus?'' And looking out I saw him, adorned with grey hair, wearing a coarse black cloak and I marvelled greatly at his humility: though an abbot, he wore such poor clothes. Never in my life had I chanced to see an abbot so poorly clad. The aforementioned father put on his cassock and, taking me, led me to the abbot. Falling at his feet I asked his blessing. He gave me the customary blessing and then questioned me, saying, ''Where are you from, brother? and what is your name? and why have you come to our monastery?'' I answered that I was from the land of Kiev, that I had come to that holy monastery to become a novice, and that my name was Petro. Hearing this he rejoiced greatly and said to me, ''I thank our most merciful God for sending you to us to become a novice. For lo, we had heretofore a novice by the name of Petro who performed the obedience of the cellarer, but he left us a fortnight ago. I give you, therefore, who have the same name, this obedience.'' Hearing this, the other venerable monk was surprised, and he said to the abbot, ''Holy Father, this brother has only just come to the monastery and knows nothing whatsoever of monastic customs. If you so bless, let him live in my cell, at least for a short while, until with some instruction from me he learns something of monastic obedience; then, as you wish, you may assign him an obedience.'' But the other answered, ''If, brother, we had another novice suited to this obedience, I should gladly fulfill your request; but since, as you know, we have no such novice, by unavoidable necessity I assign this obedience to this brother, though he has only just come to us.'' Hearing this, the venerable hieromonk did obeisance and retired to his cell. The superior then commanded that the storeroom should be opened and took me into it, explaining to me all that was therein and all the duties of this obedience: in what measure and where I was to distribute from it to the cooks the foodstuffs necessary for the brethren's table, namely, the mash, fish, oil, flour, groats, etc; and he gave me the keys to the storeroom. I fell at his feet and received his blessing. He ordered that I should live in a cell not far from his own, where, in a small room, lived the aforementioned venerable hieromonk Father Joakym, and I was to live in another, larger room with an old monk and another young novice.

I performed this obedience with fervor, but it was completely beyond my ability. For many times every day, again and again, I would have to remove the heavy stone by which the mash was pressed, and replace it, lifting it with great difficulty, beyond my strength. It was mostly from this that I ruined what little health I had. In no wise did I dare tell the abbot of this, but I endured the labor to the extent that I was able with gratitude, beseeching the Lord for strength. Now I performed this obedience in the worldly clothing in which I had entered the monastery, but I greatly desired black clothing; and when I managed to get hold of a cassock made out of simple black cloth and dressed myself in it, I did not know what to do for my ineffable joy! And when, in time, the old monk who lived in the cell with me departed to the Lord, he left behind a garment made of coarse grey cloth. Summoning me the abbot gave this to me, saying, ''If this garment pleases you, wear it.'' I did obeisance to him and received his blessing; and going to my cell, I took off my worldly clothing and dressed myself in the garment which the abbot had given me. My joy was so great that I kissed the garment repeatedly as if it were a holy thing. I wore it always, until I wore it out, thanking God for having deemed me worthy of clothing appropriate to a monastery, instead of the worldly clothing I had worn hitherto. Going about in this garment with joy I performed the obedience to which I had been assigned, beginning at matins and finishing in the late evening. At night when I was in my cell, the aforementioned venerable hieromonk Joakym sometimes called me to read the cell rule.[37] It was mostly on his account that I had gone to that monastery, in order that I might receive his counsel and instruction concerning my monastic intention; but I durst in no wise tell him of this, even had I found a suitable time to do so, putting all my hope for this in God alone.

He copies the Ladder of Divine Ascent

Sometime later the abbot ordered that Father Joakym should live in the hermitage of our holy father Onuphrius the Great which was located about five versts from the monastery, and he gave to me the little room in which he had lived. Then one day he summoned me and gave me the book of our father John Climacus, which is divided into seventy lessons, saying to me, "Take this book, brother; read it with diligent attention and be instructed in holy obedience and in every good deed, for it is a book of great benefit to the soul."[38] I made the customary prostration to the ground before him, taking this book from his hands with inexpressible gladness, and marveling at his godly love for me and his great paternal concern for the profit of my soul, I retired to my cell. Having read but a small part of this book, my soul greatly delighted in the words of this God-bearing father, filled with the grace of the All-Holy Ghost; and considering that my stay in that monastery would be a temporary one, and that after I had left it I should perhaps not find such a book elsewhere, I determined to copy it out in the silence of night, in order that I might have it for the constant benefit of my soul. Now I had no candles, for nearly all the brethren of that monastery burned splinters for light, so I also lit a splinter, which was some seven feet in length, and thrust it into a crack in the wall. Asking God's help, I began to copy the book with great difficulty on account of the smoke, for having nowhere to go it was forced downward and filled my cell. When it decended below my head I could in no wise write any longer, but would open the window of the room and would wait in the big cell until the smoke had cleared; then returning to the room and closing the window, I continued to write until the room again filled with smoke. Doing thus all night long, I had no little difficulty in this work. Later I acquired a

---

[37]   I. e., an order of prayer to be observed by a monk in his cell.
[38]   Cf. e.g., *Kirillovsk. Peč.*, no. 173.

lamp and, filling it with oil, I wrote by its light somewhat more easily; and by the time of my departure from that monastery, I had copied out the greater part of the book.

Paisij's imprudent generosity

At the beginning of my stay in that monastery and for some time thereafter, performing my assigned obedience as cellarer, I enjoyed profound peace in my soul, as long as I could in good conscience follow the orders given me by the abbot, distributing to the cooks the foodstuffs necessary for the brethren's table according to his specifications. Going to the storeroom each week, I would leave the foodstuffs where I had been instructed, that is, in the monastery courts and other places I passed on my way into the monastery. But when the brethren learned of my indulgent habits and my inclination to their requests, nearly all of them—not only the simple monks, but the hieromonks and hierodeacons as well—came to me, especially in the evening, to ask for whatever each desired for himself: flour, millet, groats, oil, and other foodstuffs. Now I had no orders from the abbot concerning the brethren, whether to give them what each wanted, or not; nor durst I ask him about this, fearing lest he should strictly command me to give no one anything without his blessing and, if I failed to follow his orders without transgression, I should lose his blessing and, worse still, should sin before God. My conscience rebuked me for giving the brethren anything without the abbot's blessing; but nevertheless, seeing such venerable and holy fathers and brethren who came with such great humility to me, unworthy and last of all in that monastery that I was, requesting foodstuffs for an evening meal for themselves or some other need, I was ashamed even to look them in the face; and, violating my own conscience, I gave them what they requested, not daring to refuse or withhold anything. Likewise the cooks, when they collected the foodstuffs for the preparation of the brethren's meals, prevailed upon me, though I was unwilling, to give them twice the amount of all the foodstuffs, lard, fish, oil, groats, and the rest, saying that there would thus be a better meal for the brethren. Persuaded by them, against my will, I transgressed the abbot's express orders in this matter, and I gave them twice the amount, or even more, of all the foodstuffs. Thereby a better and more pleasing meal was indeed laid before the brethren, and they were all grateful to me and came to love me, inasmuch as there requests had been granted in the

time of their need. Several of them told me that, because of my solicitude for them in their need and granting of their requests, there was by
God's providence an abundance greater than ever of all foodstuffs in
the storeroom. I feigned rejoicing with them in all of this, but within
my soul I had not the peace I had had before: my conscience often
rebuked me for my trangression of the abbot's commands and for my
distributions without his blessing; and as long as I remained there I
thus performed that obedience to the condemnation of my soul.

In one thing alone did my soul greatly rejoice: that as long as I
remained there I profited in my soul beholding the great and extreme
humility of that holy father, the abbot Nykyfor, who had accepted me
into the monastery. In the evening he was wont to call to himself one
of the venerable fathers of the monastery, and he often called me in
the evening as well. Upon entering his cell and seeing him sitting at
table with one or another holy father, not only would I not dare to sit
at table with them but, considering my own unworthiness, not even to
look them in the face. Bidden to do so with assurance, however, I
would sit with them and eat, albeit with great embarrassment. The
meal would consist only of one boiled dish, buckwheat porridge, or
something similar. The drink was either sour or pear kvass, the same
which was served at the brethren's table. I saw no other drink in that
monastery, neither mead nor beer, save for the vodka which was
served to the brethren on appointed days. After we had risen from
table and rendered thanks, he would dismiss me to my own cell with
his blessing. He also often bade me read the lesson during the meal in
the refectory, and at his bidding I did this. Whenever the lesson happened to be from one of the very moving Lives of the saints, as I read
with the enunciation I had learnt in school, many of the brothers were
moved to tears and stopped eating. Several of them rose from table
and stood round me listening to the lesson with emotion and weeping,
and seeing their great longing for words of profit to their souls, I
rejoiced in my soul and glorified God.

A merciless abbot

Whilst I remained in that monastery I felt joy in my soul most of
all at the sight of how the pious superior, as a loving father, directed
the brethren with great love, with meekness and humility, with patience and forbearance. If it happened that one of the brethren committed some sin, as any man might do, if he asked forgiveness, the abbot

granted it him forthwith, correcting him with the spirit of meekness
and chastising him with words of profit to his soul, prescribing for
him a penance in accordance with his ability to do it. For this reason
all the brethren lived in profound peace, rendering thanks to God. But
three months after my arrival there, an abbot from another monastery
was appointed to that monastery by order of His Holiness Lord
Antonij, metropolitan of Moldavia, who exercised hierarchical authority in Černihiv. This new abbot was the learned Herman
Zaborovs'kyj, and when he came to that monastery in Ljubeč where I
then dwelt, he administered it not as the former superior, mentioned
above, had done, but as a dictator. When the brethren came to know
his temperament, they were so frightened that out of fear several of
them ran off from the monastery, no one knew whither. And I, still
performing the same obedience, was in constant fear lest I should
commit some offence before him–the which I was unable to avoid.
For one day during great Lent he summoned me and ordered me to
give the cooks a certain sort of cabbage for his meal. I did not understand what sort of cabbage it was he wanted me to give them, but I left
his cell, not daring question him about this. I informed the cooks and,
taking the cabbage they knew to be best, they cooked it for him. But
when the cook took the dish and placed it upon the table before him,
he asked him, ''What sort of cabbage is this?'' Learning from the
cook what had happened, he said nothing to him, but summoned me to
his cell forthwith. Rising from the table he asked me, ''Was this the
sort of cabbage I asked you to give them for my meal?'' Having said
this, he struck me on the cheek with such force that I barely managed
to remain on my feet; and then he kicked me, and I fell across the
threshold of the cell. I had scarcely gotten up when he shouted at me,
''Get out, idler!'' I went out, trembling all over with fear, and I considered, if he had become so angry with me because of this, which
seemed to me no great offence, what should I suffer at his hands if
ever I offended him in something more important. Then it happened
that his servant, who lived in the same cell with me, also somehow
offended him, and he became angry with us both and boasted to others
that he would punish us with a severe beating; and these same out of
their love for us told us what he had said. His servant was frightened
by this, knowing his master's temperament all too well, and began to
consider where he might be able to go in order to escape from him.
Summoning my courage I spoke to him from my soul, telling him of

my intention to go thence across the border[39] into foreign parts, to seek a suitable place where I might be deemed worthy of the monastic habit. Hearing this he rejoiced greatly, and we began to take counsel together how we might cross the border, the river Dnieper, on which that monastery of Ljubeč was situated.

Paisij goes to Čornobyl'

Such an opportunity presented itself in the sixth week of holy and great Lent, at night, when all the brethren were asleep. Having prayed to God to help us cross the border unharmed and without hindrance, we left the monastery and went down to the Dnieper, along which there were sentries everywhere. Having found a suitable place between sentry posts, we made our way upon the Dnieper with great fear lest the sentries should observe us and seize us, for the night was then illumined by the moon. But after we had gotten away from the bank, we took heart somewhat and proceeded with ease of mind, the ice on the Dnieper being still solid. Thus, with God's help, we came without harm to the other bank of the Dnieper, but not knowing which way to go, it still being night, we rested in a place. When it began to grow light, we found our way and came to a village, and there we rested in the house of a certain man and restored ourselves with food. Then we made our way on a road which went through great forests to the town of Čornobyl', spending the nights in the villages in the forest which lay on the road. After several days' journey we arrived at the Pryp''jat', a rather large river, upon the other side of which stood the town. We durst not cross the river on foot, however, for the ice was already soft and unstable. But then several men came up to the river and made bold to cross it on foot; and taking courage we went after them, albeit with great fear and trembling, for in many places the ice had melted and the water was visible. When we got to the middle of the river we found that the ice had split in two pieces, one cubit apart, along the whole length of the river, and between them the river's depth revealed itself. More than all the other places I feared that one, lest I should be unable to cross the great chasm or should stumble, for it was quite slippery, and should be swallowed up by the deep. With

---

[39]   I. e., the border between the Hetmanate and the Polish-Lithuanian Commonwealth.

very great fear then, as though I beheld inescapable death before my
eyes, I scarcely managed to pass that frightful place, and with God's
help we crossed to the other side of the river and sat down to rest a little.

Whilst we sat there, the ice all over the river began to break up
with a great noise and became like walls floating down the river, and
fear and trembling seized us. With tears we glorified God's inscrutable providence for us, which had suffered us to cross the river
unharmed and had not given us over to sudden death. Then rising to
our feet we went into the town without any hindrance, for it was not
fortified nor were there any sentries, and there we lodged in the house
of a certain man. It was the Saturday of Lazarus when we arrived, in
the afternoon.[40]

In the morning, before the midday meal, as we went along a
street in that town, someone coming up behind us began to call out my
name and surname. Hearing this I was greatly frightened in my soul,
casting in my mind who this could be, for as a stranger there I knew
no one. But looking about I realized that the one calling me was a
countryman of mine, the son of a well known citizen of Poltava, who
approached and greeted me with words of affection; and he then took
us to the house where he was staying and received us with affection.
First he began telling me why he was there at that time: "I was sent,"
he said, "by the lord colonel of Poltava, Vasyl' Vasylevyč Kočubej,
to the administrator of this place with petitionary letters and money
for the acquisition of wood necessary for construction; and I shall
remain here until I have finished the assigned service." Then he began
telling me, "Your mother," he said, "weeps for you and mourns
inconsolably because you have left her and gone off no one knows
where. For she has only you as an heir, and now that you have left
her, all the townsmen pity her on your account." Saying this and
many similar things, he began to exhort me by all means to return to
my mother. I was seized with such fear in my soul that I scarcely
managed to say anything in answer to him. For I considered that, if he
chose to inform the administrator concerning this, he would be able to
restrain me by force and send me back to my mother, or else to detain
me until he had finished his service and then take me back home himself. He ordered that the table should be laid, and sitting together with

[40]   The Saturday before Palm Sunday.

him and my companion, I could scarcely eat because of my great fear.
When we rose from the table he dismissed us with affection, bidding
me visit him often whilst I tarried in that town. Now as I went along
the street with my companion, the latter, having realized from what
the man who knew me had said, who I was and where I was from,
began to commend me greatly. For whilst we stayed in the aforementioned monastery, not knowing who I was or where from, he had often
told me about himself: that he had spent a considerable time in the
school in my native city of Poltava and in our cathedral church of the
Dormition of the holy Mother of God, and that he had known my
mother very well, as well as me and my relations; and having heard
this from him I had taken great care that he should not recognize me,
and therefore had altered my speech. For I endeavored to speak partly
after the manner of the country in which we then were, and he had in
no wise been able to recognize me; and I had rejoiced greatly that I
had been able to conceal myself from him, for I desired that no one
should discover who I was.

On the way to the Right-Bank Ukraine

Having fully recognized me, he commended me for having left
my mother and my father's inheritance for the salvation of my soul,
and for having given myself over to such poverty and wandering for
the sake of monasticism. Seeing that I had been recognized by him
and that he so greatly praised me, I was saddened in my mind and
found his praise in no wise pleasing. Most of all I feared lest I should
be detained by the countryman who had recognized me, and I considered leaving that very day, Palm Sunday. When we came to the
house where we were staying, my companion went off for some reason, and I went off to a school near a certain church in search of a
companion who would be able to take us to the Right-Bank Ukraine.[41]
And lo, by God's providence I found a certain monk who was ready to
depart for the Ukraine. I therefore besought him with great fervor to
take us with him, telling him also about my companion. Then I went
off to call the latter, asking the monk to wait and not to leave without
us. He promised to wait for us a little while, until we should come;
but we had to be quick, for he could not wait long and the day was

---

[41]   на Оукраинȣ, i.e., lands that were part of the Polish-Lithuanian Commonwealth.

already drawing to its close. I went quickly to the house and, not finding my companion, I waited a little while. When I saw that he was not coming, however, I entrusted his care to God's providence and went off to the monk, who had already started on his way. I begged him to wait a little longer for my friend, that I might not blame myself. Thus with great sorrow I left my friend there, and the monk and I set off on our way, for the fear which I have described above did not permit me to remain in that town even for the sake of my friend. Having spent the night in a certain village, we made our way through immense forests for several days, until we drew near to the Ukraine. And it happened to me on that journey, as I had never before made such a long journey, that I had terrible pain in my left leg, and the foot and calf swelled up, as if from a terrible illness, and I could scarcely make my way by walking on my heel, stopping to rest often by sitting or lying upon the ground. This caused my companion the monk no little annoyance, and seeing how badly I limped, he was many times minded to leave me. But then, seeing my tearful supplication, he felt compassion and could not abandon me. As we came to villages along the road, we rested in them for several days at a time, until the swelling of my leg subsided and the pain abated; but scarcely had we left the village when the pain renewed itself and the swelling returned. After some time, however, through God's inexpressible mercy upon me, unworthy that I was, the pain ceased and the swelling in my leg subsided completely, and I made my way with ease.

Paisij falls ill

When we arrived at a certain little hermitage on the Dnieper below Kiev, called Ržyščiv,[42] which was once a dependency of the Kievan Monastery of St. Cyril, we asked the blessing of the superior to rest there for a while. Whilst remaining there with his blessing, I fell so ill that I could in no wise keep any food in my stomach: whatever I ate I soon eliminated by vomiting; and after a month or more I became so weak and my body so thin that, though I was not confined to my bed, I could scarcely walk because of my great weakness. I

---

[42]   The Monastery of the Transfiguration on the right bank of the Dnieper, near the border of the Hetmanate and the Polish-Lithuanian Commonwealth. Cf. A. A. Pavlovskij, *Vseobščij iljustrirovannyj putevoditel' po monastyrjam i svjatym mestam Rossijskoj Imperii i Afona* (St. Petersburg, 1907), 299–301.

besought God that He should not allow me to end my life there, for I was not at peace to die in that place. By God's providence, three foreign monks, who had been in that place for some time, now resolved to go to Moldavia. Learning of this, I rejoiced greatly and asked them with fervor to take me with them, for with all my soul I desired to go to live in that blessed land. Seeing my extreme weakness, they were in no wise willing to grant my request, but they were moved by my fervent petition, and though unwilling, they promised to take me with them.

A young Orthodox martyr

Leaving that little hermitage, we made our way with great difficulty to the high ground where there was a great level plain, and the air there was quite salubrious. Forthwith I began to feel my illness abating, and little by little I grew stronger in body and could walk with greater ease and comfort. With all my soul I rendered thanks for God's goodness, which had not forsaken me utterly.[43] But as the monks and I made our way, beginning at noon the sky grew dimmer and dimmer with very dark and gloomy clouds, and seeing this the others hurried greatly on their way in order to escape the rain. Since I was unable to go so quickly with them, however, I was left alone, and soon a great cloud came overhead with the frightful noise of hail, and a great rain poured down with frightful lightning and thunder. Hail the size of small nuts fell and covered the field to a depth of nearly four inches, and I was so completely soaked that water dripped from my clothes. With great difficulty I made my way through the hail, and it was very late in the night when I reached the village where my companions were.[44] Having spent the night in the house of a certain man, I found them in the morning in a school, where a certain cantor had given them lodging; and seeing me they rejoiced greatly. Then they began enquiring of the cantor which road led to Moldavia, telling him that it was their intention to go thither. But he began telling them, "O holy fathers, I advise you not to go there at this time, for there is great fear on the road. Soldiers are on patrol everywhere on account of the fear of brigands, and I fear lest you fall into the hands of these

---

[43] Cf. Ps. 118 (119): 8.
[44] Presumably Ržyščiv.

merciless soldiers who, if for no other reason, simply because of their hatred of the Orthodox faith, may do you the utmost harm.[45] For not long ago in this our village the following happened. There was in this church before me a cantor of blessed memory who feared denunciation by the persecutors of the Orthodox faith, and when during the liturgy he read the Creed, that is, 'I believe in one God,' and came to the part, 'And in the Holy Ghost,' he would read it thus: 'the Lord, the Giver of life, which proceedeth from the Father *true*.'[46] Reading the Creed in this manner, he escaped denunciation by the enemies of the Orthodox faith. But in time he was denounced to the administrator of the village by the blasphemers of the holy faith for not reading the Creed in accordance with their blasphemy: not 'the Holy Ghost which proceedeth from the Father and the Son,' but only, 'from the Father true.' Hearing this the administrator was greatly enraged, and taking several soldiers he came with them to the church a little before the reading of the Creed. When that blessed cantor began to read the Creed, forthwith the other drew near him to listen diligently to his reading of it. The cantor understood why the other had drawn near, and he read loudly and slowly, with boldness. When he got to the words, 'And in the Holy Ghost,' he was filled with the Holy Ghost and pronounced loudly, 'And in the Holy Ghost, the Lord, the Giver of life, which proceedeth from the Father,' omitting the addition of the word true, which he had included out of fear. Hearing this the administrator forthwith shouted like a wild beast and set upon him; and seizing him by the hair he threw him upon the ground and kicked him mercilessly with his feet. He ordered him to be dragged from the church and to be beaten mercilessly with rods. Whilst this was being done, someone went quickly to call his mother, telling her also the reason why her son was being beaten. She ran to him with tears and exhorted him not to lose heart in his struggle: calling upon God for help, he ought not shrink from giving his life over to death for the Orthodox faith. Kissing his head she said to him, 'O dearly beloved son of mine, be not afraid of this brief torment which you suffer for your confession of the Orthodox faith: persevere as a valiant soldier of Christ for His sake even unto death, that you may be deemed worthy

---

[45]   The cantor is referring to soldiers of the Polish-Lithuanian Commonwealth.

[46]   I.e., *istina* (''true,'' masc. sing. gen.), which sounds very much like *i syna* (=*filioque*).

by Him of a martyr's crown in His heavenly Kingdom.' Said he to his
mother, 'O dearly beloved mother of mine, have no doubt about me,
for I am ready, God strengthening me, to suffer not only this beating,
but ten thousand of the most cruel deaths for the Orthodox faith. Even
as God, glorified and worshipped in the holy Trinity, is one, and there
is no God but Him, so the holy faith of the holy Eastern church, in
which alone is certain hope of salvation through good deeds, is one,
and there is no other but it. How, therefore, can I not fervently desire
to suffer the most cruel of deaths for its sake?' Hearing this his mother
rejoiced with inexpressible joy and, raising her hands to heaven,
thanked Christ God that she had been deemed worthy to give birth to
such a sufferer for His sake. When that tormenter saw and heard this,
he became yet more wroth, and shouted to the soldiers to beat him
more harshly. The sufferer for Christ's sake endured this cruel beating with joy and, thus refuting the impiety of the Westerners and
glorifying the Orthodox faith by his confession of it, he committed his
soul into the hands of God.''

With the hermit Isyxij

After the monks traveling with me had heard this story, they
feared to go any further and, abandoning their intention of going to
Moldavia, they entered Orthodox monasteries located not far from the
Dnieper, two of which were under the jurisdiction of the most holy
metropolitan of Kiev and another two under that of the most holy
bishop of Perejaslav. I, too, went with them, sorrowing greatly that
for the aforementioned reason I was unable to go to Moldavia. When
we approached the hills near Mošny, where one of the aforementioned
monasteries was located,[47] I found in a village near the hills a certain
hieromonk with whom I remained, leaving my companions to go their
way. I rested in that village for several days, and the hieromonk
began telling me about a certain virtuous hermit by the name of Isyxij
who lived an ascetic life for the salvation of his soul on an island in
the river which flowed below the hills. Hearing this I desired with all
my soul not only to see this hermit, but, if it was possible, to live in
his company. I began, therefore, to beg the hieromonk fervently to

[47]   The Monastery of the Ascension, north of Čerkasy, then in the Polish palatinate
of Kiev. Cf. Pavlovskij, Vseobščij putevoditel', 297–98.

lead me to him; and inclining to my request, he took me to the hermit, who received us with great love and restored us from the toil of the journey; and leaving me there, the other went off.

Remaining there several days, I greatly profited in my soul, for he was a true servant of God and a diligent follower of His commandments. He had a great and ineffable longing for the word of God and the teaching of our God-bearing fathers, and he labored diligently in the copying of the books of the fathers for the profit of his soul. From what follows one may perceive how great was his longing for this. Once he heard that a certain book of one of the fathers, which was filled with great profit and was very difficult to obtain, was to be found in a certain monastery in the eparchy of Černihiv, located in the hills far away from Černihiv. He went thither, and with eagerness and much fervent supplication besought the abbot and the council of the monastery that he might have the book to copy; and by his fervor and the cooperation of the grace of God the book was given to him. Returning with it to his cell, he copied it with all manner of diligence; then he took it back to the monastery and, thanking the abbot and council for their great benefaction toward him, he returned to his cell rejoicing and glorifying God who had deemed him worthy of acquiring a treasure so full of profit to his soul. He reckoned as naught the long journey to fetch and return the book, which amounted in all to nearly two thousand versts: such was his longing for the word of God. From his diligent copying of the books of the fathers he had done great harm to his eyesight, to such an extent that he could then scarcely copy out books in large letters.

Seeing his great longing for the word of God and the teaching of our God-bearing fathers, I considered that if ever I gave myself over to such a servant of God in true obedience of soul and body, and obeyed him in everything, he might be able, God's grace illumining my mind, to set me upon the true path to salvation. I began, therefore, to beseech him diligently to receive me in obedience, promising to heed him in all things. But he would in no wise receive me, telling me, "My child, I am a sinful man, full of passions, and of no worth. How could I, who cannot lead my own poor soul to the path of salvation, dare receive you? This is a matter beyond my ability, and I beg you not to press me further." Now, wretch that I was, I though that it was out of humility that he was unwilling to receive me as a novice, and I begged him yet more fervently, with many tears, falling to his holy feet, to receive me; but he would in no wise do this. Seeing this, lest I should importune him excessively, I withdrew to the aforementioned village; and not finding the hieromonk there, I took lodging in the house of a certain Christ-loving man who received me with great joy. Then, after a few days, I went again to that holy elder, and he received me lovingly as a guest, but only to rest there with him for a few days. Finding an opportune time, I fell again at his feet, albeit with great embarrassment and without daring to look him in the face; and kissing his holy feet with many tears, I begged him to receive me, saying to him, "Holy Father, receive me for the Lord's sake, for I shall obey you in everything as I would the Lord Himself: if I do not obey you in everything, then you shall thrash me and drive me away like a foul cur." But seeing that he would in no wise receive me, I withdrew from him a little way and there wept and sobbed over the failure of my petition on account of my unworthiness; and from the tears and sobbing my face swelled. When I returned to him, he saw my face swollen from sobbing and he consoled me from the depth of his soul, telling me, "I beg you, for the Lord's sake, my brother, do not grieve because I will not receive you. For it is not in disdain for your salvation that I do this: my Lord who knows the hearts of men knows this.[48] It is because of the weakness of my soul that I cannot receive you. Put all your hope in the almighty providence of God, for He will not abandon you if you seek salvation with all your soul, but by His grace He will look upon your tears and will direct you upon His path."

Saying these and many other spiritual words of comfort to my soul, he dismissed me in peace. I went away from him weeping and sobbing and returned to the house of the Christ-loving man and remained there. I was at a loss for what to do, for the hieromonk had gone off I knew not where, and I durst not go anywhere alone since by nature I was timorous, but especially because of the fear of the persecutors of the holy faith, for that country was in their control.[49] I thought of going once again to that holy elder, not in order to importune him further with petitions to receive me, but only that I might be deemed worthy of learning from him whither I should go and where abide.

---

[48] Cf. Ps. 43 (44):21.
[49] I. e., Catholics of the Polish-Lithuanian Commonwealth.

It frightens me even to reminisce about what sort of journey it was to the abode of that holy elder. For in many places it was necessary to cross streams by means of very narrow planks placed across them. With great fear and trembling, then, I crossed those streams supporting myself by means of a long pole, immanent death looming before my eyes. Now, on that last trip to see the elder, having crossed all the other streams, I started across the plank over the last stream, which was wider and deeper than the rest. Before I had gotten halfway, my feet slipped from the plank, which was quite slippery, and fell into the water, one on either side of the plank; and I sat upon the plank with great fear and trembling, supposing that I should fall into the stream and be drowned. O ineffable providence of God, which did not give me over to sudden death by not allowing both my feet to slip onto the same side of the plank! For if they had slipped thus, I should have beem drowned forthwith in that stream. Moreover, by God's providence, the pole had not fallen into the water but was still in my hand. Had I let go of it, I suppose, I should thus also have been drowned, having nothing with which to support myself whilst sitting on the plank; likewise, without the pole I should have in no wise been able to stand up on the plank. Thanks be to almighty God who thus provided for me! For strengthened by His grace, albeit with great fear, and supporting myself with the pole, I managed to stand up on the plank and cross to the other side without harm.

When I reached the abode of the aforementioned elder I besought him with tears to bless me to stay with him for several days until the Lord should provide for me as He wished. He gave me his blessing and I remained with him, daring no more importune that holy man concerning my reception, as if this was an impossible thing; but standing before him with shame, I wept, beseeching the Lord to direct me upon His path. As I had done before when I stayed with the elder, I obeyed him as best I could.

Awkward in handicrafts

Now in the course of the few days that I remained there, lo, by God's providence the aforementioned hieromonk came to visit him, and the elder received him lovingly and asked him to take me to the monastery of Mošny. The other gladly promised to do this. And when the time came for me to take my final leave of that holy man, I fell down at his holy feet, kissing them, and I wept many tears and sobbed because I had not been deemed worthy, on account of my unworthiness, to remain there in holy obedience to him. He consoled me as best he could with spiritual words, counseling me to put my trust in God alone, who was able to direct my life in accordance with His divine will. I thanked that holy man for his counsel, so profitable to my soul, and withdrew. The aforementioned hieromonk then thanked him for the love he had shown us and for his hospitality, and we left him and went to the village where the hieromonk lived; and having made all ready for the journey, he took me to the monastery of Mošny. I rested there for several days and then went off with several monks to the Monastery of the Trinity called Motronyn.[50] I remained there for several days and then went off to the monastery of Christ's hierarch Nicholas, called Medvediv, located on an island in the river Tjasmyn, which was under the jurisdiction of the holy metropolis of Kiev.[51] The all-venerable hieromonk Father Nykyfor was abbot there at the time.

Having arrived at this monastery, I approached the abbot and fell at his holy feet; and having received his blessing, I began to beseech him to accept me in his holy monastery. As a loving father he understood my intention of becoming a monk and did not disdain my petition. He accepted me with love and assigned me to a cell where I was to live together with another novice, commanding me to do general obedience with the brethren. It was then the month of July and they were gathering the hay. I went out, then, with the holy fathers, first to gather the hay and then to harvest the wheat, which they instructed me to reap with them. But when they saw how I cut my fingers out of inexperience, they assigned me the task of conveying the sheaves to the threshing-floor; however, in this obedience, too, I was inept. For whilst I was conveying the sheaves, because I was unable to direct the oxen, the cart overturned and the sheaves were strewn upon the ground. Not knowing what to do, I sat upon the ground and wept. When the brethren came, they reproached me as an ignoramus and, seeing my ineptitude in this obedience as well, they assigned me the task of bringing clay and water to the threshing floor. Though this obedience, especially bringing the clay, was quite beyond my strength,

---

50   Near Čyhyryn. Cf. also Pavlovskij, *Vseobščij putevoditel'*, 301.
51   Approximately six kilometers from the village of Medvedivka, in the palatinate of Kiev. Cf. Pavlovskij, *Vseobščij putevoditel'*, 301.

nevertheless, I called upon God for help and performed the task with gladness. Each evening I would return with the brethren to the monastery, and early in the morning I went out with them to my obedience. In the monastery the abbot assigned me the obedience of reading at the lectern in church, as well as obedience in the refectory, that is, cutting and setting out the bread, bringing in the tureens of food and placing them before the brethren, collecting the dishes and washing them, sweeping the floor, etc.; all of which I performed with gladness, thanking God for having deemed me worthy to serve those holy fathers and brethren.

He takes the monastic vows

When in the month of August the fast of the most holy Mother of God began,[52] the abbot summoned me to his cell and said to me, "Seeing I intend to tonsure as rhasophore[53] the brother with whom you share your cell on the feast of the Lord's Transfiguration, go you also to your confessor and confess before him all of your offences and, having received his permission, make ready to partake of the holy Mysteries; and afterwards, go to the venerable hieromonk Nykodym and ask that he may stand as your sponsor in the tonsure." Hearing this from him, I fell at his holy feet and, receiving his blessing, I left his cell, rejoicing and glorifying God for what had happened, though I was also terrified that in such a short time the abbot would deem me worthy of the first degree of monasticism. I went to my confessor, then, and made confession of all my offences, and received his permission and blessing to partake of the most pure Mysteries of Christ. Likewise I went to the holy hieromonk Nykodym and, falling at his holy feet, I besought him to stand sponsor for me in the tonsure. Said he, "Do you ask this of yourself, or at the bidding of the abbot?" Learning from me that it was at the bidding of the abbot I came to him and asked this, he promised with all gladness to stand sponsor at my tonsure; and he bade me wash my hair, for from my departure from the holy monastery of Ljubeč, nearly five months past, I had not only not washed my hair, but neither had I combed it. I washed my hair, then, and prepared myself to partake of the holy Mysteries. On the

---

[52]   On the first of the month.
[53]   I.e., the lowest grade of monastic tonsure.

feast of the Transfiguration of the Lord, after the hours were finished, the abbot tonsured us as rhasophores, giving the aforementioned novice, with whom I shared my cell, the monastic name Platon, and to me, Parfenij.[54] After the divine liturgy, when we had gone out of the church, the brethren confused our names out of inattention: they began calling him Parfenij and me Platon. I went to the abbot and informed him of this, but he told me, "Inasmuch as the brethren were inattentive and have changed your names, calling him Parfenij and you Platon, be you so called and be not confused about this in any wise."

I did obeisance to him and withdrew; and by his command I was called Platon, though, not understanding the power of holy obedience, I was somewhat grieved by this, for I wished, had it been possible, to be called by the name given me in the tonsure. Seeing, however, that everyone now called me thus with assurance, I remained at peace, attributing the blame to my unworthiness. After a few days there came to me a very pious monk from Russia, born of noble parents, and he asked me, "Are you performing any service for the elder who sponsored you in the tonsure?" When I replied that I was not doing so, he said to me, "It behooves you, brother, to serve your elder, be it to collect wood and carry it to his cell, to make a fire when necessary, to bring water, to sweep out the cell, or perform other obediences." I rejoiced in his instruction and went to the cell of my elder. Uttering a prayer,[55] I entered the cell and fell at his feet, kissing his holy right hand; and I asked his forgiveness for not having done any service for him because of my ignorance, promising to serve him thenceforth in every way. But he would in no wise accept any service from me, saying to me, "It is enough, brother, that you go to do general obedience: there you will be given orders by the brethren. I do not require any service from you, for whilst God still gives me strength, I can serve myself." *Whereupon I did obeisance and withdrew.*[56]

The aforementioned monk, who was the sacristan in that monastery, came to me again, and learning that my elder would not allow me to serve him, he said to me, "Go to him again and ask that

---

54   According to the *Life* of Paisij by Platon (in Tachiaos, *Revival*, 172), Paisij was tonsured at the age of nineteen, that is, in 1741.

55   E. g., Молитвами святыхъ отецъ нашихъ Iисусе Христе Сыне Божїй помилуй насъ Аминь; to which the other would reply, Аминь, meaning, "Come in."

56   Omitted in Tachiaos (cf. *Revival*, 47).

he appoint for you a rule for your cell, for you ought to have direction from him in this matter." I thanked him for his instruction and, going to my elder, besought him to appoint for me a rule for my cell. But he said, "You, brother, are literate, and for this reason I will not appoint for you a rule for your cell: as God enlightens you, so keep the rule in your cell." Hearing this, I did obeisance and left his cell. My elder remained in that holy monastery only one week after my tonsure, and then he went away, God only knows where; I never discovered where he was. Thus was I left, wretch that I was, like a lost sheep without my pastor and instructor, to live all the days of my life in self-direction and free will. Nowhere was I deemed worthy to live in obedience to any father, even though, as I now understand by reflection, the temperament of my soul in my youth was well-inclined to obedience. But wretch that I was, I was never deemed worthy, on account of my unworthiness, of such a divine gift.

Whilst I remained in that monastery I performed diligently the general obedience, as well as the other obediences in the church and refectory. Furthermore, of my own will, I helped the cook somewhat, either bringing water in a small barrel on two wheels, or cutting wood, or doing some other work in the kitchen with joy. I attended the holy offices in the church with fervor; on occasion I left them in the day time in order to work, but never at night.

Back to Kiev

Whilst I thus abode quietly and peacefully in that monastery, by God's permission the heretical authorities began to persecute the monastery and the Orthodox faith. For there came to the monastery an official of the ruler of that country[57] and, commanding all the brethren to assemble in the abbot's cell, he began with multifarious arguments to exhort them to unity with his heresy.[58] But when he saw

---

[57]   August III, king of Poland (1733–1763).

[58]   I. e., to try to force the Orthodox into union with the Catholic church. On the policies of the Catholic church in the Commonwealth towards its Orthodox inhabitants during this period, see F. I. Titov, *Russkaja pravoslavnaja Cerkov v Pol'sko-Litovskom gosudarstve v XVII i XVIII vv.*, vol. 1, pt. 2, *1725–1761* (Kiev, 1907); and L. R. Lewitter, "Intolerance and Tolerance: Foreign Intervention in Early Eighteenth-Century Poland-Lithuania," *Harvard Ukrainian Studies* 5 (1981):283–305.

that they would in no wise incline to his impiety, he was greatly enraged and went off to the church. There he made a list of all the church vessels, and when he left the church he locked it and put his seal upon the doors; and taking the keys with him he left in great anger and with many threats. On this account there was no little confusion in the monastery, for when the fathers saw that the church was closed for more than a month, some of them began to go off wherever they wished.

Seeing such persecution of the Orthodox faith by the heretics, I resolved before God never to live in any country where there was persecution by the impious of God's church and the Orthodox faith. I desired greatly, therefore, to go to the Orthodox and God-protected land of Moldavia, but both because of my fear of the enemies of the holy faith and because I could not find anyone at all who could take me thither, my desire was thwarted. I prayed to the Lord that by the decrees known to Him He might set me upon His path. By God's providence the aforementioned sacristan of the monastery, Martyrij by name, and another venerable monk by the name of Kreskentij, a singer who had been a member of the choir of the most holy metropolitan of Kiev, Lord Rafajil Zaborovs'kyj, resolved to go live in the holy Kievan Caves Monastery; and I agreed to go with them. Having made ready, then, and calling upon God for help, we left that monastery and set forth on the journey to Kiev. It was then the month of December and much snow had fallen, and we suffered greatly on the way because of the cold; I especially, for I was in dire need of clothes.

Trained as an engraver

Strengthened by God's help we came to the town of Vasyl'kiv, the homeland of our pious father Feodosij of the Caves, where we were detained for nearly six weeks. Just before the sixth week was out, the orders came and we were allowed to cross the border.[59] Rejoicing, then, we went to the God-protected city of Kiev, and upon our arrival there, at our request, the authorities assigned us residence in the holy Monastery of the Caves. We gave the documents to the most pious archimandrite of the monastery, Father Tymofej Ščerbac'kyj, and until further consideration could be given, he

---

[59]   I. e., between the Polish-Lithuanian Commonwealth and the Hetmanate.

assigned us quarters in the Nearer Caves. In time we were summoned to a meeting of the monastery council, and after sufficient examination we were accepted and assigned quarters within the holy monastery. At first we all lived together in a cell assigned to us in the brethren's row of cells. Then Father Martyrij was put under the charge of the monastery's steward, and Father Kreskentij was ordered to live in the quarters of the director of the right choir, and to sing in the left choir; and I was for a while left alone in the cell. Now the aforementioned most pious father, the archimandrite, and my natural father had studied together as youths in the schools in Kiev, and they had conceived an ineffable love for each other and had become friends united in soul. They had made a pledge before God that they would preserve this same unanimity and love for each other all the days of their lives, even unto their last breath. In accordance, then, with the love he had had for my father, so to me also, unworthy that I was, he showed all-surpassing love. In his desire that I should always remain in the holy monastery and that I should not be sent anywhere outside the monastery to perform any obedience, I was assigned to the printing press, to learn from the all-venerable hieromonk Makarij, under the supervision of the most pious superior of the press, the hieromonk Lord Venjamyn, the handicraft of engraving icons on metal plates. I was assigned to live in the middle cell in the steward's row, in which a hieromonk and a hierodeacon also lived. I rejoiced greatly in my soul on account of the love shown me by the most pious archimandrite in assigning me this obedience. Whilst I lived in that cell I went twice a day to my teacher, the aforementioned hieromonk, and I learned this handicraft from him. He conceived a godly love for me, especially after he had gained complete confidence that I never told anyone else a single word of what he said in conversation with others who came to see him. For in my youth this had been, as it were, a natural habit of mine: I never told anyone anything I had seen or heard, but kept it all to myself. Confident of this, then, he would converse openly about whatever he wanted with those who came to him, having no fear of me in anything. For this reason he was especially disposed to love me and taught me this handicraft with fervor.

Every day except Sundays and feast days I went to the early liturgy, and after the liturgy until the meal, and after the meal until vespers, I would go to my teacher and practice the aforementioned handicraft. I went always to vespers and to matins, and standing behind the right choir, I listened to the offices. But just before great and holy Lent, as I stood in my usual place in church, the precentor approached me and said that the director was calling for me. I was terrified by this, casting in my mind what he would say to me; and when I came to him and kissed his right hand, he bade me come into the choir. Hearing this, I was greatly frightened and told him that I was completely ignorant of singing. But he said, "If you cannot sing, you will at least read what you are told to read." Unable to oppose his command, I thenceforth stood, albeit unwillingly, in the choir on the right side, singing whatever I could and reading, now from the Book of Offices, now from the Canons.[60] Likewise, I also read with gladness from the Canons whenever special prayer services and acathists were performed for pilgrims, and whatever else was commanded of me.

Instructed to avoid alcohol

When holy and great Lent had begun I went to the superior of the Farther Cave, the most pious hieroschemamonk[61] Ivan Kmita, the general confessor of the monks, and laid bare to him all my conscience. After he had performed the mystery of holy confession, that is, after he had read the prayer of forgiveness, he said to me with tears, "Hark, my child, I have understood from your confession that God, by the decrees which He knows, has until now preserved you, even in the world, free from any great sin; and were you to live somewhere in a monastery in the wilderness under the direction of an experienced elder, with God's help you might perhaps be able to preserve your body and soul until death, free of the worst sins. But inasmuch as you have chosen to live here with us in this holy monastery which is in the midst of the world, I fear greatly lest you, being still young, should suffer the final and utter ruin of your soul, which you escaped whilst living in the world. This ruin will come to pass if you become the friend of such as are young in age and understanding and in whose souls the fear of God has not been confirmed. You will fall prey to such soul-destroying friendship, hateful to God, if ever you use any

---

[60]   I. e., the Canons in honor of the saints and feasts of the Church which are sung at matins, contained in the *Menaion*.
[61]   I.e., a monk who has assumed the great *schema*, the third and highest degree of monasticism.

sort of intoxicating drink. If, therefore, with all your soul you desire the salvation of your soul, I advise you, for God's sake, never partake of any intoxicating drink whatsoever. In this way, with God's help, you will be able to flee from ruinous friendship and from the utter destruction of your soul. Can you, my child, indeed heed this counsel of mine?'' I told him that from birth I had never drunk vodka, for such drink was repugnant to my nature and I could in no wise partake of it, that with all my soul I accepted his counsel, so full of profit to my soul, as from the mouth of God, and that indeed, God helping me, I should heed it. He rejoiced greatly in this and said to me, "If, my child, in accordance with your promise you do indeed heed my counsel, I believe that God by His grace will preserve you from all spiritual harm. Know well that those who desire to lure you into friendship with them will greatly importune you, inviting you, bidding you, entreating and exhorting and persuading you by every means to partake of intoxicating drink with them. If you in no wise comply in this, they will abuse and disgrace you, and will become wroth and resentful of you. But strengthened by God, bear up under it all: in no wise submit to their will; and to the extent that you are able, avoid friendship with such as these, for from this proceed all evils. You will have to endure this trial for only a short while, for once they see that you will in no wise partake of any intoxicating drink, which is the reason for their useless friendship, they will cease importuning you about this and will leave you in peace; and you will enjoy the most profound peace in your soul.''

Having received from him counsel so full of profit to my soul, I rejoiced greatly and thanked him, and I went away praising God for having deemed me worthy to receive spiritual instruction from such a holy man. In accordance with his counsel I have never partaken of any intoxicating drink, but only of water and one or another sort of kvass. And all that he had said did indeed come to pass: I was not a little importuned by such young men. But afterwards I enjoyed profound peace, living quietly and peacefully in the holy monastery. All of the fathers in authority in that holy monastery loved me, the most pious lord Venjamyn, the superior of the press, most of all. Out of his great affection for me, as a loving father, he treated me as his spiritual child, and he provided for me out of his paternal mercy. For when in time my dire need for clothing came to his notice, he took care to clothe me. I had come to that holy monastery in the winter, and I scarcely had clothing enough for summer. Whilst attending church I suffered greatly from the excessive cold and severe frosts, shivering through all the holy offices for one or two months, for as a newcomer and stranger there was no one to whom I could make known my need. But God strengthened me, and I suffered with gratitude. And when the radiant feast of Christ's Resurrection drew near, the aforementioned superior of the press, as I have said above, clothed me and took care for my other needs; and I performed my obedience with gladness, giving thanks to God.

His mother's unbearable sorrow

A NARRATIVE CONCERNING WHAT BEFELL MY MOTHER
AFTER MY DEPARTURE FROM HER

Whilst I remained in this holy Kievan Caves Monastery, when summer came, my sister-in-law, the wife of my deceased brother Ivan the priest, came on a pilgrimage to Kiev with her brother Fedir and my uncle Symon Maksymenko. They came to me, and we sat down *in my cell*[62] to converse, as is the custom, and my sister-in-law began to tell me of my mother. "After your departure for school in Kiev," she said, "your mother remained in her house with me, now weeping over your absence, now consoling herself in the hope that you would not abandon her. But when, contrary to all her expectation, the news came from Kiev that you had gone off from Kiev, no one knew where, such inexpressible grief seized her soul that she wept and sobbed inconsolably. Being thus unable to console herself, she went off to Kiev in search of you, in the worst of winter; and upon arriving there, she searched for you everywhere with diligence in all the holy monasteries and hermitages of Kiev. Not finding you anywhere, she returned home with inexpressible hardship: she all but died on the way from the severe frost. Once home, she wept constantly, sobbing day and night; no one was able to console her. After some time her unbearable grief and sorrow utterly overwhelmed her soul and, unable to bear it any longer, she resolved neither to eat nor drink anything until she was dead; thenceforth no one could persuade or induce her even to taste any food or drink. After several days she grew so weak

[62]   Omitted in Tachiaos (cf. *Revival*, 53).

from not eating that her mind could no longer function. She began to
be confused, conversing now sensibly, now no one knew with what
meaning, and finally she became utterly ill, lying upon her bed and
awaiting death's imminent approach. Many of her relations gathered
and sat by her without interruption, pitying her greatly. Then she saw
some sort of vision and was terrified: she began beseeching her relations insistently that they should quickly bring to her the book entitled
the *Akafistnik*.[63] They gave this to her, and to the amazement of all she
began reading aloud, without any error, the Acathist hymn to the
Mother of God. When she had finished, she began again to read the
same Acathist hymn, and after she had read it several times, they
wanted to take the book away from her, but they could not, for she
held it firmly in her hands, incessantly reading the same Acathist
hymn. Her relations then realized that she saw something, and that
she was defending herself against it by the incessant reading of the
Acathist hymn. When a day and a night had passed, during which
time she continously read the hymn as her relations sat by, keeping
watch over her in the bed, she suddenly looked up, and her eyes were
fixed, motionless, upon a vision above for nearly half an hour. Everyone was amazed, not knowing what would happen. Then she cried out
in a loud voice, 'If such be the will of God, I shall no longer grieve for
my son.' Her relations heard this with terror as well as gladness, and
they began to ask her persistently what she had seen. She answered
nothing about this, but asked them to call her confessor. The latter
was called, and she confessed everything to him. After confession she
returned to her senses completely; and when the confessor had gone,
her relations came in to her and began again to ask her what she had
seen. But seeing the severity of her bodily weakness, they realized
that she was scarcely alive at all and could not converse with them.
First, then, they began to take care to strengthen her, pouring water in
her mouth with a spoon, and then they gave her very light food, cooking some porridge and feeding her, like a small child, by spoon with
their own hands, until little by little she began to take food by herself.
When she had become a little stronger, they lifted her and propped her
up on the bed, and sitting up she began to tell them of the vision she
had seen. 'When,' she said, 'I had become utterly weak from not

---

[63]   Cf. e.g., *Kirillovsk. Peč.*, nos. 397, 412, 530; Zapasko-Isajevyč, nos. 776, 825,
922.

eating for so long, and I expected soon to die, great terror came upon me, and I saw a multitude of the most frightful and ghastly demons attempting to attack me. Seeing this vision I was greatly terrified in my soul, and I asked you for the *Akafistnik*. Taking this book, I read the Acathist hymn to the Mother of God diligently and incessantly, putting all my godly trust in her; and by reading the hymn I defended myself against the attack of the demons. Hearing me reading the acathist they trembled in fear and, standing far off, they durst in no wise approach me. It is for this reason that, when you wanted to take the book from my hands, I held it firmly and would not give it to you, for I was in dire need and could defend myself from the demons only by reading the hymn.

"'And after a day and a night had passed, during which I read the Acathist incessantly, I was suddenly in ecstasy. Looking upwards I saw the heavens open, and the angel of God, bright as lightning, descended from heaven and stood beside me; and he said to me, "O wretch, what have you done? Instead of loving your Creator above all creation with all your soul and all your heart,[64] you have loved His creation, your son, more than Him, your Creator. Out of your love for your son, which is foolish and hateful to God, you have resolved to end your life by starving yourself, thus incurring God's eternal punishment. If your son had left you and gone astray to a life of thievery or some other injustice, even then you ought not to have despaired beyond measure, for each man will give account of himself to God on the Day of Judgment. But inasmuch as your son, by God's will, has gone away from you to lead the life of a monk, is it fitting that you grieve inconsolably and destroy your soul? Know well that your son, with the assistance of God's grace, will certainly become a monk. It is fitting that you, in imitation of your son, give over all grieving for him, and that you renounce the world and all that is in the world and become a nun. Such is the will of God. If you oppose God's will and do not with all your soul and all your heart give over this grieving and desperate sorrow on account of your son, then as Christ the Lord is my God and my Creator I shall give you up to the demons who are waiting to seize you. Let all other parents who love their children more than God be warned." After the angel of God had said these and similar things to me, I cried out, "If such be the will of God, I shall no

---

64   Cf. Matt. 22:37.

longer grieve for my son''; and forthwith the demons disappeared, and the angel of the Lord ascended rejoicing to heaven.'

''When her relations heard this from her they were terrified, and they glorified God for having delivered her, by the decrees which He knows, from such desperate grief and voluntary death, and given her instead life and health and a desire for monasticism. Rejoicing in this they returned to their own homes. And with God's help,'' my sister-in-law continued, ''your mother regained complete health; and although she often weeps for you out of her natural love for you, she remembers her promise before God not to grieve for you excessively, and restrains herself from such grief as best she can. She is now making ready with all her soul to leave the world and everything in the world and to enter the Convent of the Holy Protection of Our Lady, which is located five versts from our city of Poltava,[65] in order that she may there be deemed worthy of the holy and angelic monastic habit. Her mother, your grandmother, who is still alive, is the abbess of that convent, and her sister, your aunt, the lady Ahapija, is a nun there as well.'' My mother remained in that convent, struggling in the monastic state for the salvation of her soul for more than ten years before she departed to the Lord.

Prominent monks of the Kievan Caves Monastery

Whilst I remained in the Kievan Caves Monastery I profited greatly in my soul, for I saw there among those holy fathers great contenders for virtue. The first among these was the aforementioned superior of the Farther Cave, the hieromonk Father Ivan, whose surname was Kmita; he was the general, that is, principal confessor. This man had lived in the wilderness for three years together with the deceased father Vasylij of blessed memory, the common elder of us all, before the latter's departure for the land of Wallachia.[66] Second was the all-venerable hieroschemamonk Father Pavlo, who in his life in the world had been a priest and had led a life deserving of great praise. After he had become a monk, because of his great virtue, he was sent to China, to the monastery there; and when he had spent the

[65]   Formerly in the village of Ladyna, now part of the city of Poltava. Cf. Pavlovskij, *Vseobščij putevoditel'*, 551–52.
[66]   See below, n. 78.

determined length of time there, he asked permission to live in the
Kievan Caves Monastery. Living there contentedly, he occupied himself partly with books of the fathers. He gave me several of these to
read, and he deemed me worthy of his spiritually profiting conversation. One day I went to his cell and asked him what meekness was.
He looked at me in a menacing way and so quickly shook his hand at
me, as if to strike me on the cheek, that I was thoroughly frightened
and could scarcely remain standing out of fear, imagining that he
would strike me with force upon the cheek. Seeing that I was so
frightened, he began to speak to me in a meek and loving manner,
"God be with you, child, fear not. Behold, you asked me what meekness was, and if I had answered you with words, you might in time
have forgotten my answer. On this account, that you might always
keep this my word indelibly in your memory, I have made use of this
manner of answer. Know well that this is meekness: if anyone shall
smite you on the cheek, not only must you not become angry but, in
accordance with the commandment of Christ, you must turn the other
cheek to him."[67] Hearing this from him I marveled at his God-given
discernment, and I thanked him for his instruction. Third was the son
by the flesh of this holy man, the hieromonk Feoktyst, the superior of
the icon-painters, who led a very pious life and was meek and humble,
a great ascetic adorned with every virtue. Fourth was the Russian
hieromonk Father Ilarij who lived in a cell in the garden near the
Farther Cave, greatly mortifying his body with extreme abstinence
and fasting, so that when one looked upon his holy face, one was
terrified by the wasted appearance of it: it seemed to be covered by
skin only, and merely from beholding him did my wretched soul
receive benefit. Fifth was a schemamonk who lived in the Farther
Cave and had conducted pilgrims there for fourteen years, enduring
extreme abstinence and fasting. To the length of his waist he wore a
shirt made of thick mail with the rough side turned inward. On
account of its abrasiveness he could in no wise lie down on a bed, but
only sat when he slept, and that for very short periods. Sixth was the
subordinate blacksmith, a great ascetic and monastic struggler who
wore forty pounds' weight of iron upon his person. He loved me in a
godly way, and I would go to him frequently and profited from his
conversation. Seventh was Father Nykander, the superior of the cooks,

---

[67]   Cf. Matt. 5:39.

another great ascetic, who also loved me in a godly way and often imparted to me words profitable to my soul. He, too, wore upon his person an iron belt which weighed thirteen pounds. There were many other great ascetics and fasters in that place, and whenever I looked upon them I was gladdened, glorifying God because I had been deemed worthy to live among such holy men.

Moreover, as I looked upon the inexpressible external and internal beauty of the holy church of the Caves Monastery, which resembled heaven, upon the incomparable good order of the reading and singing of the church offices, upon the magnificent and sacred services of the divine liturgy in that great church when all the brethren assembled on feast days, and upon all the beauteous buildings of that holy monastery; and especially when I reflected that in that holy place, in that holy monastery, our pious and God-bearing fathers Antonij and Feodosij, the first superiors of the monastery and of all the pious monks of the Caves, lived after the manner of our God-bearing fathers of old, whom God glorified in this life and after their decease through divers gifts of His Holy Ghost and great miracles and the incorruptibility of their holy relics—as I considered all of this and also that, because of my unworthiness, my original intention, to leave the world and go abroad with my aforementioned beloved friends and live in holy obedience to some pious man, was not fulfilled and, furthermore, that because of my sins I had not been deemed worthy to be accepted in obedience by the aforementioned hermit, though I had sought this with all my soul, I therefore resolved with all my soul to remain forever in that holy monastery until my last breath.

Prediction about leaving the Kievan Caves Monastery

I remained in that holy monastery with ineffable joy, as I have said, for more than a year, and I had not the slightest thought of leaving it to go anywhere. But one day the aforementioned all-venerable monk, the subordinate blacksmith, called me into his cell and bade me sit down. Looking upon me with pity, he began to speak to me: "Beloved brother, I greatly commiserate with you, for you will leave us and this holy monastery and will go to another place whither God will direct you." I heard this from him contrary to all expectation, and I marveled, saying to him, "Believe me in this, venerable Father, I have not the slightest thought of leaving this holy monastery; rather, I have resolved, God helping me, to remain here forever until my last breath. I live here with joy, thanking God with all my heart for having deemed me worthy to live with the holy fathers in this holy place.'' But he said to me, "Know well, brother, that in a short time my word will become fact: it shall not be otherwise, and you shall see that I have told you the truth.'' Knowing him to be a great ascetic, I durst contradict him no more, and doing obeisance to him I withdrew. Returning to my cell, I cast in my mind how this could be, when I had not the slightest thought of leaving that holy place.

After constant reflection about this, I received a visit from one of my aforementioned friends, my dearly beloved soul mate Aleksij Fylevyč, a native of Kiev. As is the custom we kissed each other in our greeting in the Lord and sat down together, and he began to tell me, "Beloved Father and like-minded friend in the Lord, remember the covenant we made in our souls, that we should not be tonsured or live in any monastery where there was any abundance or bodily ease, but that we should leave the world and go abroad, and should be tonsured by some pious man who lived in solitude, and should remain with him in holy obedience, inseparable from one another until our last breath, obtaining the necessary food and clothing by the righteous work of our own hands. Such was the covenant which we confirmed in our souls. And lo, as I now see, you have abandoned this intention. You did go abroad, and there you were deemed worthy of the monastic habit; but instead of remaining in solitude, you have returned again to our homeland and, contrary to our covenent, you remain in this holy monastery.'' I said to him, "Such indeed, as you have said, dear friend, was the covenant we made. But when I left the world I was not deemed worthy of going abroad with even one of our dear friends. Because of my unworthiness our beloved friend Dmytro would not heed my counsel, and when I went abroad to withdraw from the world, he remained in it. I went abroad alone, then, but I was not deemed worthy of being received in holy obedience by a holy man who lived in solitude, though I begged him with many tears. I was deemed worthy of receiving the first degree of monasticism in a certain monastery in the wilderness, but because I had no like-minded friend, and for other well-founded reasons, I returned to our homeland and now abide in this holy monastery.'' He said to me, "Then have you no longer the intention of going off from here to live in solitude?'' I told him that I had not the slightest thought of this, but intended to remain in that holy monastery until my last breath. He said, "If I went abroad with you, to remain inseparably with you in the wilderness, would you come with me?" Said I, "O beloved friend, if it were possible for us to go abroad and remain in solitude, inseparable from each other until death, I would go with you straightway." Hearing this he rejoiced greatly and, rising, said to me, "O beloved Father and faithful friend in the Lord, if such is your godly love for me, that for my sake you are willing to leave this place where you have found peace for your soul and intended to remain forever until your last breath, I therefore call my conscience as witness before God and before you that, God's grace assisting me, I shall remain with you inseparably until my last breath."

Hearing this from him I told him, "Believe me, beloved friend, I had resolved firmly in my soul to end my days in this holy monastery; I had not the slightest thought of going hence. But in as much as you desire to depart with me that we may abide in godly solitude together, I therefore, following the example of your spiritual love for me, unworthy that I am, pledge before God who knows the hearts of men,[68] that I shall not leave you until my last breath. Behold, out of my love for you, beloved friend, I renounce my firm resolve to remain in this monastery forever. Contrary to all my earlier expectations, I now resolve otherwise in my soul: with God's assistance I shall straightway leave our homeland and go abroad with you, my beloved friend in the Lord." When I had said this he rejoiced greatly and glorified God with tears. We agreed that he should go to his home and endeavor by all means to find a way whereby it would be possible for us to carry out our intention.

When he had gone home, I was quite stricken with awe and marveled with exceeding great wonder that the word which had been spoken to me about my departure by the venerable father, the subordinate blacksmith, would indeed come to pass beyond all my expectation. I had begun to feel thus even whilst talking with my friend; and when I happened to meet that holy father, I was so ashamed that I could not look him in the face, seeing he had foretold the truth to me and I falsehood to him. Out of shame I durst not reveal to him the secret of my heart, and in secret I made ready for my departure.

---

[68]   Cf. Ps. 43 (44):21.

Taking the road to Moldavia

My friend took quite assiduous care for our departure and found two students from the Kievan schools who had the same intention of becoming monks, one of them being a friend of his who bore great love for him and was named Myxej. He revealed to them, then, his own intention of becoming a monk and of going abroad with me; and seeing that they greatly rejoiced in this, he took counsel with them as to the means by which it might be possible for us to cross the border with them. Inasmuch as they had been born on the other side of the border,[69] it was easy for them to obtain from the authorities a document allowing them to pass, and they made such a plan: that they would first cross the border, and there they would find someone who could take us across to them. They agreed that when they had found such a man they would send him to my friend with instructions as to how and when it would be possible to accomplish this.

Having made such a plan, then, and made ready for the journey, these two crossed the border, and after a short time they found a foreign monk, told him of our intention and besought him, for the salvation of his soul, that he should show his zeal by bringing us across the border to them. When they saw that he regarded this undertaking with zeal and gladness, they rejoiced greatly and asked him to go to my friend in Kiev and take counsel concerning this. He followed their instructions with diligence and went to my friend in Kiev, and my friend brought him to me. Seeing him I rejoiced greatly and glorified God, and with him we formed the plan that he should return across the border and find a reliable man. Engaging the latter's services, he was to send him to my friend in Kiev at an appointed time with instructions. Once he had given the instructions, this man was to wait for us behind St. Cyril's Monastery of the Holy Trinity[70] and, having shown us precisely which road led to the border, he would leave us there. Then he would cross the border and inform the monk of our departure from Kiev, and both of them, the monk and the hired man, would make their way toward us in the night and find us on our way to them. As a sign whereby we might recognize them beyond doubt, they were

---

[69] I.e., in the Right-Bank Ukraine, part of the Polish-Lithuanian Commonwealth.

[70] Located in Podil, the monastery was demolished in 1786 and the church converted for use by a parish. Cf. Sementovskij, *Kiev*, 231–33.

to whistle in a certain manner, and by this means they would find us, and we them, and they might easily take us abroad. According to the plan, then, the monk crossed the border and found such a man, and at the appointed time he sent him to my friend in Kiev with instructions. My friend then dispatched him from Kiev and told him to wait in the appointed place. Then he came to me with all the preparations.

When I saw that the time of departure on our desired journey was at hand, I made ready and prayed with my friend to our almighty Lord God Jesus Christ that, through the prayers of His most holy Mother and of our pious and God-bearing fathers Antonij and Feodosij of the Caves and of all the saints, He might prosper us in our intention. Leaving the holy Kievan Caves Monastery, I went out beyond the city, and there we hired a coachman who took us to St. Cyril's Monastery of the Trinity. There we stopped and, paying the coachman, dismissed him. We went a little way by ourselves, then, and found the man awaiting our coming. We got into his sleigh and he took us a long way, bringing us to a certain place where the road parted in two: he would cross the border by one road and we were to go by the other. Stopping in this place, he described the road in detail: we were to keep to the road on the right, along a certain river which flowed into the river which divided the borders.[71] When we came to certain dwellings, we were to make a diversion from them to the left, leaving the road and proceeding through the woods, lest anyone should see us. After we had gone a little way, thus avoiding the dwellings, we were once again to make our way to the right, along the river. "I shall cross the border," said the man to us, "and come to you there with the monk in the night. From there we shall not be far from the border, and we shall take you across without incident." Saying this, he left us and went off. When we were left by ourselves we made our way, placing all our hope in God and beseeching Him in His goodness to protect us from all untoward occurrence.

We had gone quite a distance when night fell, and the darkness was illumined by the moon. As we made our way we caught sight of certain dwellings and, in accordance with the man's instructions, we went round to the left, leaving the road, and proceeded through the woods, though with no little difficulty, for the snow was then almost

---

[71] Probably the Irpin', constituting the border between the Hetmanate and the Commonwealth north and west of Kiev.

up to our knees. Then we returned to the road. After we had thus passed several dwellings, we approached the estate of the Brotherhood Monastery of the Epiphany, which my friend knew, and we again diverted our path away from it, going through the woods as we had now become accustomed to do. After we had gone a long way, thinking that the estate was now far behind us, we returned to the road, but then realized that we had not passed it at all. We were about to make a diversion again when, lo, two caretakers suddenly met us on the road and demanded of us who we were and where we were going. We were terrified, and revealed to them the whole truth: that for the salvation of our souls we were going across the border into foreign parts to seek a deserted place where it was our intention to remain and serve God. Hearing this they praised our intention and told us that the road along the river would lead us to the very border and we ought not stray from it; thus we should cross without incident. Saying to us, "May God help you," they let us go freely. We thanked them for their benevolence and the mercy they showed us, and we went on our way, without the slightest suspicion of them in our minds. We glorified God for protecting us from any untoward occurrence.

Unexpected troubles

After we had left all human dwellings behind, having gone a long way through the woods, when midnight had long passed we heard someone whistling, and we rejoiced greatly. My friend went on ahead to see if the monk and other man had come to meet us as we had agreed. Having seen them, he came running to me with great fear and trembling and told me with many tears, "Woe is me, wretch that I am! Lo, together with the monk and the other man I saw also my cousin who lives on the other side of the border. He will detain me and will inform my mother, and she will come and take me home, and my intention will be thwarted; she will separate me from you, my beloved Father and friend." As he said this, lo, his cousin approached with the monk and the other man. Seeing his cousin weeping and sobbing, he began feigningly to console him, as though he too rejoiced in his cousin's longing to leave his mother and, for the salvation of his soul, to serve God as a monk. He began to promise that, for the salvation of his own soul, he would in no wise inform his cousin's mother, but would leave him to follow his intended path.

Saying such words he somewhat consoled my friend, and we proceeded on our way. My friend and I went ahead, and his cousin and the others came along behind as guards. When we approached the border, lo, those two caretakers caught up to us, having quietly followed us. They had taken with them nothing except clubs, for they thought that there were only two of us, without clubs or anything else in our hands, and that it would be easy to rob or even, as often happens, to kill us, for both of us wore good clothes. When they saw, however, that we were not alone, but had three guards, they despaired of robbing us and called out in a loud voice, "Who goes there? From whence come you, you who cross the border like criminals?" Hearing their unexpected cry we were terrified, and looking at them we recognized that they were the two caretakers who had met us on the road; and we realized what sort of love it was they showed us; from which most merciful God by His unfathomable decrees had preserved us unharmed. For my friend's cousin had a stick with a blade attached, and with the others he charged them, to scare them off. Taking fright they ran away from us very quickly to the guard post, crying out after their fashion, "Guard! Guard!"[72] In terror we watched, lest they should fall upon us, for their guard post was not far from us, and making our way hurriedly we soon arrived at the river separating the borders, to which we were now very close. With God's help we crossed and came to the house of my friend's cousin on the bank of the river. Taking us inside, he arranged everything for us in a loving manner. It was nearly dawn, and after such a journey my friend and I were quite exhausted, but we slept only a little: the immeasurable grief which had overcome our souls because of my friend's being recognized by his cousin did not allow us to sleep long.

Having risen the next day, we were greatly grieved, knowing well that we would soon be separated from each other. My friend's cousin had sent word straightway in secret to my friend's mother that she should come to him in haste across the border and take her son home. He took great care for us and afforded us every comfort and ease, falsely consoling his cousin in every way and exhorting him not to grieve, but to take heart, promising very lovingly to send him on his way with me in all comfort in three or four days' time.

[72]   In the original, каравул, a Ukrainianism.

Now the monk who had led us across the border, realizing that my friend was the cousin of this nobleman who had come with him to meet us in order to take us across the border, feared greatly lest he should suffer some misfortune on the part of this cousin or my friend's mother, and he went off no one knew where. My friend then began to ask his cousin insistently how he had learnt of our coming. He did not conceal anything, but told him the whole truth. ''The monk,'' he said, ''with whom we brought you across the border, came often to my house after he had returned from Kiev, and drank vodka with me. One day, when he was drunk, he began to boast that he was going to bring across the border a young monk from the Kievan Caves Monastery, together with a young nobleman from Kiev who had the intention of becoming a monk. ''Upon hearing this,'' he said, ''I began to ask him insistently who this was, of what family, and what his name and surname were. But he kept silence and would in no wise tell me who it was. One day, then, I put him at rest and began more insistently to ask him who it was, promising him that no one would learn of this secret except him and myself. Trusting my word, he told me the whole truth: that the nobleman's name was Aleksij, and that his surname was Fylevyč. Hearing this from him I rejoiced greatly, in no wise revealing to him that I was your cousin, and I besought him insistently that he might in friendship include me in this holy matter, in order that with him and the other man I might bring you across the border, for I feared lest you might in some way suffer harm from someone. I now rejoice and glorify God that I was there when you crossed the border. Who knows what you might have suffered without me at the hands of those caretakers, or from that monk or the other man, for I was not certain that they would take you across the border without harm.'' Having thus informed his cousin, he exhorted him not to grieve, but rather to rejoice, promising to let us go with joy; and leaving us, he went about his business. But we were greatly grieved, knowing that the time of our separation was soon drawing near.

Parting from his friend Aleksij

When the two aforementioned students from the Kievan schools had crossed the border, they learned of our crossing and came to us. Learning the reason for our sadness, they grieved greatly and wept over the immanent separation from their friend. With me they exhorted him not to grieve over this to the point of despair, even if his mother were to take him home, but, in his intention to leave the world and become a monk, to keep unwaivering hope in the almighty providence of God who by His wondrous decrees would bring his intention to fruition. Nor was he to cease seeking by every means a way whereby, with God's help, he might be able to leave the world; and once having left it, he was to seek us in the monastery of Motronyn. We promised to wait there until he came to us.

After this and similar conversations of profit to our souls, the other two friends returned to the house where they were staying at the time, and I was left with my friend to await the coming of his mother. She arrived on the second day. Seeing me and thinking that I had deceived her son and led him away from her, she began to reproach me with great anger, boasting that she would have me beaten without mercy. My friend, her son, scarcely managed to assuage her wrath, laying all the blame on the other monk who had led us across the border and then run off, saying that he was the cause of his leaving, not I. Only barely could she restrain herself from reproaching me. I saw that the time of bitter separation from my friend had come. I bade him farewell with many inconsolable tears, whilst he too wept and sobbed, and I left him and went off to the aforementioned students. Having made ready, we set out on our way, often looking back at the house where our friend was, for it was not yet far in the distance, and when we had gone about a verst, lo, we saw our friend running after us. Approaching us, he wept and sobbed loudly and inconsolably, throwing himself upon the ground and beating his breast, intending to do the impossible: with many tears he besought us not to leave him, but to take him with us. We likewise wept and sobbed with many inconsolable tears and, bidding him farewell, we begged and implored him to return in good time to his mother. We told him that it was impossible for us to take him with us, and that men would come running forthwith, sent by his mother, to take him from us by force; furthermore, we feared lest they should do us harm, on his account. But he would in no wise return, and whilst this was happening we looked and, lo, his cousin was rushing toward us with others on horses. When they reached us they took him as he wept and sobbed desperately, unwilling to be parted from us, and they returned him to his mother. Fearing lest they should do us harm, we went on our way, weeping with many tears over our separation from our beloved friend. With God's help we arrived without incident at the aforementioned monastery of Motronyn, where the founder of the monastery, the most venerable schemamonk Father Ihnatij, received us with great joy.

With Father Myxajil

We arrived there at the beginning of great and holy Lent, and found the most venerable hieroschemamonk, the elder Myxajil, a man most experienced in the understanding of divine Scripture and the teaching of the God-bearing fathers and in spiritual discernment, who remained in solitude in a certain hermitage not far from the monastery. We went to him often and enjoyed his spiritually profitable words, glorifying God who had deemed us worthy of seeing such an elder so full of spiritual wisdom. He had many books of instruction and of the fathers, and out of his inexpressible love for me he gave me some of them, especially from among those of the fathers, in order that I might read them. We would all go together to see him in his cell, and I would also go by myself, and I received no little benefit in my poor soul from spiritual conversations with him.

This elder of blessed memory had lived for some time in the wilderness in Russia, then for a while in the hermitages of the aforementioned monasteries of Motronyn and Mošny, and later he had gone with other zealots of such a life to the Moldavian and Muntenian[73] lands. He remained there for a long time with his disciples, and then returned to the Motronyn monastery for a while, with the intention of returning to the land of Muntenia. It was then that I was there and, as I have said, I profited greatly from his spiritual words. I told him of my designs: that I had the intention of going to these aforementioned lands, to remain there wherever God pleased. The elder greatly rejoiced in this, and praising my intention, he advised me to go to the land of Muntenia, to the hermitage called Trăisteni, not far from the city of Focşani,[74] where his disciple, Father Dometij abode with his brethren; and there I was to await his arrival, for he intended, with God's assistance, to return to that hermitage.

Hearing his counsel I rejoiced greatly and awaited the end of great and holy Lent. After the radiant feast of Christ's Resurrection, the time for my departure having come, I went to the holy elder to

---

73   I.e., Wallachian.
74   Cf. Păcurariu, *Istoria*, 2:581.

receive his blessing for the journey, and I besought him diligently on behalf of my aforementioned spiritual friend Aleksij: if God by His unfathomable decrees should take him from the world and bring him to the holy elder, I besought him to take him to himself as a spiritual child, like a loving father, and to bring him along to the aforementioned hermitage. I told him about my friend in detail, from the very beginning until my most tearful separation from him, which I had already sufficiently described when I had first come to him with the aforementioned students from school. These latter remained with the elder, to await my friend's coming. With all joy the elder promised to carry out my request, and rejoicing I thanked him for this. When I asked for his blessing for the journey, he said to me, ''I shall go, my child, to my cell in the wilderness, which stands apart from the monastery, and you and your companions shall come to me in that hermitage, and there with them you shall receive my blessing for the journey.'' I did obeisance to the elder and, leaving him, went into the monastery. I then came to an agreement with the venerable monks Antonij, Feodul, and Jerofej, and after several days' preparation for the journey, we received the blessing of the builder and founder of that holy monastery, the most venerable schemamonk Ihnatij, and we set out on our way. In accordance with the elder's command, we went to his wilderness cell, and he received us with great love and took double care for us, providing both bodily nourishment and spiritual conversation of profit to our souls. Then he dismissed us with a prayer and his paternal blessing. Falling at his holy feet, we kissed his holy right hand, and we went on our way with dread and trembling, fearing harm from the adversaries of the holy faith.

In the hermitage of Dălhăuţi

Protected by God's assistance we traversed the Ukraine without harm or incident, and when we crossed the Dniester by boat below Mohyliv and arrived in the land of Moldavia, we were filled with inexpressible joy. For by the grace of God we had been deemed worthy to come to an Orthodox country, and giving over all fear, we went our way, glorifying God in all joy. After we had crossed the Orhei, we came to a hermitage belonging to the holy Monastery of St. Cyprian called Condriţa, where the superior was the venerable hieromonk, Father Mykolaj. The latter received us with joy and looked after us in a loving manner. Two of my companions, Fathers Feodul and Jerofej, remained there, whilst Father Antonij and I, taking leave of them and thanking the father superior, continued on our way. With God's assistance we arrived without incident at Nicoreşti, and then crossing the river Siret we came to Odobeşti. There we crossed the border into the land of Muntenia and arrived with all rejoicing at the hermitage of the holy Archangels, called Dălhăuţi,[75] which was under the spiritual direction of the schemamonk and elder Father Vasylij of blessed memory, for he was then still alive. The superior of the hermitage was the venerable hieromonk Father Dorofej, a disciple of Father Vasylij, and receiving us with great joy, he accommodated us as guests.

Remaining there several days, I profited in my soul from the example of the pious life of the holy fathers there: from the holy offices performed by them in all good order and fear of God, their meals eaten with reverence in silence and fervent attention to the lessons, and from their good order in all things. God also deemed me worthy of seeing several fathers who abode in reclusion. One of these latter was the hieromonk Rafajil, a most blessed man, filled with the fear of God, who lived quite near the hermitage. He occupied himself in the copying of books of the fathers and thereby obtained the necessities for his bodily nourishment. Another man most experienced in spiritual discernment and understanding of the teaching of our God-bearing fathers was the monk Dosyfej, who together with another like-minded zealot, the schemamonk Tymofej, lived further off from the hermitage, on the other side of a hill. There, in a deep valley between the hills, in a small but most beautiful glade, they sowed maize and a great variety of corn and greens, and thus they obtained their sustenence. In time I was deemed worthy to visit them and with my own eyes to see that place and their life of solitude there. This man, full of spiritual understanding and discernment, was driven by godly love for his neighbor and, seeing me to be young and lacking in knowledge, often imparted to me many words of profit to my soul concerning the keeping of God's commandments and the rules of the holy Church. I listened to his words and joyously accepted them with all certainty, without any doubt, as if from the mouth of God. Throughout my life I have kept these as a way of inclining my thoughts correctly and wisely according to the teachings of God's holy

---

[75] In the *judeţul* of Vrancea. Cf. Păcurariu, *Istoria*, 2:581.

Orthodox church, and I thanked God for having deemed me worthy
during my life to see such a prudent man who, even in his external
appearance, was so comely and reverent that I received no little profit
in my soul just from looking upon him. All of these monks were disciples of the aforementioned elder and instructor of us all, the
schemamonk Vasylij.

Living in the hermitage of Trăisteni

After remaining for several days with my companion, the monk
Father Antonij, in the aforementioned hermitage, we thanked the
father superior and, receiving his blessing for our journey, we set off.
In accordance with our intention, we arrived with joy, God assisting
us, at the hermitage of Christ's hierarch Nicholas, called Trăisteni,
which lay nearly one day's journey from the hermitage mentioned
above. The superior there was the aforementioned hieromonk Father
Dometij, who received us with great love. It was in this hermitage that
I was first deemed worthy to see the holy offices performed, with all
good order and great piety and fear of God, partly according to the
rule of the holy mount of Athos. I rejoiced in this greatly in my soul
and glorified God for having deemed me worthy to abide there with
the holy fathers. Twelve of these brethren abode in common in the
hermitage, whilst the other fifteen dwelt in reclusion nearby, obtaining
all their necessities, of food and clothing, from the righteous work of
their hands. For the holy offices they all gathered together, both those
who lived in common and those in reclusion. Among the latter was
Father Proterij, a Ukrainian by birth, from the city of Rešetylivka in
the regiment of Poltava, who had been a goldsmith during his life in
the world. Whilst he stayed in the monastery he made the most beautiful spoons and sold them, and he received visiting monks with inexpressible love. In his mercy he nourished the many divers birds that
flew in the air, providing them with an abundance of food at a suitable
time. They would gather at his cell every day, and would await the
time when he would come and open the window; and flying into the
cell with no fear whatsoever they would eat the food he gave them.
He took into his hand any of them he wished, stroking them and let-
ting them go: they in no wise feared him. When they had had their
fill, they flew off. As he went to the holy office, many of the birds
would gather and accompany him to church, some sitting on his head
and shoulders, others flying round about him and singing in their

divers voices. As he entered the church doors, they all flew up onto the church and awaited his coming out. And when he came out of the church they flew down and sat upon him, accompanying him to his cell in a like manner. Seeing this with all the others I marveled with great wonder and glorified God for having deemed me worthy to see such a servant of His. Another of the recluses was the schemamonk named Ivan, a Russian by birth. This man, whenever he provided a meal for all the brethren out of the righteous work of his own hands, would go before the meal to each of the brethren with a vessel suitable for the washing of feet; and stopping at each cell and washing the feet of all, he would give them all a kiss of love. Others of these recluses copied books of the fathers and thus obtained their sustenance.

Now at this time the brethren who dwelt in the hermitage were constructing cells, and the superior himself was the first to labor with the brethren in this and every other work. But seeing that I was ill and weak, he assigned me lighter work, and I took assiduous care to perform this as best I could. I lived in the refectory which, because of the lack of cells, was also the kitchen and the bakery. Living there, I watched the monks who were assigned the holy obedience of cooking the food or baking the bread, and I feared greatly in my soul lest somehow I should at some time be assigned this holy obedience: not that I despised it—heaven forbid!—but because I was in every way ignorant of this holy work and thought that I should in no wise be able to do it. Nor was I to escape that which I feared. For one day it happened that all the brethren were making ready to go off for several days with the superior into the forest to prepare wood for the construction of cells, and the superior called me and commanded me to cook the meal for the brethren at a certain time. Because of my utter inexperience I was terrified, and with great shame I told him of my complete ignorance of this holy obedience. Understanding this, he left with me one brother to show me the rule of this obedience. The latter gave me partial instruction and then went off to the brethren in the forest. But I was utterly ignorant, and in my great inexperience I forgot his instructions, not knowing what to do first and what afterwards. When the cooking boiled over, in my desire to take it off the fire, I burned my hands and upset the pot, and the food spilt out. I sighed over this and wept; and again I prepared the greens and put the pot on the fire and set the food to boil. When the brethren came at the usual time and did not find the food ready, they were somewhat grieved and,

finishing the cooking themselves, they prepared the meal. There were
-other times when I laid utterly unsuitable meals before the brethren,
which they ate of necessity, complaining to me on account of my
ignorance. Many times did they show me how to cook, and I was
greatly grieved with myself because. I was not deemed worthy to
please the brethren with my service. With all my heart I heeded their
instruction, and with God's help and their holy prayers, little by little,
I learned to perform this holy obedience. What joy I felt in my soul
when I was at last deemed worthy to please the holy fathers and
brethren with my service! I could, however, in no wise bake bread.
But seeing that I had learned somewhat to cook, the superior desired
that I should also learn to bake bread.

Paisij is an awkward baker

When everyone had gone off to the forest, then, to do the
aforementioned work, the superior called one of the brethren who was
the most experienced of all in the baking of bread and ordered him to
show me the procedure for baking bread; and he ordered me to bake
the bread, that it might be ready for the meal. This brother showed me
in detail the procedure: pouring water into a cauldron, he showed me
the the pans of flour and the jug of kvass. He told me, ''After you
have heated the water, pour it into the flour in the pans and begin to
knead it; then pour all the kvass from the jug into the dough and knead
it all together.'' Having said this, he went off to the brethren in the
forest. But wretch that I was, after his departure I heated the water
and poured it in the flour, completely forgetting to add the kvass.
When I began to knead it, there was too little water, and too much
flour. Having no experience, I did not know that it was possible to
heat more water and add it, but thinking that once the brother had
measured out so much water and flour it was in no wise possible to
add or take away from it, I labored with great toil to knead all the
flour; and the dough became so hard that it was impossible to put my
fingers in it. At a loss for what to do with all the remaining flour, I cut
the dough in pieces with a knife and placed it on the table. Sprinkling
flour upon it, I beat it with a piece of wood and thus scarcely managed
to knead in all of the flour; and placing all the dough in the pans with
the greatest of difficulty, I scarcely managed to set them on the oven,
so that the dough might rise more quickly in the warmth. I waited for
quite a while, and then I lit the oven so that it might be ready, but after

I had burnt a great quantity of wood, the dough had still not risen. I was grieved by this, not knowing why it would not rise, but remained hard and immovable like a rock. In the afternoon one of the brethren came from the forest, not the one who had shown me how to bake the bread, but another, sent by the superior to learn whether the bread was ready or not. He asked me, "Why is the bread still not ready?" Answering him with a sigh, I told him that it still had not risen. He and I then took the pans off the oven and, feeling it with his hand, he found that it had been kneaded hard as a rock. Learning the reason for this, he smiled and said, "You ignoramus! When you saw that there was too little water you ought to have added more without hesitation, or else taken away some of the flour, and thus you would have kneaded the dough as one must needs do." Then he asked me, "Did you add kvass to this dough?" What fear and shame came upon me when I heard this! I scarcely managed to answer that I had forgotten to add the kvass. But seeing that I was terrified, and being a sensible man, he began to console me with spiritual words: "Do not grieve over this," he said, "for it was not from contempt, but from your inexperience in this work that you have erred." He heated some water and poured it upon the dough, and he and I began to knead it, adding the kvass. With great difficulty we scarcely managed to knead it somewhat, though it was impossible to knead it thoroughly on account of its great hardness. Then, having given me instructions what to do, he went back to the forest. I waited a rather long time, and when I thought the dough had risen somewhat, I made it into loaves and placed them on the table. After sufficient time I built up the fire in the oven, and it grew so hot that it emitted sparks. I swept these up carefully and, allowing the oven to cool a little, though not as much as was necessary, I put the bread into it, thinking that it would bake well. But because of the oven's great heat it turned black forthwith and began to burn, and it was burnt nearly two fingerbreadths from the top and bottom. At a loss for what to do, I fell into great despair, firstly because through my ignorance I had made such a mess of things in the bakery of the holy hermitage, and secondly because the holy fathers would not find anything to eat when they came back from the forest. Taking the bread, then, completely burnt, from the oven, I awaited with fear the arrival of the brethren. And when they returned from the forest and saw what I, wretch that I was, had done in my ignorance, what great fear and shame came upon me! Not knowing what to do, I fell down at their holy feet with tears and asked forgiveness. The father superior and all the brethren, imitating Christ's mercy, forgave me. Cutting one of the loaves, they saw that it was in no wise fit to be eaten; and they boiled corn mush[76] and made a meal of this. No more did they bid me to bake the bread. But once having endured this, I thereafter watched diligently how the bread was baked and, with God's assistance, I learned to do this. I describe here how I suffered because of my inexperience in this matter for the sake of the brethren who come now to our community, that they may not be frightened because of their inexperience in this or a similar obedience. For through God's help and their own fervor they will be able to gain experience in the obediences assigned them.

Paisij declines ordination

Whilst I abode in that hermitage, the aforementioned most pious monk Father Dosyfej, came there to visit the brethren. He was a great zealot of the canons of the holy Church, and he had previously taught me much that was of profit to my soul. Seeing me, he took me aside and said to me, "Beloved brother in the Lord, if you will receive counsel from me, I shall give you this same in accordance with the purport of the sacred canons of the holy Church, to the benefit of your soul." I told him that I should in all certainty receive his counsel as from the mouth of God, and rejoicing greatly, he said to me, "I tell you, my brother: our common father and instructor, the elder and schemamonk Vasylij, had a disciple named Paisij, of blessed memory, who departed to the Lord three years ago. He had grown up with the elder from childhood, and the elder loved him very much, for he surpassed all others in the practice of Christ's commandments and in the right and true understanding of divine Scripture and the teaching of the holy fathers. Because of the serious lack of priests in his community, the elder persuaded this Paisij, though he was unwilling, to receive the rank of priest before the age established in the canons by the saints.[77] Upon his death, the elder grieved and wept very much, both because there was no other brother to be found like him, and because there was again a serious lack of priests. This our elder, then, will

76   мамалигȣ (Romanian *mămăligă*).
77   I.e., the age of thirty years.

soon come here to visit the brethren according to his custom; and when he sees you, he will surely want to take you to himself. Through confession he will enquire of you, as a spiritual father, whether there is any obstacle to you receiving the priesthood in accordance with the sacred canons. If you are found not to have any obstacle, he will by all means exhort you to go to live in his community; and if you go, because of the lack of priests, the elder and the brethren will forever exhort and urge you to receive the priesthood. And if you thus, even unwillingly, receive the priesthood before the proper time, you will never have peace of conscience in your lifetime on account of your transgression of the sacred canons, which the Holy Ghost established in the holy Church through the holy apostles, the holy general and local councils, and the holy fathers. Thus, in order that your conscience may always be at peace, I counsel you to strive with all your heart and soul to keep the sacred canons of the holy Church without transgression, as the apple of your eye. For this reason I give you the following counsel: if you trust that you will be able to observe the prescription of the sacred canons in the aforementioned matter, then go to live with our holy elder; if not, remain here, where the Lord will help you, at least until the age prescribed for the priesthood by the holy Church. Then, after you have attained the proper age, you may go off to live with the elder, and it will be of profit to you.'' He spoke these and many more words to me, and I thanked him for his counsel so full of profit to my soul. I told him that I had resolved, the Lord helping me, never to assume the rank of priest to my very death. Hearing this from me, he was gladdened, and he said, ''May God help you, my brother,'' and left me.

After a short time our common teacher and instructor, the most pious and holy elder and schemamonk Vasylij,[78] did indeed come there to visit the brethren. He had lived for a long time in Russia, and in the hills of Mošny, and in other deserted places with great zealots of the monastic life, and had then come with his disciple, the aforementioned most venerable elder Myxajil the hieromonk, to live in the land of Muntenia. This pious servant of God far surpassed everyone in his understanding of divine Scripture and the teaching of the holy fathers, in spiritual discernment, and in his thorough knowledge of the sacred canons of the holy Church and interpretation

[78] The elder Vasile of Poiana Mărului. Cf. Păcuraiu, *Istoria*, 2:579–80.

of them in accordance with the commentaries of Zonaras, Theodore Balsamon, and others.[79] The fame of his teaching and pious direction toward the path of salvation went out everywhere. When I saw him, I glorified God because He had deemed me worthy to see such a holy man. The father superior and the brethren received him with inexpressible joy, and with them I fell at his holy feet and was deemed worthy to kiss his holy right hand. And seeing me, he rejoiced greatly. After he had been there several days, he called Father Dometij, the superior, and bade him ask me in confession if there was anything to hinder me from receiving the priesthood. When, after I had revealed my conscience to the other, he learned that there was no great obstacle to hinder me from receiving the priesthood, he rejoiced, and bade the other by all means to exhort me to go live with him. Performing this obedience, Father Dometij diligently exhorted me to do this. But I retained the counsel of the aforementioned man firmly in my soul, and I kept silent, not agreeing to do this. The elder learned of this and, reasoning that I would not agree to go live with him lest I should somehow be compelled by him to receive the priesthood before the age prescribed by the holy Church, he promised me, through the other, that he would not compel me in this matter until the appropriate time, but would wait until the established age in all gladness. But I informed him through the other that even after I reached the proper age, if I was still alive, I had resolved never, to my very death, to assume such a fearful and terrible dignity. Being a man full of spiritual discernment, the elder attempted no more to call me, but left me free in my purpose. It was for this reason that I was not deemed worthy to live with such a holy man, for had I lived in obedience to him, I should certainly not have been able for long to avoid the dignity of the priesthood, which I feared and trembled at on account of my unworthiness.

Whilst the elder remained there I was several times deemed worthy to hear the words of profit to the soul, filled with spiritual discernment, which he spoke to the brethren; I profited greatly and it seemed to me that these were words of the life everlasting. After he had remained a short time, all the brethren having shown him hospitality as was the custom, he returned to his own abode.

[79]   In the collections of Nomocanons. Cf. e.g., Zapasko-Isajevyč, nos. 133, 140, 188, 351.

His friend Aleksij's adventurous story

Not long after the elder's departure there came the gladsome news that the aforementioned all-venerable elder Father Myxajil, the hieroschemamonk, and his disciple the hieromonk Aleksij and my beloved friend Aleksij were approaching the hermitage. Hearing this, the father superior and all the brethren in Christ rejoiced greatly and went out to meet him, and, falling at his holy feet, they were deemed worthy to receive his paternal blessing. I, too, wretch that I was, the very last of all of them, was deemed worthy to receive his blessing with inexpressible joy. Then, as was the custom, they went into the church and gave thanks to most merciful God for their safe arrival, and went out. Everyone was joyful and glad beyond expression. After their needs had been seen to, I called my beloved friend aside; and after we had given each other a kiss in the Lord, I begged him to tell me how the Lord had deemed him worthy to leave his homeland. With all gladness he told me in detail, saying, "O most beloved friend in the Lord," he said, "after that bitter parting, deserving of much weeping and sobbing, when my mother seized me by force and took me home, I felt such grief and unbearable sorrow in my soul that I fell into a feverish illness, and I besought God with tears, by the decrees which He knows, to take me, wretch that I was, from this world. And lo, by His almighty providence, one of the students from school, my beloved friend and namesake Aleksij, surnamed Meles', came to our house to visit me, unworthy that I was, having heard that I had fallen ill. He revealed to me that he had a longing for the monastic life not unlike my own. Hearing this, I rejoiced greatly and begged him to come visit me often; and whenever he came, out of his love for me, we took counsel concerning our departure from the world. By his advice, I concealed from my mother the aforementioned grief which I felt always in my soul, and she loved him greatly for this, for she thought that through his instruction I had given up my intention of becoming a monk, and she rejoiced in this exceedingly. We waited until the spring, my friend having taken diligent care for our departure. With God's assistance he found a foreign monk and, revealing to him our intention of leaving the world to become monks, he begged him fervently, for the love of God, to help us leave the world. Out of godly love and for the salvation of his own soul he promised to do this, and proposed that we should buy a boat, for by way of the Dnieper he could very easily take us to the monastery of Motronyn, which stood at a distance from the Dnieper. Hearing this I rejoiced greatly and glorified God who by His divine providence had arranged for us such an easy departure from the world.

"We bought a boat, then, and having taken the necessaries for travel and prayed in the church of Christ's hierarch Nicholas for a safe journey, we sat in the boat and went on our way; and merciful God, through the prayers of the hierarch Nicholas, at that very moment delivered me completely from the feverish illness. We sailed down the Dnieper without incident, but when we had passed Trypillja, we saw working men on patrol, and they called to us in a loud voice to come to them. We were greatly frightened lest upon careful examination we should be detained by them, for we had no documents concerning our journey. Unable to go past them, we rowed toward them with great fear, praying to God with all our souls that by His almighty providence He would prevent us from being detained by them. But as we drew near, the monk accompanying us looked at them carefully and, recognizing several of them, he said to us softly, 'God be with you. Do not fear: several of these men are acquaintances of mine.' When we reached them, they recognized the monk, and greeting him they asked, 'Where are you going in this boat, Father?' and he said, 'I have been sent a second time by the abbot to see to the administration of a certain village which belongs to St. Cyril's Monastery of the Holy Trinity; as you know, I have been sent there before.' This was indeed the truth, for the monk had lived for a short time in the aforementioned monastery, and his obedience had been the administration of that village. Then they asked him, 'And these who go with you, who are they?' He answered, 'These are my clerks, given to me for assistance by the abbot.' Having said this, he gave them each a good drink of vodka, pouring some more into a bottle for them: we had brought the vodka for just such a contingency; and he also gave them bread and other foodstuffs, as well as some money. Thanking him for this, they gladly let us go. Having left them we thanked God with tears for protecting us by His divine providence from any untoward occurrence.

"Sailing down the Dnieper we kept close to the bank on the right side, and after several days' sailing without incident we came ashore directly on the bank of the monastery of Motronyn. We sold the boat to some men who happened to be on the bank and made our way with inexpressible joy to the aforementioned monastery. When we arrived there, we received the customary blessing from the builder and founder of that holy abode, Father Ihnatij the schemamonk, and he received us with joy in the holy monastery until our intended departure for Moldavia, of which we informed him. With his blessing we went to the all-venerable hieroschemamonk Father Myxajil, who lived in a hermitage near the monastery. When he saw us he was filled with great joy and received us as a loving father does his spiritual children, keeping us by him, directing us through the word of God to the path of salvation and nourishing us doubly, both in our spiritual and bodily needs. I found there also those students from school, including my friend Myxej, with whom we crossed the border, as you know, when my mother forced me to return with her. With them I remained in the elder's hermitage and awaited our departure thence for Moldavia. When the long-expected time came, having made everything ready, our holy father and godly instructor took us to the all-venerable founder of the hermitage; and bidding him farewell, he asked his blessing for himself and for us on our journey, and we set out on our intended way. With God's assistance, then, we traversed the Ukraine and Moldavia and came without incident to this Orthodox and God-guarded land of Hungrovlachia,[80] to this holy elder's hermitage of Christ's hierarch Nicholas, called Trăisteni; and here I have been deemed worthy most joyfully to see you, my beloved Father and friend in the Lord, who arrived here before me and have joyfully awaited my coming. Likewise, I thank God with tears that I have also been deemed worthy to live in obedience with such a holy man, for after such a grievous, albeit temporary, separation, brought to pass by God's decrees, He has deemed me worthy not only to see you again, but also to dwell in the same abode with you.''

I listened to this with many tears, glorifying God, who by His wondrous decrees brings to fruition the intentions of those who truly desire monasticism, even if there should be divers obstacles, as those which had come to pass for my dearly beloved friend. For after my most sorrowful and involuntary separation from him, I was most joyfully deemed worthy to see him, contrary to all expectation. We conversed, then, about matters of spiritual profit to us both, and then we parted and went to perform holy general obedience. I was greatly amazed that as long as this my friend lived in the world he had been very weak and sickly in body, but after he left the world for

---

[80] I.e., Wallachia.

monasticism and lived in obedience in the aforementioned hermitage, he grew so healthy and strong in body that he performed even heavy work with great ease. He carried wood from the forest for the communal kitchen by himself, and it was of such great weight that I was terrified just watching him work. I thanked God for having given him such strength.

One day the all-venerable hieromonk Osija came there to visit the all-venerable elder and the brethren; he had been on the holy mount of Athos. After his visit, he received the elder's blessing upon leaving the hermitage, bade the brethren farewell, and set off. Having gone but a little way, he returned to find the elder and the brethren at table, and the three novices, my friend Aleksij and his two friends, Aleksij and Myxej, who stood before them. Said the elder Osija, "Holy fathers and brethren, abide with God! And you too, holy youths, abide with God!" And he went his way. The elder was amazed and said, "Holy fathers, he called these our three brethren simply 'holy youths,' but in so calling them he had in mind the first letters of their names, which are the same as those in the names of the the three holy youths, that is, Ananija, Azarija, and Mysajil,[81] and Aleksij, Aleksij, and Myxej." And when, in time, he tonsured these three as rasophores, he gave them these names, according to their age: Myxej, the eldest, was called Mysajil, the other Aleksij, Azarija, and my friend Aleksij, the youngest, Ananija. Thus was the hieromonk's prediction of their names fulfilled.

Disappointed by Aleksij's silence

Whilst I remained in that hermitage with my friend, before he was tonsured, I waited with great expectation for him to begin a conversation about the resolution which we had made whilst still in the world and which, indeed, we had made before God, in the Kievan Caves Monastery: that after our departure from our homeland we should remain inseparable from one another until our last breath. It was for this reason and no other that I had left the Caves Monastery: I abandoned my intention to end my days there in the expectation of remaining all my life with my like-minded friend, each of us rousing the other to zeal and monastic struggles and every good deed,

[81]   Cf. Dan. 3:12.

occupying ourselves ceaselessly in the reading of divine Scripture and the teaching of the holy fathers, and obtaining food and all necessities from the righteous work of our own hands.

I waited for such a conversation about this our resolution with inexpressible desire, but because of my unworthiness I was not deemed worthy to hear even a word about this before his tonsure or, moreover, after it. Seeing that he showed not a trace of being thus disposed, I was not a little amazed at how he had consigned our resolution to utter oblivion. Not knowing what to do, I partly regretted my departure from the Kievan Caves Monastery, inasmuch as, by God's unfathomable decrees, I was not to be deemed worthy to live out my poor life with my beloved friend. I durst in no wise remind him of the resolution which we had made before God, for in my youth I was wont to be extremely timorous and bashful, but I entrusted myself to the almighty providence of God, and I prayed to Him to do with my life as it pleased Him in His holy will.

Now my resolution to remain inseparably with my friend was not such that we should separate ourselves from the holy fathers and brethren in a place where we should remain without obedience to and counsel of a spiritual father, or that I should be his instructor—heaven forbid!—but that we should remain in obedience to a man inspired by God in holy Scripture and the teaching of our God-bearing fathers, rousing each other to every good deed. Such was my intention, not otherwise. But because of my unworthiness, I was not deemed worthy even of this.

Father Myxajil instructs the monks

I had not the slightest grievous thought against my friend because of my failure in this resolution, but attributed all the blame to my unworthiness. For the while I remained in that hermitage, performing general obedience and heeding diligently the words which came from the mouth of the hieroschemamonk and elder Myxajil of blessed memory. It was his custom on Sundays and feast days to sit on the grass under the orchard trees which had been planted round about the church. The brethren came and sat by the elder, and he would talk to them; and they listened to the elder's spiritual words with great attention and the fear of God, asking him many questions of their own. He answered these by means of his God-given spiritual understanding of the teaching of the holy fathers. He conversed on divers topics: for instance, how one must follow the catholic way of thinking and teaching of the one, holy catholic and apostolic Eastern church; or concerning the Orthodox faith and good works, that is, concerning the diligent keeping of Christ's soul-saving commandments, the traditions of the apostles, and the commandments of the church, as well as the observance of the holy fasts handed down by the apostles and all the church of God, and other requisites for salvation. These conversations so profitable to our souls took place not only on feast days, but also in the night, whenever it was illumined by the moon. Then the brethren would gather in the same place with the elder and converse until the middle of the night; and with them I, too, the least among them all, would sit, and listening to what was said, I rejoiced with inexpressible gladness and glorified God with tears because He had deemed me worthy in my youth to hear words filled with such spiritual profit from the mouth of such a spiritual man. These have been a source of instruction to me throughout my life.

Aleksij and friends take monastic orders

On the feast of the Dormition of the most holy Mother of God, after the all-venerable hieromonk Father Aleksij had served the divine liturgy, the aforementioned elder, the hieroschemamonk Myxajil, tonsured as rhasophores my friend Aleksij together with his aforementioned friends Aleksij and Myxej, and I was deemed worthy to be present and witness their tonsure. He gave them the names Ananija, Azarija, and Mysajil, though in the order aforementioned, taking their age into account. I rejoiced with great gladness that I had thus been deemed worthy to see my friend receive the first degree of the monastic state, that of rhasophore, which I then held, even though I had not been deemed worthy, on account of my unworthiness, to abide together with him in accordance with our resolution.

Paisij's predilection for grapes

At the appropriate season the venerable superior of the hermitage, Father Dometij, assigned me the obedience of tending the hermitage's vinyard, which was on level ground above the hermitage, at a distance of nearly one verst. He commanded me in no wise to dare eat any grapes until I had eaten at least a small piece of bread; but provided I ate the bread, he gave me his permission and blessing to eat as many grapes as I wished, before or after the daily meal. He did this for two reasons, firstly because grapes were few in the country where I was born, and I had scarcely ever had the chance to taste them, and secondly, out of indulgence to my weakness, for he realized that I had a great desire to eat grapes and that I could not get my fill of them. Having received his command and blessing, then, after eating a bit of bread, I ate grapes often, both before and after the meal, choosing the ones which grew sparsely, that is, not close together, for these were sweeter than the others. My passion for eating grapes came to such a pitch that I wanted no other food. When I went to the meal in the hermitage, I ate very little of anything else, but I ate grapes in abundance and with great relish. Having partaken of almost no other food that whole season until the harvest, I suffered no small illness of body, and my face grew thin as if from some disease. But after the harvest, when I ceased eating grapes and partook of the usual food with the brethren, I began to feel stronger day and night; and in a short time I was restored to my previous state of health.

Paisij fails to wake for matins

Before the grape harvest, the father superior had given me a cell on a stream not far from the hermitage. From this cell the church could not be seen. Whilst I was living there it happened once that I did not hear the banging on the gong for matins; it was Sunday. When I awoke, I went forthwith to the church, and I heard them read the Gospel and begin singing the Canon.[82] Not daring to enter the church out of shame, I returned to my cell lamenting and grieving over this unexpected trial which had befallen me. Such inexpressible grief came over me that I was in no wise able to go to the divine liturgy, and leaving my cell I sat on the ground and wept. After dismissal from the divine liturgy, when the time came for the meal, because the all-venerable elder and the superior and the brethren had not seen me at matins or at the divine liturgy, they wondered at my absence. "I pray you, for the Lord's sake," said the elder to the brethren, "wait a little for the meal, until we discover what has become of our brother Platon." Having said this he sent the monk Afanasij, a copier of the books of the fathers, in search of me. He found me without difficulty,

---

[82]   I.e., in the midst of matins.

weeping, and asked me the reason for my tears. Out of shame I could not answer him, still weeping; and after great exhortation from him I scarcely managed to tell him the reason for my grief. But he consoled me spiritually and begged me fervently not to grieve over this, and "to come quickly to the holy fathers in the hermitage who," he said, "await you before they will begin eating." I was scarcely able to speak to him: "Holy Father, how can I go to the holy fathers? How can I look them in the face after committing such an offense to my eternal shame before God and before them?" I begged him with tears to leave me and not compel me to go to the fathers. But he comforted me, fervently bidding me not grieve; and he prevailed upon me, though I was unwilling, to go to the hermitage. I rose, then, and went with him weeping and sobbing. When we arrived at the hermitage and I saw the elder and all the brethren sitting at table, what fear and immeasurable shame overcame me! I fell to the ground before them, weeping and sobbing inconsolably. The elder rose, and the superior and brethren raised me from the ground. When they learned from the monk who had brought me the reason for my weeping, the elder began to console me, like a loving father, with spiritual words, bidding and praying me not grieve over such an involuntary incident. Rendering thanks to God that they had found me, they began eating, and bade me sit with them at table and eat as well. But because of the shame which had overcome me I could in no wise eat. Even after they had risen from table I scarcely managed to eat even a little food. Thereafter, as long as I remained there, I durst never sleep at night lying down, fearing a similar incident, but slept what little I did sitting on a bench.

I have written this in order to rouse the holy fathers and brethren who abide with me, especially the young, to fervor in rising from their sleep and attendance of the holy offices. But woe is me, wretch that I am! For the following narrative will show how short-lived was my zeal for this in my youth, and how great was the sloth and insatiable desire for sleep to which I later succumbed.

Moving to the hermitage of Cîrnul

In the month of October there came to the aforementioned hermitage of Christ's hierarch Nicholas, where I abode, the all-venerable schemamonk Father Onufrij, from the hermitage of Christ's holy archangel Michael, called Cîrnul. That hermitage was in the mountains, above the river Buzău, at a distance of about two hours. Onufrij had also lived for a time in the wilderness of Moldavia and in the highest mountains of Hungrovlachia, but he now abode in the wilderness near the aforementioned hermitage, at about an hour's distance. He came now to visit our all-venerable elder, the hieroschemamonk Father Myxajil, and the father superior and the brethren. With the elder's blessing he conversed with the brethren, describing the beauty of the place where he abode, the salubrity of the air and water, and the other benefits of life, and he stirred a longing for the life there within my wretched breast. For I saw that there was no longer any hope of abiding together with my dearly beloved friend in accordance with the resolution we had made, and I thought of going to another place for a while, until the providence of God should bring all to pass for the good of my soul.

When the brethren learned that I intended to go to the other hermitage with the aforementioned schemamonk, several of them, namely my friend's two friends, Mysajil and Azarija, as well as Afanasij, a copier of the books of the fathers, and the aforementioned Jerofej from the hermitage of Condriţa, who had come to stay in our hermitage shortly before this time, and Symon of the monastery of Motronyn, also resolved to remove to the hermitage of Cîrnul. Seeing that we were all, save Father Symon, still young, the blessed elder and hieroschemamonk Father Myxajil, had mercy upon us and gave us his long-time disciple, the hieromonk Father Aleksij, for spiritual instruction throughout the winter. With tears we thanked that holy man for the great love he had shown us, and we thanked the father superior for having received us in his holy abode and lovingly kept us for so long a time. Then we received their blessings for the journey, and took our leave of the brethren, I especially of my beloved friend, weeping and lamenting my parting from him, and we set out upon our way through great forests and fields and beauteous mountains. With God's help we arrived on the third day at the aforementioned hermitage where the superior, the all-venerable hieromonk Father Feodosij, received us with all joy. After making the customary obeisance in the church and kissing the holy and venerable icons, we left the church and the father superior restored us from the toil of the journey with all the ease and comfort he could manage. In the morning he assigned us cells in the wilderness to live in, some near, others rather far off from the hermitage, and each of us went off to his cell. To me he gave a cell near the hermitage together with Father Azarija; and after I had lived there for a while, he gave me another on ground above the hermitage at a distance of about half a verst.

This hermitage was called Cîrnul. The church, not very large but exceedingly beautiful, was built of stone. It had been founded by the pious ruler of Hungrovlachia Ioan Mircea the voivode[83] in the name of Christ's archangel Michael. The air in that place was quite salubrious, and the water also very salubrious and light; there was a great stream which flowed constantly, as well as smaller ones with the same good water. There was an enormous apple orchard, where there grew as many as fifty different kinds of apples, an immeasurable multitude of the biggest and sweetest plums, a great abundance of Wallachian nuts, and every sort of vegetable in great abundance.

The elder Aleksij

The rule in this hermitage resembled that in use in the hermitages on Mount Athos: only on Sundays and feast days did the brethren gather for the offices in the church, and after the divine liturgy a common table was laid for all; but after vespers they all went to their separate cells and each said the office there by himself. Then, on the following Sunday or feast day, they gathered together again for the common office as described above. When someone happened to give charity, that is, for a requiem service on the fortieth day or some other donation, the superior and the brethren who lived near the hermitage would also then gather to sing the office in the church, but the other brethren who lived farther off would come as they wished, save on Sundays and feast days when, as said above, everyone gathered for the offices in church.

Whilst I remained there I went with the other brethren at an appropriate time to the all-venerable hieromonk Aleksij. Sometimes he would read to us from the books of the fathers and explain to us in lengthy conversations the purport of the words he read, and at others he spoke to us with the inspiration God had given him, instructing us with his spiritual counsel in every good deed, not only in word but in deed, for he was a meek and humble man, merciful and loving of his

---

[83] Mircea II, *vodă* 1543–1554 and 1558–1559. The hermitage was restored by Matei Băsarab (1632–1654). Cf. Păcurariu, *Istoria*, 2:217.

brethren. He had the gift of words of consolation and could comfort a soul afflicted with even the most terrible grief. At other times he would take us to the aforementioned venerable father Onufrij, the solitary who lived in a cell in the wilderness above the monastery at a distance of about half an hour. The way thither went through a beautiful forest, and his cell was on the summit of a mountain. From there one could see the rugged mountains in the distance, and the hills and valleys covered with great forests, and beneath his cell a stream flowed constantly, and thither he descended and ascended by stairs to draw water.

He occupied himself in prayer and reading and in psalmody and handiwork. His handiwork was of every sort: spoons, dishes, cups, and large and small baskets with lids made of linden bark. The brethren would sit round about him, and he told them in detail of his life in the farthest wildernesss. In the summer months he would go off thither, taking enough food to suffice for eight months, and during that time he would not see the face of any human being. To Father Aleksij he would impart yet other words of profit to the soul, and hearing these I, too, was deemed worthy of no small comfort to my soul. After sufficient conversation we took our leave of him and returned to our cells.

The elder Varfolomej

I remained there during the spring, and when summer drew near an order came from the all-venerable elder Father Myxajil to his disciple, the venerable father Aleksij, summoning him to return to him without fail and informing him that he intended going thence to Moldavia, to the hermitage of Poiana Voronă.[84] The elder then returned, and with him went also the monks Azarija and Misajil. I lamented greatly their parting from me, and took leave of them with many tears, asking the blessing of the all-venerable father Aleksij. I was left there, like an orphan, with Fathers Afanasij, Symon, and Jerofej, bereft of spiritual instruction. At that time the superior, Father Feodosij, also left the hermitage, and the brother of Father Onufrij the solitary, named Varfolomej, took his place. He had been a disciple of the all-venerable elder and hieroschemamonk Father Stefan from childhood,

---

[84]   In the *judeţul* of Botoşani. Cf. Iorga, *Istoria*, 2:179.

and had lived for many years in the wilderness in the region of
Černihiv. But when it was forbidden in Russia to live as a monk in
deserted places, he came to the land of Hungrovlachia together with
the all-venerable elder and schemamonk Vasylij and other zealots, and
settled in a hermitage called Valea Stiopului, where he ended his days.
Whilst there, he made his aforementioned disciple Varfolomej a hieromonk through the offices of the most holy bishop of Buzău. From that
hermitage, then, Father Onufrij brought his brother to be superior in
the hermitage of Cîrnul with the hierarch's blessing. When he
assumed the dignity of superior he treated the brethren with the
appropriate love, for he was a man who greatly loved all his brethren.
Since there was no cell there in which he could assemble the brethren
for conversations of profit to their souls, which might also be used for
a refectory, he began himself to work upon the building of such a cell;
and all the others, of their own free will, helped him in this construction as best they could. When they had finished this cell, we all often
took our ease in it together, sometimes in conversations of profit to
our souls, sometimes as a refectory. Instead of bread the brethren ate
only corn mush, both at common meals and by themselves; nor was
any fish ever to be found in that hermitage; only once in the whole
time I remained there did I chance to taste a bit of fish, the father superior having brought it from elsewhere.

The products of the hermitage's lands

In the spring I had sown a few haricot beans and broad beans and
onions. Because the onions had been sown in an inappropriate place,
they yielded but little. The broad beans grew profusely, but the mice
ate nearly all of them. I got one box of haricot beans. The apples and
plums grew in great abundance. All the brethren, together with the
superior, gathered the nuts and dried them, and then distributed them
equally among themselves, including the superior. One portion of all
the fruit was given to the superior for the use of guests. The many
apples which were left over after they had been gathered and distributed among the brethren, as well as the plums which had not been
gathered, of which there were a great many, were sold by the superior
for eight *lei*[85] to a merchant. He took away twelve carts of apples in

---

85   Romanian unit of currency (sing. *leu*).

all, and with sticks he shook down about fifty buckets of plums. For each of the brethren there were eight thousand nuts, and four or five sacks of the most beautiful dried plums. The brethren sold none of the nuts, and only some of the dried plums. The value of the nuts was four *paras*[86] to the thousand, and of the plums one *para* to every four okes.[87] Among themselves the brethren set aside four thousand of the nuts and, crushing them, divided the resulting four okes[88] of pure oil. Whenever any of the brethren lacked bread, they would, with the superior's blessing, ask pious Christians for maize and other grains, and these latter gave it willingly, with great fervor; and thus soliciting donations for themselves they gained their sustenance, praising God.

I obtained all the implements necessary for the making of spoons, and though I had scarcely learnt this handicraft, I worked very hard at it, even if there was no one to encourage me in this.

Having passed the winter in that hermitage, when the summer came, I went with the superior's blessing....

---

[86]   Turkish silver coin worth 1/40 piastre.
[87]   Turkish unit of weight (*okka*) equal to 2.75 lb.
[88]   The liquid oke was equal to 2/3 of a quart.

The *Biography* of Paisij Velyčkovs'kyj by Mytrofan

On the 15th day of the month of November: The Life and ascetic labors of our blessed father the elder Paisij: His flight from the world, his wanderings, the gathering of the brethren about him, and his life with them.

Introduction

The praising of noble men and weaving of crowns for them, and the extolling and exalting of their virtues is profitable and beneficial, and speaking of them to the best of one's ability wins over the listener. We see that worldly and transient things, which are visible only in matter, as well as praises of these things, disperse like smoke. Like the flame of a fire which disappears as soon as the matter is consumed, so the praises and honors paid to worldly things, which in pursuit of vanities very quickly dissolve into nothingness, disappear, according to Scripture, and their memorial is destroyed with a noise.[89] But we know that the lives of those who have lived a godly life and have shone forth in virtue are the cause of great profit, for the very praises of those who have heeded God rouse their hearers to imitation of the God-pleasing struggles being described; and to those who have chosen to write these praises is grace bestowed in return by the saints, as well as recompense and reward. Moreover, since God is pleased by such things, He bestows breadth of wisdom upon those who compose such praises. For praise of the saints is wont to pass on and be referred to God Himself. He says, "Them who honor me will I honor,"[90] and this is indeed meet, inasmuch as the Lord and Master of all thus clearly decrees, speaking of the apostles, "He that receiveth you receiveth me, and he that receiveth me receiveth Him that sent me."[91] For the laudations and praises of the saints do not take their beginning and foundation from things which are base and low and have nothing firm or certain in them, but from things of old which are divine and remain the same forever. As when one desires to erect a costly house: unless he first dig and excavate the earth, and lay a firm foundation, putting down hard rocks, he will see his construction

---

[89] Ps. 9:6.
[90] 1 Kings 2:30.
[91] Matt. 10:40.

come to naught. For the house will fall apart, and its small foundation will disappear with it. Thus must we think concerning those other praises and the lowly things set forth in them with all manner of show and vainglory by those who praise such things after the manner of secular wise men: they charm and delight only the ear with eloquence and adornment of speech. Wherefore praises of such things are given over to the abyss of oblivion, whereas the true memorials of the saints, laying down the foundations of virtues, derive their beginning from that imperishable chief cornerstone which is Christ.[92] It was in truth from thence that he who is now being praised, the radiant subject of this narrative, our blessed father Paisij, took his beginning and foundation, as the following narrative will show.

As for me, I learned from him, that is, I was his disciple and spent no short span of time with him; and having been his spiritual servant with all joy, I desire to compose an account for my brethren who have entered our community of late, who have not seen his face, and for the benefit of all others who will read it. Taking bits, then, from what I saw when I was with him and heard from his mouth, from his letters, and from the narrative in his own hand concerning himself and the community, which he began writing in his youth; and taking bits also from what I have heard from the brethren concerning his great accomplishments, I should have liked to adorn them in worthy language, whereby with praises I might have made a fitting offering to our father. But inasmuch as it is dear to God to do the best one can, and naught is deemed so praiseworthy by a teacher but that a disciple honor him in return for the debt he owes him, it is right that I should compose this account, my ability notwithstanding. Thus it behooves us to begin the narrative, putting our hope in the succor of the holy and divine prayers of our father of eternal memory. To the extent that it is possible I shall set forth the facts of his life with simplicity, as a choice relish, profitable to the soul, for those who live a godly life and embrace virtue, who practice truth and regard his accomplishments with zealous longing. Thus do I begin, having laid the foundation, and it is meet to attend that which will be said.[93]

---

[92]   Cf. Eph. 2:20.

[93]   Mytrofan borrowed this preface from the *Life* of St. Gregory of Sinai, apparently from a translation by Paisij. Cf. A.-E. N. Tachiaos, Ὁ Παΐσιος Βελιτσκόφσκι (*1722–1794*) καὶ ἡ ἀσκητικοφιλολολογικὴ σχολὴ τοῦ. Publications of the Institute of

Two years before the death of the great sovereign of blessed memory Peter the First, emperor and autocrat, the father of Russia and conquerer of many lands, that is, in the year 1722, this our blessed father, the hieroschemamonk Paisij, was born of noble Orthodox parents in the Ukrainian city of Poltava....[94]

* * *

On the way to Mt. Athos

Whilst he remained in the hermitage of Cîrnul he imitated the prudent bee. For the latter gathers from divers flowers and makes sweet honey, laying it up and sealing it in its treasury, and our blessed father, collecting the spiritual honey which flowed from the tongues of the holy fathers of old, delighted himself to satiety in it and, laying it up in the treasury of his heart, sealed it with silence for the time; and then he would delight and fill to satiety the souls of those who cleaved unto him in godly faith and obedience, rousing them to virtue. In that hermitage he learned what activity was, and vision, and true mental solitude. There he not only learned sobriety and attentiveness and mental prayer performed by the intellect in the heart, but also delighted in the divine and constant activity it causes in the heart.[95] For he would not have been able gratefully and easily to bear all the sorrow and extreme poverty which he endured as he abode in solitude there, nor to rejoice that he had been deemed worthy to imitate our Lord, who was poor in heart, had his own heart not been inflamed by divine prayer to the love of God and his neighbor. He had acquired these latter even in the beginning of his monastic life, like a divine seed, from his reading of the books of our God-bearing fathers. Dwelling there among those true ascetics he cultivated in his heart the keeping of God's commandments and the diligent practice of moral virtues and constant mental prayer; and shedding many tears he blossomed and shone forth with divine radiance of the mind, which filled

Balkan Studies, 73 (Thessalonica, 1964), 81–82; and Introduction, pp. xxix–xxx. For the Greek original, see I. Pomjalovskij, *Žitie iže vo svjatyx otca našego Grigorija Sinaita* (St. Petersburg, 1894) (=*Zapiski Istoriko-filologičeskogo fakul'teta Imperatorskogo Sanktpeterburgskogo universiteta* 35), 1–3.

[94]   See Introduction, p. xxx.
[95]   I.e., hesychast prayer.

his soul with ineffable joy and roused him to longing for spiritual struggles and utter solitude, as the hart earnestly desires the fountains of water.[96] Since, for the aforementioned reasons, he could not remain there with the holy fathers, though he desired this with all his heart, he visited and took leave of all of them who lived in the hermitage and those who abode in solitude without, asking their blessing for his journey and thanking them for the mercy and love and paternal spiritual instruction they had given him. What words, what prayers, what counsels did those holy fathers not employ! For they did not want to lose their companion in monastic struggle, whom among themselves they called the young elder. But then they prayed and blessed him and, entrusting him to God's will, dismissed him in peace. For who hath known the mind of the Lord, or who hath been His counselor,[97] when by His divine providence He took His true servant, our blessed father Paisij from his homeland, leading him through many countries in order that he might gain great spiritual wealth through spiritual commerce? When he came to these blessed Orthodox lands there were many rich spiritual merchants here, and seeing that he fervently desired to buy from them, they bestowed upon him without cost their precious spiritual pearls, for they knew that they would make the buyer rich and would themselves not lack for anything.

After he had collected the spiritual bounty here and filled the recesses of his heart, God's providence took the blessed one off to the holy mount of Athos, that he might also do commerce there, to increase his treasure and give unstintingly to all who had need of the profit of his spiritual teaching. In this way God's grace prepared him to become an imitator of our pious and God-bearing father Antonij of the Caves Monastery, his forefather and countryman, for the Ukraine[98] produced both of them. Just as our pious father Antonij traveled through many countries and came to the Holy Mountain, where he assumed the great and holy angelic monastic habit and lived for many years, having been deemed worthy of great spiritual gifts, and was then returned by God to his homeland, that he might implant and foster the monastic life there and create a city of heavenly inhabitants (as indeed came to pass, for by his teaching he enlightened those who

[96]   Ps. 41 (42):1.
[97]   Rom. 11:34.
[98]   *Malorossia.*

were in darkness and brought forth fruit unto God not by a hundred-fold, but by the thousands upon thousands), even so did our blessed father do in his life. He become rich in heavenly wealth, increasing his fruit even to sixty souls, and with these same he was brought back by God's grace to these God-guarded lands, that he might renew the enfeebled monastic life here by reviving the cenobitic rule, which had fallen into dissuetude, and implanting in it thrice-blessed obedience, and might enlighten with his teaching those who sat in the darkness of ignorance and bring them to understanding through the correction and translation anew from the Greek into his own language of the theological books of the fathers. But just as it is fitting, after one has left a subject, to return to it, so it is right that I should return to the the subject at hand.

Having visited all the holy fathers in the hermitages there, as well as those who dwelt in solitude, he took leave of them all and asked their blessing for his journey, thanking them for the mercy and love they had shown him. Then he went off to seek companions for the journey to the Holy Mountain. He hoped to find there an experienced spiritual father dwelling in solitude, to whom he intended to commit himself in obedience of soul and body for instruction in the spiritual life; otherwise, he would find a like-minded friend with whom he might live in careful attention to Scripture and the teaching of the God-bearing fathers, each helping the other to renounce his own will, and thus seeing some fruit of obedience in his soul, he might satisfy his longing. He had naught but twenty *paras*[99] for the journey, but he had no concern for this: just as he had done at the beginning of his travels, so now he put all his hope in the almighty providence of God and sought a traveling companion. He found a hieromonk by the name of Tryfon and, coming to an agreement with him, they took to the road rendering thanks to God.

When they reached Galați they embarked in a ship. How many privations, how many frightful, deadly incidents, from the sea, from hunger, from lice, and especially from brigands, did the blessed one suffer! When they arrived in the Imperial City[100] they rested there for several days, and finding other traveling companions they embarked in another ship. After several days' sailing with ease on a calm sea they

---

[99] Cf. above, n. 86.
[100] I.e., Constantinople.

came to the Holy Mountain, to the quay of the Great Laura. There
they disembarked and entered the holy Laura on the eve of the feast of
the holy Athanasius.[101] They stayed there, celebrating the feast and
rendering thanks to God, and restored themselves from the journey.
But who can relate the sorrowful story thereafter? Now, outside the
Monastery of the Pantocrator there dwelt certain brethren who spoke
the Ruthenian[102] language. The subjects of our narrative had to go
there in order to get counsel and instruction from their countrymen.
The Monastery of the Pantocrator was at a distance of eight hours
from the Laura. The journey there was very rough: the way was hilly
and rocky and went through much forest land. The heat of the sun at
that season was such that all the grass was scorched by the sun, as it is
in these lands by frost in winter. They were unaware of the customs
there, how one must protect oneself from the poisonous air of the
place; and even if anyone advised them to beware, it appeared
unnecessary to the newcomers from these parts.

Thus after they had left the Laura and had worked up a great
sweat, they rested in their sweaty clothes in the forest, sleeping on
stones in order to keep cool. They drank cold water on the way, not
knowing to avoid it, and they spent the night in their sweaty clothes in
the forest. And after a day and a night they fell sick with a deadly,
incurable disease. In great need they scarcely managed in their illness
to make their way to their brethren at the Monastery of the Pantocrator. When two of these latter saw the newcomers from their homeland
they rejoiced with great gladness at their coming, thinking that their
illness was due to the sea, this being much more easily cured. But
when they learned that they had fallen sick on the Holy Mountain they
lamented bitterly for their immanent death. What did they not try in
their desire to cure them! They lighted a fire to warm them, and they
rubbed and wiped them with spirits. They were able to warm our
blessed father somewhat before the fire, but they could not cure the
hieromonk Tryfon at all, save by summoning a confessor and giving
him to partake of the divine Mysteries. He died on the third day.

---

[101] The founder and patron saint of the Great Laura, commemorated on the fifth of
July. According to the *Life* by Platon (Tachiaos, *Revival*, 206), Paisij remained on
Athos for seventeen years. Since Platon also informs us that he and the brotherhood
left for Moldavia in 1763 (ibid., 207), he must have arrived on Athos in 1746.
[102] *russkii.*

What did these loving fathers do then for our blessed father? They prepared a good meal and forced him to eat, and to drink wine, which he had never drunk. When he swallowed it, his stomach was convulsed by the unaccustomed drink and he vomited. Again they forced him to drink wine, though he was unwilling, and again he vomited; and by vomiting he rid himself completely of the poison. Thus by God's mercy he regained his health over the course of several days. Afterwards he dwelt in a hut near the other brethren, and whilst he remained there he went round to the the monasteries and hermitages seeking a spiritual father who dwelt in solitude and attention to himself, to whom he might commit himself in obedience. But he found no one, for few of our Rus' brethren[103] there knew holy Scripture; and thus failing to obtain his soul's desire, he commended himself to God's providence and dwelt alone.

Ascetic experiences shared with companions

Who could count the prostrations upon his knees which he performed in solitude at night? And how great was the blessed one's abstinence! He ate only once each day, and then only a few rusks. His poverty was extreme: he had no garment save one cloak, and that a very old one, for he could not practice handiwork, lest he should take time away from the holy offices. His bed was a bare board. He delighted in his poverty as no one could delight in wealth. He thanked the Lord Christ always that he had been deemed worthy to imitate His poverty in every way. His ascetic struggles consisted in profound humility, constant self-reproach, gratefulness for everything, contrition of the heart and tears which ran in streams, ceaseless prayer of the heart, love of God and his neighbor, indelible remembrance of death, and the singing of the Psalms and reading of Scripture. From the Serbian monastery[104] he procured books to read. But he grieved and wept that he was deprived of the divine grace of obedience, having found no father who would receive him in obedience.

The blessed one remained in solitude and proceeded from spiri-

---

[103] *rossiiskogo naroda*
[104] Hilandar.

tual strength to strength, making ascents in his heart.[105] He was inflamed with divine zeal for greater struggles, delighting in solitude for two and a half years.[106] Then there came to the Holy Mountain a certain brother from the land of Muntenia who, after he had gone round to certain of the monasteries there, asked to be received by him in obedience. The blessed one did not even want to hear of becoming a superior to another: he wanted to commit himself to a superior, not to be a superior. This brother, however, besought him to receive him yet more fervently and with tears, and the blessed one, seeing such humility and tears on the other's part, was moved and agreed to receive him, not as a disciple, but as a companion. God then granted him a greater understanding of Scripture; and He granted them both to reveal His will to each other, to struggle for the keeping of His commandments and for every good deed, to renounce their will before each other, to obey and heed each other, to have one soul and one heart, and to have everything in common in the condition of their lives.

Thus they began to live in union of the soul, following the Royal Path.[107] This brother's name was Vysarijon. The blessed one rejoiced that by Christ's grace he had found the much-desired rest and consolation of his soul in obedience, through his and his companion's renunciation of their own will in the presence of each other; and in the place of a father or superior they had the teaching of the holy fathers. They dwelt in divine love. But they did not delight in such a life for long before other brethren who had left the world for monasticism saw the life they led, which greatly appealed to them, and longed with great zeal to take part in such a life. They began to importune the blessed one with fervent entreaties that he should receive them, to live with him and to be his disciples. For a long time the blessed one refused, fearing and trembling to receive them in discipleship, berating himself and saying to them, "This is a matter for those who are perfect and

---

[105] The goal of hesychastic prayer.

[106] The *Life* by Platon (Tachiaos, *Revival*, 193) relates that when Paisij was twenty-eight years old, thus in 1750, the elder Vasile (cf. above, n. 77) visited Athos and, at Paisij's request, "clothed him in the mantle," i.e., bestowed on him the second degree of monasticism, changing his name from Platon to Paisij.

[107] Also called the "Middle Path": the hesychastic term for the semi-eremitical life in small hermitages (sketes) where a monk might combine obedience to a superior with dedication to constant prayer.

without passion, whereas I am weak and full of passion.'' He would not receive them for a long time, but later, either because of their fervent entreaties, or else because he was won over by the tearful entreaties of the brother who lived with him, he began, albeit unwillingly, to accept them to live with him, revealing to each of them the power of holy obedience through holy Scripture and the teaching of the holy fathers. Seeing that they had ineffable faith and love for holy Scripture and for him, and peace and unanimity among themselves, and that they gave themselves over to him wholeheartedly in soul and body in blessed obedience, he rejoiced greatly in his soul on their account and praised God. He commended himself to the ineffable providence of God for their spiritual and bodily nourishment, receiving one after the other. It then became necessary to buy another hut, one which stood on higher ground, at a stone's throw from the lower one. But when the number of the brethren increased and there was no longer room enough in the two huts, they bought the Cell[108] of St. Constantine, which had a church, at a distance of about two stones' throws.

There was need of a priest, and the brethren began to importune him with fervent entreaty to accept the priesthood and dignity of confessor, but the blessed one in no wise desired this, saying that it was for this reason that he had fled from the aforementioned holy fathers in the land of Muntenia, lest he should have been forced by them, unwillingly, to accept the priesthood. But as often as the blessed one refused with tears, saying that he was unworthy of such a great dignity, the others again and again fell at his feet with tears, begging him and entreating him not to despise their request, presenting him with many sensible reasons. Furthermore, the venerable confessors of the Holy Mountain exhorted him with fervent entreaty not to refuse, saying that he would be guilty of disobedience if he despised their counsel, for they knew that he was worthy and able to bring many souls to the Lord through his instruction, to enlighten with his teaching those who sat in the darkness of ignorance, to invigorate the enfeebled cenobitic life, and to plant in it the tree of life—thrice-blessed obedience, the soul, as it were, of the cenobitic life. The aforementioned fathers would not relent in their entreaty and counsel, or in the charge of

---

[108] Greek κελλίον. Originally the cell of an individual hermit, this had grown into a hermitage for several monks (σκήτη).

disobedience, and they said to him, "How can you teach the brethren obedience and the renunciation of their will and discernment, when you yourself disobey and despise the counsel of so many who entreat you? From this it is clear that you love your own will and trust in your own discernment more than in that of those who are your elders both in years and in understanding. Do you not know what disobedience has wrought?" Then our blessed father, seeing himself to be in inescapable straits on all sides, though he did not wish to obey, said with tears, "God's will be done." And he was ordained to the priesthood and the dignity of confessor.[109] There was great rejoicing, not only among his spiritual children, but also among all the other monks of the Holy Mountain who had come to him before for the profit of their souls and to whom he would now also be a spiritual father.

The foundation of the Hermitage of Elijah the Prophet

During the years that the blessed one had lived in the huts with the brethren who spoke the Romanian language, they had read the holy office in that language. But after they had removed to the Cell of St. Constantine and had lived there for a time, brethren who spoke the Slavonic language began to join the community, and they began to read and sing the offices in church in that language as well, for they did not have all the neccesary church books in the Romanian. They lived a life of privation, obtaining their daily food from the labor of their hands. When the Lord increased the number of the brethren and there was no more room there (for there were already twelve brethren, seven who spoke Romanian and five Slavonic) and, moreover, other brethren importuned the blessed one with fervent entreaty to be received, the blessed one took counsel with the brethren and bought the empty Cell of Elijah the Prophet which belonged to the same Monastery of the Pantocrator. Putting all their hope in the providence of God, they began to build everything from the foundations: a church precinct, and cells around the precinct, all built of stone, through the donations of Christ-loving men and the boundless labor of the brethren. With God's help they built a very beautiful church, a refectory, a bakery, a kitchen, a reception room, and sixteen cells; and they

---

[109] According to the *Life* by Platon (Tachiaos, *Revival*, 201), Paisij was thirty-six years old when he was ordained priest.

made provisions to supply the hermitage with water. The blessed one was resolved in no wise to receive more than fifteen brethren, and hence the number of cells built. The Hermitage of Elijah the Prophet[110] stood at a distance of half an hour from the Cell of St. Constantine.

They all dwelt in common in the hermitage, thanking and glorifying God who by His inscrutable decrees and infinite mercy had blessed their progress from the Royal Path to the cenobitic life. They divided the holy office in church between the two languages: in one choir they read and sang in Slavonic, in the other in Romanian. Now the blessed one had hoped that after such boundless labor and concern for the construction of the hermitage he would be able to rest a little, but greater troubles came upon him. For many brethren of the Holy Mountain and those who had newly arrived from Russia[111] and from these lands[112] in their desire to serve God in the monastic habit, when they saw the good order of the reading and singing in church, the cenobitic obedience, the handiwork in solitude, the piety, peace, and love among the brethren, their humble dutifulness and faithful obedience to the blessed elder, and also his careful assignment of tasks, his compassion for those who were weak and sincere love for all—seeing all this, they wished to join in such a life. By their fervent entreaty and tearful petition one after another they persuaded him, though he was unwilling, to receive them. Commending himself to God's providence for their spiritual and bodily nourishment the blessed one received them, and seeing that they wholeheartedly gave themselves over soul and body in blessed obedience, he rejoiced. Not only did he not fear difficulty, but he was ready to give his life for the brethren.[113] Since they had no cells, the brethren by their own labor built cells beneath the hermitage, attaching them to the walls as swallows do their nests. Soon the number of the brethren increased greatly.

All of them, the blessed one too, toiled in handiwork, making spoons which they sold and thereby fed and provided for themselves, receiving and looking after visitors as well. Now our blessed father

---

[110] Paisij founded the Hermitage of St. Elijah in 1757. Cf. Pavlovskij, *Vseobščij putevoditel'*, 35–36.

[111] *s Rossii*, i.e., the Russian Empire, including the Hetmanate.

[112] I.e., Moldavia.

[113] Cf. John 10:15.

labored in handiwork, doing twice as much as the brethren, and at night he copied books. Throughout his life he kept a vigil at night, being unable to sleep more than three hours. He had besought this from the Lord in his youth.... I heard this from his own mouth. His fame spread throughout the Holy Mountain, and all held Paisij in honor and love, marveling at his divine gifts. Others came to him for the benefit of their souls, especially for confession, and there were always so many visitors that there was no time for his own brethren to tell him of their thoughts, and some of them were troubled. He was the confessor of many on the Holy Mountain, even of the most holy patriarch Seraphim,[114] who lived in the Monastery of the Pantocrator. He often came to the hermitage to visit the blessed one, and listened to him with delight. The blessed one was an example of the virtuous life to all on the Holy Mountain, and a new restorer of the cenobitic monastic life which had fallen into dissuetude, he was an instructor and teacher of divine obedience, a true leader to salvation for those in obedience to him, a new miracle.

An enemy of the hesychastic prayer

The devil was distressed when he saw that he had been defeated by the blessed one, and that many souls were snatched away from him by the other's mouth and brought to God by his teaching; this was unbearable to the evil one. The blessed one, protected by God's grace, was unassailable to him, but he found a Moldavian schemamonk, a certain Afanasij, whom he moved to envy; and through him he began to sow his evil tares in the ears of many, calling the blessed one not only a liar and deceiver, but also a heretic. Furthermore, he blasphemed holy mental prayer. The blessed one regarded this with forbearance, and he waited for it to develop. The fruit of evil flourished. It was not enough for this light-minded Moldavian Afanasij to slander the blessed one, but, marveling at transient fame, he was inflamed to greater envy against him, for he did not know that glory flees from those who pursue it, whereas it lies at the feet of those who

---

114 Seraphim I, patriarch of Constantinople 1733–1734, deposed and exiled to Mt. Athos. Cf. M. Gedeon, Πατριαχικοὶ πίνακες. Εἰδήσεις ἱστορικαί, βιογραφικαὶ περὶ τῶν πατριαρχῶν Κωνστατινουπόλεως ἀπὸ ᾿Ανδρέου τοῦ Πρωτοκλήτου μέχρις ᾿Ιωακείμ Γ᾿ τοῦ ἀπὸ Θεσσαλονίκης. 36–1884 (Constantinople, 1890), 632–34.

shun it and is the herald of their struggles and virtues.[115] He was roused to an unbearable pitch and sent the blessed one a letter, in the guise of friendly instruction in the beginning; but then there followed much vomit: abusive blasphemy and various other subtleties of his own, all contradictory to the holy Church and Orthodox faith. But he was bound by the very things whereby he desired to ensnare the blessed one: he dug a pit and fell into it; his trouble returned on his own head.[116]

When the blessed one received the letter from his pretended friend, he read it before the brethren, rejoicing in the beginning. But when he got to the middle, he began to weep bitterly for the other's ruin and was silent. Taking all into consideration, he went to his confessor and read him the letter. Then he and his confessor went to the other confessors. These latter took all into consideration and determined that the blessed one was innocent of the charges. Furthermore, they were grieved that the other had boasted that he would drive the blessed one from the Holy Mountain, and they commanded the blessed one to write a reply to him refuting his delusion. If he would not repent and ask forgiveness for his delusion, he would be condemned by a council. The blessed one did as the confessors bade him, refuting in sixteen chapters the other's ignorance and subtleties contradictory to the holy church, exposing his delusion, and disproving his blasphemies and slanders; and he sent it to him. When the other read it, he realized his sin and condemned himself in repentance; and he came to ask forgiveness. The blessed one forgave him and dismissed him in peace with words of instruction.

Paisij settles in Dragomirna

Whilst they remained in that hermitage, their number continued to increase, and the venerable monks of the Holy Mountain counseled the blessed one to occupy the Monastery of Simonopetra. This latter monastery was in debt and there were few brethren in it. The blessed

---

[115] Mytrofan is paraphrasing here from Paisij's translation of Homily 57 of St. Isaac the Syrian, in *Svjatago otca našego Isaaka Sirina episkopa byvšago ninevijskago, slova duxovno-podvižničeskija perevedennyja s grečeskago...* (Moscow, 1854), 340.
[116] See Ps. 7:15–16.

one presented a petition for this to the Council,[117] and its blessing was
soon granted. The blessed one removed to the monastery with half of
the brethren, leaving the rest in the hermitage. After he had been there
a short time, the creditors[118] heard that a community of monks had
gathered there and they came forthwith to demand the amount owed
them. The blessed one innocently paid seven hundred *lei*, but fearing
other creditors, he abandoned the monastery and returned to the hermitage.

Seeing the crowding of the brethren in the hermitage and the
difficulties of the place, he considered that such a large community as
his would not be able to establish itself on the Holy Mountain, in such
a difficult and harsh place. Furthermore, he feared the power of the
Hagarenes, lest they should impose on his poor community taxes similar to those of the other monasteries on the Holy Mountain.[119] He
heard from many that this would happen, and he feared, for these reasons and others, lest his community's way of life should be utterly
destroyed. Thus, he and the brethren took counsel and began to make
preparations. Seeing this, the most holy patriarch Seraphim and the
other monks of the Holy Mountain grieved greatly over the imminent
departure of the blessed one, and they exhorted and besought him not
to leave them; but they in no wise succeeded. The blessed one gathered all his community together and left the Holy Mountain, and he
came to this Orthodox land of Moldavia. For God in His providence
had taken His servant, our blessed father, to the holy Mountain of
Athos in order to show him there the true path of the monastic life,
that he might become an example of virtue to all and introduce the
cenobitic life, and then return here to confirm and enlighten and
instruct many in a life of virtue by his words and deeds. He came here
and was received by the pious governor and the most holy metropolitan, and they gave him the monastery of Dragomirna with all its pos-

---

[117] I.e., the council of monks which governs Mt. Athos.

[118] I.e., the Turks.

[119] By 1660 the taxes levied by the Turks on all the monasteries of Mt. Athos
amounted to 700,000 *aspra*. The next year it was decided by the council of monks
that every monastery would have to meet its own obligations, without help from the
others. Throughout the seventeenth and eighteenth centuries the monasteries often
had to borrow money from the Jews of Thessalonica or sell church plate in order to
pay the taxes. See E. Amand de Mendieta, *Mount Athos* (Berlin, 1972), 113–14.

sessions,[120] though it was poor in movable property on account of the many invasions and depredations of the barbarians. They found few books in it, and only five cells. The refectory was without a roof. There were six oxen. It was, however, extensive and quiet, and quite suitable for the community and the establishment of the cenobitic rule. The monastery was far removed from any secular dwellings, surrounded by a great and beautiful forest. It had many gardens, wherein grew all manner of vegetables; and there were fast-flowing streams. There was a mill before the gate, and an abundance of fodder for the beasts of burden kept by the monastery. At a distance of six hours, in the steppe, the monastery possessed choice hayfields, where the beasts grazed, and there were fields for sowing grain, and for apiaries as well.

The blessed one settled there with the brethren, and they thanked and praised God, for by His inscrutable decrees and His boundless mercy He had brought all to pass through the prayers of His servant, our blessed father, in such a way as they could not fathom with their minds. The most merciful Lord then inclined all to love and mercy for the strangers, and the pious voivode[121] became the first benefactor, building from the foundations two rows of cells, especially for the blessed elder, as well as a reception room; and he discharged the brethren from all taxes, confirming by letter that the monastery should be free of all imposts. Certain Christ-loving nobles donated beasts of burden, and others cows, sheep, and vines; others gave clothing and shoes, and still others wheat and wine. Other pious Christians gave whatever they could, of their own free will, for no one importuned them or required of them a donation: they themselves supplied these things with gladness, and rejoicing they thanked God for bringing His servant and the brethren to their pious land. They revered him and the brethren as angels and protectors of their land through their prayers.

---

[120] According to the *Life* by Platon (Tachiaos, *Revival*, 206–7), upon their arrival in Moldavia, Paisij and the brethren first lodged in the hermitage of Vărzăreşti (near Iaşi), where there was not enough room for them. Paisij then went to Iaşi to petition the metropolitan Gavriil (Callimachi, 1760–1786) and the hospodar Grigorie Callimachi (1761–1764; 1767–1769), and they granted him the monastery of Dragomirna. The year was 1763. Platon also relates that shortly afterwards Paisij's old friend Aleksij, now a hieroschemamonk in the hermitage of Poiana Mărului in Wallachia, came to Dragomirna and bestowed on Paisij the great *schema*. About the monastery of Dragomirna, near Suceava, see Păcurariu, *Istoria*, 2:109.

[121] I.e., the hospodar Grigorie Callimachi.

After our blessed father and the brethren had rested in the monastery from the toil of the journey, he began to establish an order for the cenobitic life in accordance with the rule of our God-bearing fathers: from that of the great Basil, whence the great Theodosius and Theodore the Stoudite, the leaders of the cenobitic life, took their rules. The blessed one did not create this rule from the start here, for he had already created and maintained such a rule years before on the Holy Mountain, but he made a new beginning here. He established the order of the holy offices in every way like that on the Holy Mountain, ordaining that the singing on the right side should be in Slavonic and on the left in Romanian. He ordained that none of the brethren should ever call anything "mine" or "yours," but should have in common everything given by God, for thus unanimity and love would thrive among them. Necessities were given to all in common, in order that obedience to the elder and to one another, and the renunciation of their own will and discernment, and dutifulness with the fear of God might be preserved.[122]

Life in Dragomirna

Within the monastery the obediences in the kitchen, bakery, and the rest were done by the brethren themselves, making no use of servants or hired men. The brethren were to perform handiworks necessary to life in fear of God, serving one another as they would the Lord Himself. Disobedience, contradiction of commands, and arbitrariness in tasks of general obedience, whereby the commandments of God were violated, were to be eliminated; piety, humility, unanimity, and love were to reign supreme in the community. Slanders, condemnations, envy, grumbling, and the bearing of grudges could have no place. Silence was to be kept, with prayer on the lips, during general obedience. The blessed one himself often went out with the brethren and worked alongside them in the fields and in other obediences, setting an example to all and ordaining that no one should be idle, for from idleness proceeds all evil. In their cells the brethren were to read the books of our God-bearing fathers and to maintain mental prayer, performing it mentally in their hearts, expertly and with care, even as

---

[122] Paisij's *Rule* is still unpublished. Cf. Hieromonk Leonid, "Literaturnoe nasledstvo Paisija Veličkovskogo," *Žurnal Moskovskoj patriarxii*, 1957, pt. 4:58 n. 4.

their breathing, for this is the true source of the love of God and of one's neighbor and of every virtue. The brethren were to make confession of their thoughts every evening, either to the blessed one himself or to the confessors appointed for this; and the brethren were to be under their supervision, knowing that this is the foundation of salvation, peace, quiet, and common love. These and all the other rules for the brethren were established by the blessed one in accordance with the rule of the holy and great Basil and the other fathers who lived the cenobitic life, and he ordained that they should be kept without violation. Upon all his spiritual children our blessed father poured out his paternal mercy, fostering them in sincere love, even as a hen warms her nest, assigning the obediences with careful attention, according to each brother's ability; and he showed compassion for illness, healing the sick in the infirmary, and giving them rest with all solicitude, suffering with them as if he himself were ill.

When the time for reaping came, he assigned the obedience of reaping the wheat in the steppe sometimes to seventy, sometimes to eighty, of the brethren, for they reaped and ground the wheat and other grains by themselves with the horses every year. With them he sent also a confessor who said the holy office and saw to other spiritual needs, keeping the divine Sacrament by him. He often sent a doctor also. And our blessed father himself would come to visit his spiritual children, remaining with us for three or four days. Blessing our labors, he consoled himself, and he consoled us and counted us blessed, for by our labor we imitated the holy fathers of Egypt of old who went out every year to reap. Thus having instructed us concerning obedience and labor, unanimity and love, patience and gratitude, and concerning the confession of our thoughts, he would depart rejoicing and rendering thanks to God that he had seen us and our obedience, praying that God should strengthen us through His grace, that we might complete the task and return in good health to the monastery. Bidding him farewell and kissing his hands and feet, we returned rejoicing and glorifying God, who had deemed us worthy of seeing the angelic face of our father on his visit to us, and we shed joyous tears out of our love for him. As many as had become ill from the labor and the heat of the sun were made healthy by his visit; and as many as had grown weak out of faintheartedness toward labor, even as that man of old who was healed by the Lord and took up his bed and

walked and glorified God,[123] so did these brethren forget their faintheartedness: rising from their despair as from a bed, they took up their
sickles and cried out, "Rise up, brethren, let us to our obedience go!"
They all took up their sickles and brandished them, and the glitter of
the sickles shone like the weapons of soldiers going off to war; and
they said to one another, "Let us strive, brethren, that strengthened by
the prayers of our holy father we may finish quickly and return to the
monastery." Thus they spurred one another on to work, striving diligently to the end and forgetting their illnesses and weaknesses in their
joy.

Our blessed elder commanded that we should enjoy all manner
of rest there, so much so that rarely did we rest in the monastery, even
on feast days, as we did every day in that place. When we had reaped
a certain part of the wheat, forthwith those brethren who had been so
assigned made a threshing floor and began the threshing. Having
cleaned the new wheat, we ground it and baked fresh bread. When the
reaping was finished, ten brethren remained to do the grinding with
the horses until the completion of the obedience, which occupied
another fortnight. All of the rest of us then left and returned to the
monastery, thanking and glorifying God who had given us the strength
to complete the obedience. The journey took seven hours by horse,
ten by ox. When the others had finished the grinding, all of the
brethren assembled in the monastery.

Spiritual instructor and teacher

Our blessed elder always instructed the brethren who came to
him in his cell in matters of bodily and spiritual need, explaining the
power of God's commandments and imparting an understanding of
holy obedience from holy Scripture and the teaching of our holy
fathers, and exhorted and spurred them on to every good deed. He did
this especially when all the brethren assembled after the completion of
their obediences in the fields upon the advent of the holy fast of
Christ's Nativity.[124] He would begin his admonition of the assembled
brethren in the first week of this fast, and continued until the Saturday

---

123   Cf. Matt 9:2–7.
124   The fifteenth of November.

of Lazarus,[125] unless some illness in the winter interrupted. Every
evening except on Sundays and feast days the brethren assembled in
the refectory, candles were lighted, and our blessed father would come
sit in his accustomed place and would read a book of the fathers:
either that of St. Basil the Great on fasting, or of St. John Climacus, or
of St. Dorotheus, or of St. Theodore the Stoudite. One evening the
reading would be in Ruthenian,[126] and the brethren who spoke
Romanian would read complin; the next evening the reading would be
in Romanian, and the brethren who spoke Ruthenian would read
complin. If anyone knew both languages he would attend both readings. The blessed one would use one book in one language, and
another in the other, though sometimes he used the same for both
languages. In his commentary he would cite testimony from holy
Scripture and from the teaching of our God-bearing fathers. In the
course of each reading he would present some moral admonition for
the correction of whatever offences had been committed, obliquely
exposing them in order that those who had committed them might be
ashamed and repent, and the others might beware such inclinations.
Thus he benefited all, correcting some and protecting others. His
commentary was such that the simplest of the brethren could understand the purport of his words. Our holy father had such a gift that he
could rouse the most despondent of the brethren to zeal and could console the most mournful. If he was unable to conciliate a brother with
his words, he did so with his tears: no one went away from him
without healing. Who could describe his eloquence? We would all
have been ready to stand before him every day in order to enjoy the
sight of his countenence and the great sweetness of his words. The
discernment of this blessed man was such that whenever a brother
came to his cell, after he had formed an understanding of the other's
problem, he gave him his blessing and began speaking to him, divert-
ing the other's thoughts with his sweet words, not allowing him to
talk. His conversation took into account the character and temperament of the brother, or his skill in reasoning, and introduced some
lofty words from Scripture and commentary upon them; to this he
would add something else sublime, combining it with the simplest of
things from the brother's craft or work. Thus he altered the other's

---

[125] The Saturday before Palm Sunday.
[126] *russkii* in the original, although the readings were most probably in Slavonic.

state of mind and comforted him so greatly that he forgot himself, in the sweetness of the blessed one's words, and the very reason for which he had come. Then reflecting within himself, the brother would see that his soul was filled with peace and joy, that the darkness and grief which had been there had vanished like smoke in the wind, and he remembered nothing. Upon receiving the elder's blessing, he would depart rejoicing and thanking God. This happened also to me, many times.

Now the foundation of the blessed one's teaching was that all the brethren, with all their heart and soul, should strive zealously to keep the commandments of God and the traditions of the holy fathers. If some quarrel arose among them, there was to be ceaseless and sincere reconciliation all the day long, according to Scripture: "Let not the sun go down upon your wrath."[127] If anyone grew harsh and was unwilling to be reconciled, the blessed one would separate him from the rest, forbidding him to cross the threshold of the church or to read the "Our Father, which art in heaven...."[128] He would make himself appear as a harsh judge against such a disobedient brother, for though he was very meek and approachable to all, he provided for salvation by all means, according to the Apostle, right and left.[129] To obedience outside the monastery he assigned only those of the brethren from whom no scandal might result, and whose souls might not suffer harm. If there was any matter which would result in the violation of God's commandments, he ordered that it should cease, and that it was better that it should not be done, rather than violate God's commandments and incur eternal condemnation. He strove always that there might be peace and love among the brethren, as well as the renunciation by each of his own will and discernment before the others. If there happened to be a disagreement about something, he would make it an obedience for the one who had disagreed to yield, that there might not be a quarrel, from which enmity and grudges would result. In the event that his commands were not obeyed, others of the brethren were simply to report this to him, for the sake of the brother's correction, not revenge; and he would correct him according to the understanding given him by God.

[127]   Eph. 4:26.
[128]   Matt. 6:9.
[129]   Cf. 2 Cor. 6:7.

Our blessed father toiled day and night. All the day long he directed spiritual matters and the external economic affairs of the monastery, and sometimes the doors of his cell were not closed until the tenth hour. Some of the brethren came to him because of bodily needs, others because of spiritual ones: with one he would weep, having corrected him, and with another he would rejoice, as if he had never felt any sorrow. This blessed man was like an innocent child in the temperament of his soul: he was in truth free of passion and holy. I lived in his company for thirty years (I did go off to the Holy Mountain for some time, but I returned to him), and I never saw him grieve when he was told anything, even if some great calamity had occurred. He was grieved only when he saw others transgress the commandments of God; he would have given his life for the slightest of the Lord's commandments, and he was like fire against those who did not keep them. He would say, "Let everything be destroyed, even our bodies, but the commandments of God must be kept."

The monks' spiritual endeavors

Throughout his whole life every night was a vigil for the blessed one. All night long he would translate from the Greek into the Slavonic books of the fathers and of theology which theretofore had not existed in our language. The blessed one greatly loved the reading of books and exhorted us to the copying and reading of them and to other spiritual struggles.

And in our monastery one saw a cenobitic monastic life which bore traces of the cenobitic life of the holy fathers of old. To the extent that we were able, weak as we were, we strove to follow and emulate them and preserve their rule in these wretched times deserving of weeping and sobbing. The brethren had completed all the necessary structures: a second, warm church (for the main church was very cold), cells, a reception room, an infirmary, and the rest. Entrance to the monastery was forbidden to the female sex. After they had rested a little, the brethren began to practice ascetic labors and urge one another on to the love of the Lord and the keeping of His life-giving commandments: to cleave to their father in godly faith and love, to carry out his teaching in their actions, to renounce their own will and discernment before him and before one another, to strive to be of one soul and one heart with their father and all the brethren, and to perform their obedience with the fear of God. They were to be diligent in preserving prayer in their mind with all their heart, praying seriously and expertly. They were to strive for every good deed and progress in spiritual struggles through the grace of Christ. And within the community there was sinless robbery and spiritual plundering among the brethren, for those who robbed abounded in good things, and he who was robbed was not impoverished; those who plundered got rich, and he who was plundered possessed his treasure entire. They all enriched one another and joyously gave leave to whoever wanted to plunder. One plundered humility from another, and that one obedience from yet another. One robbed another of the renunciation of one's own will, and that one in turn robbed him of self-reproach and tears. One robbed another of patience in time of repraoch and trial, and that one yet another of the remembrance of death and fear of God. One robbed another of brotherly love, and that one yet another of silence and gentleness. They would delight and rejoice in such enviless battle and praised God. Our blessed elder rejoiced also, seeing his spiritual children so earnestly struggling, and thanking God with tears, he prayed that He might strengthen them through His grace for even greater struggles. Admonishing them ceaselessly, he urged them on to greater struggles and fervor, saying, ''Be not downcast in making your purchases, my children, now is the accepted time; now is the day of salvation.''[130]

Disorder resulting from the Russo-Turkish War

Whilst we thus dwelt there, lo, there arose a dreadful storm and a terrible conflagration: the whole of the world was consumed, the mountains, forests, and steppe were in flames. For the two greatest empires on earth, the Russian and the Turkish, were at war with each other,[131] and the Moldavian and Muntenian lands were shaken; their inhabitants trembled with fear of death and scattered, and the mountains, forests, and monasteries were filled with them. Noblemen and commoners who had become refugees contended with one another for a place where they might hide from the Turks and Tatars. Ours was the best fortified monastery in all Moldavia, situated in a great forest and an inaccessible place, and now, in the first weeks of the fast of

[130]   2 Cor. 6:2.
[131]   The Russo-Turkish War of 1768–1774.

Christ's Nativity a countless multitude of people, rich and poor, came running to us, considering the protection of the prayers of the blessed one and all the community better than the strongest fortress. They so filled the monastery that it was impossible to walk about, and likewise the forest surrounding the monastery. When the elder saw the inexpressible privations and poverty of the people, for it was winter and there was snow, and they were half-naked and barefooted, having escaped only with their lives and their children, he gave over half of the monastery to them, keeping half for the brethren. There were then three or four or even five brethren to a cell where there had been only one before. The refectory was large and warm, and he gave this over to the simple people, especially poor women.

Like a father, the blessed one felt compassion for all of them. He poured out his mercy upon all as though he suffered with them and was himself in need. He ordered the cellarer, the baker, the cook, and the other brethren who saw to the foodstuffs that they should give without reluctance whatever food they had to all who came and asked, regardless of who asked for what, whether he was staying inside the monastery or outside, whosoever might come. Some took away raw food and cooked it themselves, others warmed the prepared food and bread which the brethren ate and took this away for themselves. The brethren were constantly baking bread and cooking food in their desire to take care of those in need. The nobles took wine also. Here one saw the grace of God operating through the prayers of the blessed one, for the foodstuffs and beverages which the brethren had laid up for themselves for a year sufficed for this great multitude of the needy, as well as us, during the necessary period. This great throng inside and outside the monastery remained for nearly fifty days before they went off to their homes, though the nobles remained in the monastery. For the light of God's grace shone, and the moon was obscured, and the enemy were thrown into confusion and fled in terror. Directly the Russian army had entered Moldavia, the godless Hagarenes trembled and took flight. The people returned to their homes without fear, rejoicing and praising God, though the nobles were frightened and stayed in the monastery more than a year.

When by the mercy of God we were delivered from fear of the Turks, and all strangers left the monastery, we again enjoyed peace. But not long afterwards there came new troubles: a new disease and mortal fear, the plague, and with it also a three-year dearth of grain.

By God's grace these pestilences also passed, and we regained quiet and returned to our former way of life.

After six years of war, peace was made between Russia and the Ottoman Porte.[132] But when the Russian army returned to its homeland from Moldavia, the Roman[133] empress Maria Teresa began forthwith to demand from the Porte that part of the Moldavian land which had been promised to her for the help she had given in the war against Russia; and this was given her. The Moldavian and German[134] rulers began to fix the border, and our monastery stood at a distance of three hours from it. Now, even before this time the devil had always set his wily snares, and he might well have wreaked havoc upon the community and brought our blessed father to grief, had God's grace not protected them through the blessed one's prayers, preventing the evil one from finding help. But now he found the Germans, and with his legions he dwelt in them and roused them to seize more land than had been apportioned to them, in order that they might also seize control of the monastery of Dragomirna. The wily Germans extended their border with this purpose, but the Moldavian nobles would not agree to this, conceding to them no more than what had been apportioned to them, for they wished to defend the monastery and to protect the blessed elder and the community. They were unable, however, to resist the great power. They then resorted to entreaties and promises. What words did they not employ? What presents did they not give? But they were unable to prevail, and the monastery was left completly in the power of the Germans.[135]

Paisij receives the monastery of Secu

Our blessed elder then shed many tears, and the brethren also, and they grieved for the monastery. It had grown very beautiful during its inhabitation by the community of brethren. They wept for the destruction of their labor, for they had shed bloody sweat in the construction of the cells and other necessary things, and it was now under

---

[132] The Treaty of Küçük Kaynarca (1774).

[133] I.e., Holy Roman.

[134] I.e., Austrian.

[135] The Austrians severely curtailed the rights and privileges of the Orthodox monasteries in Bucovina, which remained under military rule until 1786, when it was united with Galicia (until 1849). See Iorga, *Istoria*, 2:166–73.

the control of heretics with whom there could never be peace; great havoc would now befall the brethren, and bloody toil, and it would be difficult to escape from the Germans. They wrote a letter to the most holy metropolitan and to the pious governor Grigorie Ghica,[136] complaining that they would be unable to live under the power of the Papists[137] and asking that they should mercifully grant them the monastery of Secu.[138] The metropolitan and governor felt great compassion for our blessed father and the community of brethren and granted them the monastery which they requested, confirming the grant with an official letter. After the blessed one received the letter, he took care for the removal of the church furnishings; and with God's assistance, they removed everything through the good will of the guards. Then the brethren left, under the guise of being sent on obediences. One hundred and fifty of them remained in the monastery, and our blessed father also left there two confessors, one who spoke Romanian and the other Ruthenian, making the former a sort of abbot, in order that he might deal with the authorities and direct affairs in Romanian; the other was to assist him for the time. He did this lest there should be any trouble if he left the monastery empty straightway, and also because there were few cells in Secu. When the elder had disposed and arranged everything as was fitting, he went to the church, weeping bitter tears and sobbing, to pray to the Lord, reluctant to leave the monastery and the remaining brethren. Giving them the peace and his blessing he took to the road. Arriving at the border, he gave the Germans to believe that we were only going as far as the mill, and they allowed him to cross the river. Then he waited by the mill until all the brethren whom he had sent off, as if on obediences, should assemble. When they had all assembled they departed thence and arrived at the monastery of Secu on the fifteenth day of the month of October in the year 1775, and thanking God with tears, they established themselves there. The brethren then in the community numbered a little more than two hundred, apart from the novices not yet tonsured. One hundred and fifty had remained in Dragomirna with

---

[136] Grigorie-Alexandru Ghica, hospodar of Moldavia 1764–1767 and 1774–1777. The metropolitan was still Gavriil Callimachi (1760–1786).

[137] *papistami.*

[138] In the Carpathian Mountains in southern Moldavia, not far from the monastery of Neamţ, see below, n. 140.

their elder spiritual brethren, one of whom spoke Ruthenian and the other Romanian, as confessors. But just as children by the flesh whose parents have left home for the time, though they may be comforted by their elder brethren with loving words and the expectation of their parents' return, almost never cease weeping, nor find the food given them sweet, keeping their tearful eyes constantly upon the road by which they will see their parents return home, when they will rejoice in the sight of their faces and in their sweet conversation— incomparably greater was the constant grief and bitter sighing of the brethren who were left in the monastery in Dragomirna because of their ardent love and godly faith in their holy father, even though they were comforted and consoled by the loving spiritual words of their elder brethren and confessors and by the expectation of their immanent departure to the place where their blessed father was. They looked upon the road by which he had departed from them and wept for the loss of the sight of his holy face, the light of their eyes as it were, and of his sweet spiritual conversation, the joy and delight of their hearts. They constantly imagined to themselves the face of the beloved one, some deriving solace from this, others grieving all the more. To some the blessed one appeared in their sleep, consoling them with the expectation of the imminent reunion of all the brethren in the monastery of Secu.

But how great was the grief and weeping of the blessed one himself because of his separation and the division of his beloved spiritual children? For he no longer saw them all before him. When in times past he had looked upon them all, he thought he saw angels of God, and his holy soul was filled with ineffable spiritual joy out of his love for the brethren. He would say, "I fit you all within myself without crowding, in imitation of the holy apostle Paul, who said to the Corinthians, 'Ye are not straitened in us.'"[139] Such was the love of our holy father for us and for all Christians. In his instruction to us the blessed one many times said also this: "When I see my spiritual children struggling and striving to keep God's commandments, to renounce their own will, disregard their own discernment, and progress in their obedience with the fear of God, I feel in my soul such an ineffable spiritual joy that I could desire no greater joy in the Kingdom of Heaven. But if I see any of them neglecting God's

[139] 2 Cor. 6:12.

commandments, following their own will, trusting their own discernment, despising divine obedience, stricken with sloth through arbitrariness and self-gratification, and filled with grumbling, then such great grief seizes my soul that it could not be worse for me if I were in hell, until I see that they have repented and corrected themselves.''

Difficulties in Secu

The brethren who remained in Dragomirna had cells enough to live in, but those who had come with the blessed father to the monastery of Secu endured great privation because of the lack of cells. There were in all only fourteen cells, and there were more than fifty brethren, in addition to several old monks of Secu. They crowded, three, four, even five of them into each cell, and they endured terrible, terrible sufferings throughout the winter. Their one and only consolation and joy was the sight of the face of their holy father, and his spiritual instruction lightened every grief and the crowding, and they endured all that befell them glorifying God. When the spring came the brethren from Dragomirna began removing to Secu, and then the crowding was so great that they had nowhere to lay their heads.

Again there was grief and confusion, seeing that they were to suffer the spiritual harm which would result from the immense labor of the construction of cells. But there was no avoiding this: they had to build them with their own hands. Commending themselves, therefore, to God's help and the prayers of their blessed father, they began work. Some built cells in the towers within the monastery, others attached them to the walls like swallows' nests, others built them outside the monastery because of the lack of space within, and still others in the forest. They shed their sweat in their toil. The blessed elder helped also by giving each of them money, in order that they might find workers from among the laymen to help them. For three years the brethren took care and concerned themselves with the founding and construction of cells, some living two to a cell, others alone. With their own hands they built as many as one hundred cells, within the monastery and without. And then the brethren were reunited, only a few remaining in Dragomirna.

They left the monastery of Dragomirna, then, giving it over to the Germans as it behooved them to do, and they all came to the monastery of Secu, where the church was dedicated to the feast of the Decollation of the holy Prophet and Forerunner John the Baptist. The

brethren then had nearly a year's respite from the immense toil and
labor of constructing the cells. The place was very peaceful and quiet:
on both sides there were mountains covered with forest, and below
there was a small river on which the monastery was built, in a valley
between the mountains. The founder of the monastery, of blessed
memory,[140] in provision for the safety of its inhabitants from attacks
by the barbarians, the Turks and Tatars, had made it very difficult of
access from the level plain and the other river into which the one near
the monastery flowed, for the way to it was very difficult and rough,
over the mountains, across the river, and through a great and dense
forest; it was in no wise possible to approach it by road. The journey
was made unavoidably troublesome: first one had to cross the other,
larger river called the Neamţ, which flowed through the foothills and
upon which stood the monastery's mill; thence, from the level plain,
began the path to the monastery through a great and dense forest in the
mountains, crossing in five places the second river which flowed down
from the mountains, called the Secu. The journey on the rough path
from the level field and the mill to the monastery took three hours by
oxcart when it was dry; but when the rivers, which were swift and
rocky, were swollen by the frequent rains in that place, washing out
the path, and in wintertime, the journey took six hours for those who
toiled greatly to bring necessities to the monastery from the plain or
flour from the mill. This journey was accomplished with great loss
and even fatal accidents, especially on the first river, the Neamţ, for it
was wide and in it there were many rocks, large and small; the current
was very swift, and it easily overturned and carried downstream the
oxcarts and men, and, in mortal fear, they scarcely escaped drowning.
There was constant need to travel this path, especially to the mill. But
in spite of all the difficulties and great privations, the blessed elder and
the brethren were grateful, for the place was peaceful and quiet. Even
though the church was small and could not hold such a large community, they nevertheless persevered in expectation of the renovation of
another, warm church in the refectory. The blessed one was content
that no one importuned him with visits, for though all of the great
nobles wholeheartedly desired to visit and see the holy man, in order

---

[140]   The monastery was founded by the elder Zosima and his disciples from Neamţ in
the sixteenth century, and the buildings erected by the boyar Nestor Ureche in 1595.
See Četverikov, *Moldavskij starec*, 173.

to be deemed worthy of his blessing and enjoy his spiritual conversation, they feared the rough and difficult journey.

Remaining in Secu, then, after we rested somewhat from the care and labor of the construction of cells, we dwelt in solitude, pursuing the spiritual life which we had had formerly but had lost as a result of the troubles with the Germans, the removal to Secu, and the three-year effort of the construction of cells and resulting toil and tumult. We thanked God for our return to solitude, and seeing us progress in our spiritual struggles, rousing one another to ascetic achievement, the blessed father rejoiced.

The community grew day by day, for the blessed one could in no wise refuse to receive those who came in tears, entreating him to receive them in obedience and discipleship. What did he not propose, what did he not invoke in order to dissuade them? The lack of cells. The difficulty of obedience. The want of bodily necessities. The scarcity of everything. But whenever he refused and dismissed them, they would fall to his feet again and again, weeping and sobbing, begging to be received. Persuaded by their tears, our merciful father, who was filled with love for his neighbor, would receive them. Thus he fulfilled the word of the Gospel: "Him that cometh to me I will in no wise cast out,"[141] for he received all, revealed God's will to all, and set all upon the path of salvation. Throughout the winter he would gather all the community in the refectory and would admonish them from Scripture in the keeping of God's commandments and in obedience and other spiritual struggles. One evening the admonition would be in the Slavonic language, the next in the Romanian. Likewise, his conversation in his cell was always on the same subject, and he commended himself to God's providence for his bodily and spiritual nourishment.

Thus through his teaching the brethren returned to the spiritual life they had had formerly in Dragomirna, and through God's grace and the blessed one's prayers they attained peace and progressed in their spiritual struggles. Our blessed father, too, was quite at peace in Secu. He thanked God with tears for having delivered him unharmed from the dominion of the Papists, and he exhorted all to endure every hardship for the sake of the solitude in Secu. He had not the slightest thought of seeking another, larger or more suitable monastery; rather,

---

[141] John 6:37.

he rejoiced in the poverty, privation, and difficulty which his blessed soul had loved from his youth for Christ's sake and in which he instructed us all. Whence came the confusion which followed, God only knows.

Prince Moruzi offers Paisij the monastery of Neamţ

One day, as the illustrious and pious and Christ-loving prince Constantin Moruzi[142] sat with all his illustrious and virtuous council, there arose a discussion concerning our blessed father and his community of brethren. The pious and Christ-loving prince asked his council what sort of monastery it was the elder Paisij dwelt in with his brethren. One of the chief councilors, who had been to the monastery of Secu and knew all about it, rose and said, "Your Highness, the elder Paisij now dwells with his brethren in prison, as it were." The prince was amazed at the words and asked, "How so in prison?" Said the other, "Because the monastery of Secu is confining, and the church small; it was not built for such a large brotherhood. The place is very difficult, and the way to it very rough and impractical for conveying to the monastery the necessities of life." The Christ-loving prince said to the council with compassion, "Is there not, then, in our dominion such a monastery in which we should be able to accomodate the holy elder Paisij and his brethren?" Said the council, "In all the land there is no monastery greater in expanse, nor with a more magnificent church, or more beautiful situation, or easier access for the conveyance to the community of necessities from without, than the monastery of Neamţ,[143] at a distance of two hours from Secu." The illustrious prince rejoiced greatly, and he wrote to the elder Paisij bidding him remove to the monastery of Neamţ without hesitation, regardless of anyone else. When the blessed one read this letter, its effect was indeed like a disturbance at sea. For when an unexpected storm comes on, the sea churns, the ships are tossed about, and everyone is frightened; and so it was then.

When the blessed one read the letter and saw the Christ-loving prince's unexpected command to take charge of the monstery of Neamţ, his soul was tossed like a boat. His peace was lost, the calm

---

[142] Hospodar of Moldavia, 1777–1782.
[143] Cf. N. Iorga, *Mănăstirea Neamţului* (Neamţ, 1925), esp. 39–64.

and quiet he had had in his heart fled. A storm of grievous thoughts fell upon him, woe and immeasurable sorrow overcame his soul. He wept bitter and inconsolable tears until he was exhausted, not knowing what to do. The brethren, too, were thrown into confusion when they saw the unexpected wind which would ruin the state of their souls, destroy the peace they enjoyed in their solitude, eliminate to the last all attentiveness in their minds and hearts, and also the sobriety and prayer, all of which they had attained after a respite from the troubles in Dragomirna and the cares and labors in Secu. Some of them, however, rejoiced as though they had obtained some lordly realm, the monastery of Neamț, but these were the the least serious and most inept in discernment, who did not trouble themselves with sobriety or prayer, nor did they value solitude highly, deriving no profit from spiritual solitude; they marveled at fame and loved luxury and ease; whose God was their belly and whose glory was in their shame.[144]

What then? Our father's grief and sorrow increased, to an extent he had never known in his life. He wept and sobbed bitterly, firstly because of the division of the community that was sure to follow: he would be unable to see before him all of his spiritual children, who were his consolation and the sight of whose faces was the delight of his heart. His conversations with them were sweeter than honey and its comb, and thus the division of the community was bitterness for his soul. He foresaw the ruin of their spiritual life, the destruction through confusion of the prayer and attentiveness that they had attained in Secu after the many struggles in the labor of constructing cells. He foresaw also exhaustion and grief, and snares prepared for the weak: for the monastery of Neamț was held in reverence because of a miraculous icon of the most pure Mother of God, and the entrance was always open to everyone, of both sexes. Considering the confusion this would cause in that monastery, the complaints and reproaches and curses of the superiors, the grief and indignation of the subordinates, and many other things, the blessed one wept and mourned greatly until he had exhausted himself. Further, he considered that his common admonition of the brethren, which he gave them when they gathered in the refectory every evening in winter, would also be disrupted, either because it would be impossible for all of them to gather together to listen, since they would be divided and

---

[144] Phil. 3:19.

this would only cause them greater grief; or else, as the blessed one himself told me later in Neamţ, because there would be important laymen staying there as guests, and it would be impossible to forbid them to come and listen. Thus the moral teaching which he had been accustomed to conduct after each instruction from Scripture, in order to correct whatever offences were committed within the community, would also be disrupted. He used to denounce such offences, without revealing the persons involved, in order that the offenders might be ashamed, and in their fear might correct themselves and repent, whereas the innocent might take greater care to guard against such offences. For the disruption of this teaching he grieved inconsolably day and night.

Now, just as the blessed one made ready to write his prayerful refusal to the illustrious prince, lo, there came to him the superiors of the monastery of Neamţ. For they had heard news of this matter from certain persons and were greatly troubled, and they began to implore him with fervent prayer and humble petition not to wrong them nor destroy their lives. They had lived in Neamţ from youth to their old age, and had expended their labor and sweat in all manner of service in the monastery; and now, they said, "Where are we to go? If oppressed by you, our other brethren will also cry out against you, and of what benefit will this be to you?" The blessed one could scarcely bear to hear these words which wounded his holy soul more cruelly than fiery darts, for he was indeed peace-loving and meek, and desired the benefit of peace and salvation for everyone; he had never wronged or brought anyone to grief, nor had he wished trouble upon another, but rather, he treated those who had wronged him without resentment. He began speaking to them, weeping bitterly: he described the great and unexpected trial, the unbearable sorrow and inconsolable grief, the violence and coercion, and the confusion of the brethren in their removal from Dragomirna; the toils and sweat expended in Secu, the short respite from their labors and calm and peace of their souls. "But lo," he said, "an unexpected storm; lo, billowy waves forcing and pulling us in their wake, though we hold our sails right as best we can, not indulging our inclination to follow the waves. Behold, holy fathers," he continued, showing them the letter from the prince, "This is the reason for our troubles and grief and for yours: behold coercion and burden beyond our strength. May the Lord Christ grant you assurance that it never entered my thoughts to perpetrate such an injustice by force and thus bring your souls to grief, thereby incurring eternal condemnation for transgressing God's commandment.[145] You yourselves know, holy fathers, that we do not occupy Secu by force; the former abbot, the venerable Father Nyfon, seeing our troubles under the control of the Germans, summoned us himself out of his love for us, and gave over the monastery even before anything was written to those in authority. Moreover, he desired to remain here with us, and so it came to pass. Then in loving agreement we wrote to the most holy metropolitan and the other authorities, and our request was granted. How could I have dared to perpetrate such an evil deed? How could I look upon your holy faces, if I stood accused and judged for an offence against my neighbor by my conscience, which throughout my life has striven to be at rest, in peace and love for everyone through God's grace? How could I have approached God's altar to partake of the awesome divine Mysteries, if others wept and cried to the Lord against me because of the wrong I had done them?[146] Heaven forbid that the Lord should allow me even to think of such an evil deed! I shall write to His Highness asking and begging tearfully that he leave us and you to abide in peace in our monasteries. For in our monastery of Secu, by God's grace, we now enjoy profound peace; and though there is difficulty in bringing necessities to the community on account of the bad state of the road, and it is very difficult in winter and when the rivers flow in spate. Nevertheless, we endure all with joy, thanking and praising God for the solitude and quiet.''

Paisij rejects the prince's offer

Reassured by these and many other words, the superiors of Neamţ withdrew. The blessed one then wrote a tearful letter to the prince; and what words of imploring did he not employ? What sensible reasons did he not present on the part of both monasteries? What tearful petitions from the entire community of brethren did he not bring forth in expressing their refusal to accept the monastery of Neamţ and their gratitude for the quiet and solitude of Secu? He begged him not to trouble his old age, and to have mercy upon him in

---

[145] Cf. Ex. 20:17.
[146] Cf. Matt. 5:23–24.

his illness, lest from the immeasurable difficulties and toils of the removal to Neamţ he should be overcome by even greater concerns for the spiritual harm to the brethren which would result, the disruption of their quiet and solitude. Then, too, he would be concerned about the disruption and confusion of the community of Neamţ, their murmuring and irreconcilable enmity and hatred: from all this great spiritual harm would result on both sides.

Thus having written the letter, he sent it with the chief confessor of his Romanian brethren, who spoke Greek as well, and another brother also, in order that they might add a precise explanation of the whole matter, begging tearfully for mercy, that they might be left to remain without trouble in Secu. The brethren were to wait there for the answer, in the expectation that their request would be granted. Now this petition was written in such a way as to soften and touch the heart not only of a merciful benefactor who had conceived a godly faith and love for our holy father and the community, but of any ruler at all; it would have been impossible to be disinclined to grant his request. God alone knows why it came to pass as it did, for who has known the mind of the Lord, or who has been His counselor?[147] He does whatever He desires, in His divine and inscrutable providence.

Those who had been dispatched, then, came with the letter to the prince who, upon the announcement of their arrival, bade them approach him. Upon entering they did fitting obeisance and gave over the letter. After it had been read, they began explaining everything in their own words, and falling at his feet in tears, they implored the illustrious prince, with many arguments, that he should abandon his plan, allowing the elder and brethren to remain without trouble in Secu, and should not disturb the community of Neamţ, lest enmity and spiritual harm to both monasteries should result. But they could in no wise persuade him. The prince had already promised to give another monastery to the community of Neamţ, and he commanded that the elder should remove thither. He asked the confessor, "Do you obey your elder?" Said the confessor, "By all means does it behoove us to heed and obey him and all the brethren, even unto death, as we promised at the time of our tonsure before him and before God." "Well then," said the prince, "if your holy father expects such obedience from you, ought he not to obey us at least once? For if he himself

147 Rom. 11:34.

persists in disobedience, what sort of example of obedience can he give to teach it you?'' He commanded that a letter be written to the elder, wherein in addition to other things he said, ''Be obedient: go to Neamț and think no more about it.'' Confirming the letter with his signature and seal, he gave it to the confessor and dismissed him in peace.

Paisij finally succumbs to the prince's will

The blessed one was in expectation of a merciful answer from the prince and, lo, the brethren arrived with the letter. But when he read it and saw written the word ''obedient'' and the command, he wept bitterly and knew not what to do. His immeasurable grief so increased and overwhelmed his soul that he could not eat or drink or sleep, and he became very weak in body. We were all in great sorrow and confusion lest he should die from his immeasurable grief and we should be left orphans prematurely. Then the elder brethren from among the confessors gathered and went to him in his illness, entreating him to give over such immeasurable grief and to fortify himself with food: ''For of what profit will it be to us if you die an untimely death and we are left orphans without you? What shall we do then? If such be the will of God, it is not right to oppose it. Though the illustrious prince disregards your letter and denies the request you have made, nevertheless, how great is his benefaction toward us without any request! For he provides us with all manner of clothing and victuals, materials, and many other things. How could he have disregarded his great love for you, unless some divine providence had not urged him on to this? What shall we accomplish by opposing him? God's will be done: let us go.'' Being a prudent man he heeded the words of his spiritual children and, raising himself from his bed, he stood up. Crossing himself he bowed to the icon of the most pure Mother of God, and said, '' 'Before two or three witnesses shall every word be established,' saith Scripture.[148] If you speak thus, brethren, then God's will be done: let us go, albeit unwillingly.''

He took some nourishment, but still he could not sleep. Calling three confessors and several other brethren he sent them to the monastery of Neamț, giving them the prince's letter, that it might be

---

[148] 2 Cor. 13:1.

read there. They were to prepare a cell for him and for others of the most important of the brethren, the priests, and the singers. This was done before the eve of the feast of the Dormition of the most holy Mother of God, and when the brethren had done as commanded, they returned. The blessed one determined who was to go with him to Neamṭ and who to remain in Secu, as well as all the other necessary matters. Then in tears he went into the church to pray, and having kissed the holy icons, he came out. He gave everyone his blessing and, weeping, he went out of the monastery, sat in a carriage, and set out on his way. Like a military escort we surrounded the carriage, some preceeding, some going alongside; and we arrived at the monastery of Neamṭ on the eve of the feast of the Dormition of the most holy Mother of God in the year 1779, on the fourteenth day of the month of August. The blessed one entered the church, and after the singing of "It is meet...,"[149] and a litany, he did reverence to the icons. Approaching the miraculous icon of the most holy Mother of God, he wept bitterly, and he commended himself and the brethren to her succor, preservation, protection, and sustenence, placing all his godly hope for everything in her. After he kissed the icon, he went to his cell and rested a little, but he was still unable to sleep because of his great grief, even though he had passed many days and nights without any sleep.

When the time came for the vigil, he went to church, albeit with great difficulty on account of his illness and weakness, and sat listening to the singing; and he prayed the most pure Mother of God to grant him a bit of sleep. Whilst vespers were ending and matins beginning, sleep began to come upon him, and leaving the church, he went to his cell to rest. He quickly fell asleep for three hours. When he awoke he felt relief from the pain in his head, as well as a certain renewed health in his body, and his grief had vanished. He thanked God and God's most pure Mother. After the liturgy he gathered all of the former superiors of Neamṭ and conversed with them in a loving manner, promising to see to their every need and not to violate their authority in any way. He accepted from them all of the property of the church and the external property, whatever they gave into his control, without questioning them about anything; and in this way they were sincerely reconciled. Many years later one of them assumed the

---

[149] Hymn in praise of the Virgin.

great *schema*,[150] surrendering all his property to the community, and departed to the Lord a few years thereafter. Another of them, by the grace of Christ, is still alive. Several of the younger ones went away, but all the rest joined the community, giving themselves in obedience. There was now one community from two, and all enjoyed spiritual peace.

The blessed one then wrote to the most illustrious prince concerning his taking charge of the monastery, the reconciliation and union with the former community of Neamţ, as well as the need for cells. For though the community was a small one, there were in all only about twenty cells, and there was not room enough for all the brethren. Reading this letter from the blessed elder, the prince rejoiced greatly because of the former's obedience and because of the reconciliation and union with the community of Neamţ; and with him all the other councilors rejoiced as well. Only the most holy metropolitan was displeased, for the receipts which the metropolis always had had from the monastery were now cut off. No levy was made on our community, neither for the metropolis nor for the general taxation, but all was remitted to the community by former princes and by this Christ-loving prince on account of our poverty and very great expenses. The prince commanded that a document should be written and that it should be confirmed by the signatures of the metropolitan, the prince, and the council, and also their seals, and he gave this to the brethren who had been dispatched. He added also a message of his own to the elder, thanking him for his obedience and prudent reconciliation and union with the former community of Neamţ. He bade him pray for his health and salvation, for his worldly dominion, and for the health and welfare of the land, promising to build a number of cells and to give assistance in other matters of need. That blessed prince of eternal memory did all this in the course of his reign in Moldavia. The community had no other benefactor like him, either before or after him. May the Lord rest his soul in His Kingdom!

Neamţ flourishes under Paisij's guidance

When our blessed father received the document and letter from the prince, he began the task of directing the affairs of the two

---

[150] Cf. above, n. 61.

monasteries. His cares and labors were now twice as great as before, and again the brethren undertook labors and concerns, busying themselves in the construction of cells. Others, too, now came, leaving their former monasteries, and tearfully begged to be received, promising to construct cells for themselves with their own hands. The blessed one was unable to refuse them and received them all, and all labored in the construction of cells within the monastery and without, for there was not room enough for all within. They built also a hospital and a hospice. For the old, the lame, and the blind who had nowhere to lay their heads came to him weeping and sobbing, begging him to have mercy upon them for Christ's sake, and he took pity upon them. The blessed one received these as he did the healthy ones, assigning them to the hospital and looking after all of them as best he could, as a loving father. He ordered a doctor to attend those who required treatment, and he commanded the brethren who served to look after the the old, the lame, the blind, and the sick as if they were serving the Lord Himself. They were to wash their hair and clothes and cleanse them thoroughly every Saturday; to clean the beds with hot water, lest the lice should multiply; to hang the bedclothes in the sun and air often; to maintain cleanliness in the hospital; to burn frankincense or some other incense in order that the air should not become heavy; and to prepare food more pleasing than usual, and likewise bread and wine. All were grateful and praised God with tears, and they thanked their true father always for the care he took for them. Monks from elsewhere came and stayed as long as they liked, for a fortnight or a month, and no one said anything such as, "Why do you sit idle, eating the common bread?" Others asked to stay the winter, and the blessed one would not turn them away, but would receive them with a blessing. Upon their departure he asked them no questions, and sending them on their way, he dismissed them in peace. By the grace of Christ this practice is maintained in the community to this day.

After several years the number of brethren in the monastery of Neamț and the neighboring hermitages increased to more than three hundred. At Secu there were always one hundred and sixty, and sometimes as many as one hundred and eighty, for the blessed one would summon some of the brethren from thence and would send others thither. The brethren in Secu had no concern for cells, for there were enough there, but in Neamț there was constant construction.

Around the monastery one saw a sort of city. The place was expansive and level, with forested hills in the distance. There was an abundance of all necessities. There were beauteous hayfields near by, with easy access. Our blessed father also built a second church within the monastery, dedicated to the holy Great Martyr George, and adorned it with wondrous beauty; this in addition to the main church of the Lord's Ascension. On the day of that feast, from time immemorial, a countless multitude of both sexes would gather. They came not only from Moldavia, but also from far-off lands, in order to venerate the miraculous icon of the most pure Mother of God. There were rich and poor, monks and laymen, and in his hospitality this second Abraham[151] strove to accommodate all as best he could. The expenses were great, and the receipts scarcely made up for half of them. The brethren would then be very crowded for three or four days. Then, if the others remained after the feast, they would stay in the hostelry. But for those four days the blessed one had no rest: from morning until evening the doors were open without discrimination to all who desired to see him. He lovingly greeted all who came and thanked them for their visit, assuring them of reward from the Lord and the Mother of God for their toil in undertaking the journey. Blessing them, he would then dismiss them to the hostelry and the other cells prepared for their accommodation. He himself thought of food only at night, eating nothing all day; for if he ate even a little it behooved him to rest, and thus he remained hungry as he conducted affairs throughout the day. This man filled with divine wisdom also did the following: at the beginning of the feast he would appoint the most pious of the brethren, those filled with the fear of God, to oversee the other brethren; to go round the monastery day and night, lest any scandal should occur. Knowing their father's will, the brethren thus watched over one another. When the feast had passed, the blessed one in no wise begrudged the expense to Her who had deemed him worthy to celebrate Her bright feast, and he prayed that he might be deemed worthy to live to celebrate it the following year.

---

[151] Cf. Gen. 18.

The second Russo-Turkish war

We had been in Neamţ for about nine years, having rested somewhat and recovered from our labors when, lo, a frightful storm exhaling fire, lo, mortal fear, a sword held over the heads of the old, and thongs and ropes in the hands of the enemy, ready to bind the young and carry them off into captivity: a savage war broke out among the three empires.[152] The steppe was filled with armies; the sea was covered with ships; cities and villages were left empty; everyone fled wherever he might hide from the wrath of the Turks. Fathers and mothers sought their lost children, weeping children their parents, husbands their wives and wives their husbands. All lost their wits out of fear and ran by road and across field, trampling upon one another, hurrying to the hills and forests to hide. The monastery of Neamţ was then filled with people, within and without, of high and low birth. The Germans[153] reached the town of Neamţ before the Turks and occupied it, and this somewhat allayed everyone's fear. But after a few days had passed, lo, the Turks came against them at dawn. Seeing them coming from afar, the Germans in their fear abandoned all of their equipment and fled for their lives whence they had come. Entering the town, the Turks gained victory without fire or bloodshed, and added the Germans' equipment to their booty. They killed three men who opposed them but left the others alone. Whilst they remained there, they were minded to go to the monastery, which stood at a distance of three hours, and everyone in the monastery was half-dead with fright: no one was completly certain whether the Turks were still in the town or had gone off. The nobles dispatched their soldiers, but they were perplexed and, fearing greatly for their lives, durst not approach the place. Some said that the monastery should not be shut up, and that an embassy should be sent to the Turks, entreating them to do no harm; but others would in no wise comply, advising that the monastery should be shut up, in order that they might make a stand there against the Turks and check their approach. In the midst of this confusion, a monk from among the cenobitic brethren came to our blessed father and received his blessing to go straightway to the town to see whether the Turks were there or had gone off. Choosing a horse

---

[152] The war of 1787–1791 between Turkey and the Russo-Austrian alliance.
[153] I.e., the Austrians.

which he knew, he mounted and rode off to the town straightway. Entering it, he passed through it, hither and thither, without fear, and saw not a single Turk. Finding a certain man, he learned from him that they had gone off, and he returned with the good news and everyone rejoiced. But on the following day, upon hearing that the Turks had returned, the nobles and the elder fled to the monastery of Secu, and the brethren scattered in the forest, since there was not enough room for all. The weather was then very cold, being the second week of great Lent, and they suffered terribly in the forest; but they remained there until the coming of the Germans, who drove the Turks off and took control. The strangers in the monastery then returned to their homes, and although the brethren suffered great hardships from the Germans, the mortal fear had passed.[154]

Longing for the past

Such was the life of suffering of our blessed father and of those who abode with him: in removals, confusion, tumult, labors beyond our strength, and times of fear for our lives. Oh, how hapless we were! Through the envy of the devil and on account of our sins we were driven from the monastery of Dragomirna by the Germans, or rather, we betook ourselves away, lest because of our Orthodox faith we should suffer harm from the leaders of heresy and their worldly authorities, as those monasteries and worldly and spiritual authorities who remained there did indeed suffer at the hands of the heretics. Oh, the vain hope we cherished! Oh, the spiritual harm and havoc we suffered because of all the moving, the tumult, the wandering, the poverty, and the hardship! Just as a tree which is too often transplanted will wither and dry out, so indeed did the tree of our community suffer from trans-plantation and the changing of monasteries. O Dragomirna, Dragomirna! The remembrance of life within your walls is the sweetness and solace of our souls, though perhaps it were better to be silent, lest our hearts be filled with grief because of the loss of you. When we removed to Secu, our resolve withered, and our spiritual longing to bear up under suffering grew weak through all the

---

[154] According to the *Life* by Platon (Tachiaos, *Revival*, 238), the archbishop of Katerynoslav, Amvrosij (Serebrjakov; d. 1792), arrived in Iaşi with Potemkin and the Russian armies (in 1790); and having obtained permission from "higher authorities," he visited Paisij at Neamţ and raised him to the rank of archimandrite.

tumult and cares and labors in the construction of cells and the rest.
Even though the melifluous spiritual springs which issued from the
holy mouth of our father watered our hearts, they soon grew cool and
hard, and even he was unable to warm and soften them or to make our
minds—dimmed because of the reasons aforementioned—sober and
quick, so that we might bravely have warded off the enemy's attacks,
cutting them off, as with a fiery sword, through constant mental prayer
performed in the heart. For we had lost the latter: it had fled us
because of our tumult and cares. Our spiritual veins had been cut, and
they withered, even as the roots of a tree wither. O Dragomirna, Dragomirna! It is fitting that we remember you and our life within your
walls only on feast days, for you were to us like a paradise of sweetness. You were like a garden planted by the waters which soon takes
root and gives forth divers fragrant flowers and fruits. Within your
walls a fragrance of divers virtues was produced among the brethren:
their godly love for the holy father and for one another was like the
rose and their purity of conscience like the lily. Within your walls the
mortification of one's own will and discernment became as myrrh; the
fragrance of constant prayer wafted like sweet-smelling incense; obedience progressed with self-reproach, humility with innocence; the
shedding of tears from the brethren's eyes reigned supreme. Within
your walls those who suffered the passions of the flesh found relief,
for no entrance was allowed to the female sex. Alas for our suffering
after we departed from you! Alas for us! How great was the spiritual
wealth we lost! What great spiritual treasure we should have amassed,
if only we had stayed within your walls with our holy father until his
death, not having gone off elsewhere! Alas for our misfortune! Oh,
what havoc the enemy wreaked in his envy! It was not in vain that the
devil roared at night from the column in the eastern tower,[155] tor-
mented with envy and seeking the destruction of our way of life there.
For the adversary gained this, by God's permission, having found his
vessels in the Germans.

Whilst we abode in Secu, then, in tumult, our spiritual gardener,
our blessed father, toiled in clearing and watering the garden of our
souls with the divine teaching he conducted when we went to him in

---

[155] It is unclear exactly what Mytrofan refers to here. It would appear that the roar-
ing occurred in a tower at Dragomirna. There are in fact five towers in the
monastery's walls, including one at each end of the eastern wall.

his cell. In winter he gathered all of us together in the evening in the refectory, reading and explaining the commandments of God and other necessary and profitable things. But he had little success, on account of the broken defences of our souls: we had no strong guard, no sober mind, to occupy our hearts in constant prayer, whereby as with a weapon we might have warded off the beasts and birds, the evil thoughts resulting from the confusion and tumult. When we abode in Dragomirna we stood high, as if on steps. But then we moved thence, away from our thriving spiritual life, and the blessed one labored incessantly admonishing us, especially in assembly. For although certain of the brethren often went to his cell with some problem, receiving words of profit from him, others chanced to visit and converse with him only once a year. For this reason admonition was also given by assembly, in order that all might listen to him and receive correction every evening throughout the winter. After four years, when we had found respite from our tumult, our hearts began putting out roots to collect moisture, and then branches. But lo, there was a sudden frost and the branches drooped in our removal to the monastery of Neamţ, and our way of life fell still lower than it had done before. The melifluous spring of divine teaching which issued from the mouth of our holy father was shut up: those who happened to be in his cell might by chance hear something from him, but the others heard not a single word from his mouth—his admonition of the assembled brethren having been discontinued for the reasons aforementioned—and they could gain spiritual profit only from the reading of books, if they were able and desired to read. Wherefore our blessed father worked all the harder upon new translations of books and upon the correction of corrupt ancient ones, in order to leave them for the benefit and instruction of us who desired to struggle in heeding the teaching of our God-bearing fathers. The blessed one often regretted the monastery of Secu, remembering the quiet there. Here in Neamţ, however, there is shame and danger for the young who do not keep careful guard. For the way was opened to the high born: they came to Neamţ both to venerate the icon and to visit the blessed one. Both sexes came with their domestics, young and old, and stayed as long as they liked in the hostelry within the monastery; and everyone was together in church. For the young who did not keep guard over their senses, the snares of ruin were ready; for the old who did not want even to hear of their coming, they were a nuisance; and for the blessed one they were an importunance and caused him pain and grief because of their harm to the brethren. Nor was it possible to stop women coming or to forbid them entrance to the monastery, for from olden times it had been a place of pilgrimage on account of the miraculous icon. For this reason the blessed one could not give admonition to the assembled brethren. He would have denounced in it the weak, frightening them with God's wrath and planting in their hearts the fear of God and the safeguarding of their senses, as well as the confession of evil thoughts and vigilence against them. Thus would the weak in soul have been corrected, and the strong confirmed and roused to greater struggles and the fervent keeping of God's commandments and the traditions of our holy fathers, who taught the true monastic life. Thenceforth our way of life declined, even as the blessed one himself told a foreign hieromonk who stayed with us in Secu.[156] This monk had asked him, ''Father, how does your present life compare with that in Dragomirna?'' And since the blessed one always loved the truth and was a stranger to deceit and vainglorious hypocrisy, he answered, ''It grows worse every year, and strive though I do, it is impossible to prevent this in any degree. The cause of all this is the unrestricted entry of women into the monastery and the discontinuance of admonition of the assembled brethren.'' How, then, can we not weep for Dragomirna? For it is a cause of wonder to those who joined our community afterwards and have heard from the elder brethren about our way of life there. Let no one disbelieve what is written here, for the Lord shall destroy him that speaks falsehood.[157]

The blessed one often said this also: ''Brethren, if you will persist fervently in reading the books of the fathers and heed the teaching in them, there will flourish among you obedience, peace, unanimity, and love for one another, and our community will endure as long as it pleases the Lord; and strive as the enemy may to destroy it, he will have no success. But if you shun reading the books of the fathers, then will it soon be destroyed, and there shall not be left one stone upon another.''[158]

---

[156]   Thus in the original, but Paisij's answer seems to be referring to the conditions in Neamţ.

[157]   Cf. Ps. 5:6.

[158]   See Matt. 24:2.

Working with superhuman endurance

Therefore he worked with great care in the translation of books from the Greek into the Slavonic language, and the brethren who spoke Romanian translated them from our language into their own. Throughout each day the blessed one would conduct spiritual and worldly affairs, and throughout the night he would write, laboring beyond the limits of nature. If he had not been given strength by the grace of God, it would have been impossible for his constitution to endure such labor. Moreover, he was infirm and suffered greatly from sores. For he had sores all along his right side, on his abdomen and leg, and he could not lie on that side. The manner in which he wrote is to be marveled at. The bed upon which he rested was strewn all about with books: innumerable lexica, the Greek Bible, the Slavonic Bible, Greek and Slavonic grammars, the book from which he was translating, and in the midst of all of them, a candle. Sitting there, bent over like a small child, or reclining, he would write throughout the night, forgetting his illnesses and weariness. When thus occupied he could in no wise reply to any questions, nor did he hear anything, regardless of what was said to him or what happened outside his cell. The brother who served him never allowed anyone to see him at this time. If there happened to be some urgent matter, this brother would go in to ask him, but though he would speak to him many times seeking an answer, he would hear nothing; and if the blessed one was forced to answer, he could scarcely do so, with pain and sighing, unable to take his mind from his writing. Our father often told us, "There is no labor more difficult for me than when I am busy translating and it is necessary to answer some question: I break out in a sweat when I must take my mind from my writing." Once when I was with him, another brother came in and a converstaion began. The other brother said that he was confounded by his many thoughts. The blessed one smiled and said, "Why are you thus mindless? Do as I do. I involve myself and treat with you all day long: with some of you I weep, with others I rejoice, and I conduct all the affairs of the two monasteries. But after I send all of you out of my cell, I send all thoughts out with you as well; and when I take up a book, I then hear nothing, and I practise solitude as if I were in the desert of Jordan." O man most free of passion and holy! O soul united with God! From his youth he cleaved unto God in love, and he poured himself out in his love for his neighbor, commiserating with him in everything as if he himself suffered.

Paisij's spiritual and moral values

Now one of the brethren stood in need of correction and had been reproved by the holy man several times. One day when I was in the holy man's cell, this brother said to him, "Father, I am grieved by you: my thoughts tell me that you bear hatred for me, for you are so often filled with wrath against me and reprove me before the brethren." The elder sighed and wept, and he said, "Beloved brother, wrath is alien to the life of the Gospel, and anyone who hates another incurs utter ruin. If the divine Gospel commands one to love even one's enemies,[159] how shall I hate my spiritual children? Heaven forbid! As for my reproving you with wrath, may the Lord grant you to have such wrath. For I take upon myself the state of mind of each of the brethren: before some of them I am forced to appear wrathful, an emotion which, by Christ's grace, I myself never feel; before others I am forced to weep, in order that by both ways, right and left,[160] I may afford you benefit. But I never find myself in bondage to the passion of wrath." Then the brother fell in tears at the feet of the elder and asked forgiveness. The holy one added: "When I was seven years old I began to learn to read. For two years I studied only the Primer, the Book of Hours, and the Psalter, and thereafter I began reading books with ease. First I read, with great fervor and attention, holy Scripture, the Old and New Testaments, and then the *Pearl* of St. John Chrysostom, and the works of SS. Ephrem and Dorotheus in which they speak of accusation and condemnation, and I realized what a great sin this was. At that time, still in my youth, I made such a vow before God: "Lord, if ever I should accuse my brother, even if I see him sin with my own eyes, let the earth open and swallow me." I placed a restraint on my mouth, that I should never say even one word to anyone about anything I have seen or heard, and by Christ's grace I kept this vow all my life, until I began to live with brethren; and now, albeit unwillingly, I have become your judge. The brethren have taught me to speak and involve myself for their benefit; formerly I said nothing."

---

[159] Cf. Luke 6:27.
[160] Cf. 2 Cor. 6:7.

Who with understanding will not be amazed upon hearing about this blessed man filled with divers divine gifts from his mother's very womb. Who will not tremble at his efficacious words which teach the keeping of God's commandments? From his youth he was a chosen vessel of God and a perfect keeper of His commandments, and his words were therefore potent and effectual, filled with grace; they came from within his soul and discriminated evil from good; they eradicated passions and instilled virtues in the souls of those who heeded them in faith. Who will not marvel at this account: a ten-year-old child reading holy Scripture, the Old and New Testaments, Chrysostom's book, the *Pearl*, about the unfathomable mysteries of theology, the books of Ephrem and Dorotheus and others? A ten-year-old child reading Scripture! Let everyone consider for himself: what did you do at the age of ten? What sort of understanding did you have then? What were you inclined to do? Even under compulsion, did you not run away not only from reading, but also from any learning, to play at children's games? But as a child the blessed one would shut himself up and read, not wishing to speak to anyone, so that even his mother seldom heard him speak, and then only a very few words; and those his own age thought that he had been born dumb, for they never heard a word from him. Who among you reading this with great fervor and attention will not be amazed at hearing this and even more wondrous things about the blessed one? O marvel! Whence came to this youth such great fervor and attention in reading Scripture if not from an understanding of the mysteries therein? And who was his instructor? The grace of the All-Holy Ghost dwelt in him from his mother's womb and used him as His pure and chosen vessel, and this increased yet more after the blessed one laid such a firm foundation for the keeping of His commandments. He read with great fervor and attention, for from fervent reading comes attention, and from attention desire; and then an ineffable longing roused his soul to love God with all his heart and all his soul, and to leave the world and all that was in the world, including his mother, who then loved him so willfully, weeping bitterly and sobbing inconsolably, and was stricken with immeasurable grief to the point of bringing death upon herself, as recounted above.

The blessed one read Scripture because of his love for the Lord and in his fervent desire to serve Him in the monastic state through the keeping of His commandments. Now the reading of the Old

Testament is forbidden not only to the young, but also to the old who
are not wise, lest their faith should suffer harm by reading of God's
great and awesome miracles among the unruly race of the Hebrews.
Likewise also the reading of the prophets and the Song of Songs. Nor
do the holy doctors of the Church in any wise enjoin these same to
read theology, lest in their ignorance they should be mistaken in even
the slightest matter of dogma and fall into heresy. But the blessed one
read fearlessly, having within himself God's grace as his instructor—
he was a small child in years, but an elder in understanding and wisdom. Subjugating anger and desire to reason, he directed his senses
away from the beautiful and pleasant things of this world and considered them all as rot. As for his tongue, an organ not easily restrained and which sins with the greatest of ease, he kept it tied so
securely with silence that he was thought by many to be dumb. He
fastened his mind on Scripture and united his soul with God through
love and prayer: he was crucified unto the world, and the world
crucified unto him.[161] Shutting himself up in his room he practiced
solitude as if in the desert of Sinai. In truth was this wondrous man,
our blessed father, in all ways like the holy fathers of old who loved
God from their youth and desired to serve Him as monks. How shall
we, brethren, who have been the disciples of such a luminary, our holy
elder Paisij, answer before God for our sloth? Not only are we unwilling to imitate his virtues, but we will not even read the books of the
fathers, some of which he corrected and others translated anew.
Through these we might be brought to an understanding of our
infirmities and, looking upon ourselves, each of us might weep before
God and repent. But even if some of us do read these books, it is from
habit only, without paying them any attention.

Whence did our blessed father acquire his divine fervor and
heavenly understanding? Was it not from the reading of books? All
the saints teach this. Moreover, the Savior Himself said, ''Search the
Scriptures, for in them ye think ye have eternal life.''[162] The Lord
enjoins searching, He bids us probe the depths of meaning, not read in
a cursory manner. Wherefore we are condemned for forgetting the
labors of our father and his teaching concerning the reading of books:
like wood on the water we are carried downstream. It is as though we

---

[161]   See Gal. 6:14.
[162]   John 5:39.

never heard the word of God. For this reason have I mourned for Dragomirna. But let us rouse ourselves and recover our sobriety of mind.
Let us make a beginning and the Lord will help us. No one can
describe the blessed one's quickness of mind and his memory
strengthened by grace. He could very quickly comprehend the loftiest
dogmatic matters, and once he had read anything, it remained stored
in his memory forever. I was once in his cell when there was a
conversation about books, for it was my obedience to copy books of
the fathers according to the rules of grammatical orthography.[163]
Another brother came in who knew the Greek language, and the
blessed one asked him the meaning of a certain phrase. The other
answered, "Our teacher explained it to us, Father, but I cannot
remember." Said the blessed one with a happy, smiling face, "Once I
read something, I never forget it until I die."

Comparing Paisij to the ancient fathers

Our father had such a gift for copying books as is rarely found
anywhere in the world. He had copied the book of St. Dorotheus in
his youth. This is a very large book, but he fitted all of it on three
sheets of paper: he folded each sheet into eight leaves, and thus there
were twenty-four in all. On each page he fitted in seventy lines of
writing in uncial letters as thin as a hair. The letters were not
obscured by any smears, but were quite neat and clear, and the upper,
lower, and side margins were perfectly even. Marveling at this, I
asked him, "Father, with what sort of pen did you write this book? A
dove feather?" "No," he said, "a goose feather." Our blessed father
was endowed by the Lord with so many excellent gifts, internal and
external, that no one could describe them; and if one tried to demon-
strate how great his virtue was, one would only obscure rather than
elucidate it. For this great man was full of grace, and everything about
him was miraculous. If anyone was to liken him to the God-bearing
fathers of old, he would indeed not miss the mark: he was lacking in
none of their gifts. If we compare him with the holy desert fathers

---

[163] по художеству граматическаго правописания. The technical term for the systematic correction of Slavonic manuscripts, which had been one of the favorite
activites of fourteenth-century hesychasts in Bulgaria. Cf., for instance, H. Goldblatt.
Orthography and Orthodoxy: Constantine Kostenečki's Treatise on Letters, Studia
Historica et Philologica, 16 (Florence, 1987).

who lived alone in solitude, it will come as no surprise that he so greatly delighted in prayer and united himself with God. But it is a wonder that in the midst of such tumult, worries, confusion, and griefs he was always able to keep his mind clear. And after he had finished conducting the common affairs, he would dismiss all thoughts about them, shutting himself up in the quiet of his cell as in the desert of Jordan: enrapt in his love and union with God he heard nothing that might happen outside his cell, as if nothing ever did happen. If love be the consummation of all God's gifts, then he was filled to abundance with this, as a most pure and chosen vessel of God. Even as the holy desert fathers kept an all-night vigil, so he kept awake all the night throughout his life. In none of the spiritual struggles of those God-bearing fathers of old was he found wanting.

Likewise, if we compare him with the holy cenobitic fathers of old, we shall see that this comparison, too, is valid in the case of our blessed father. In written accounts we have seen the divers divine gifts and many virtues in those great saints of old, but in our own Israel, not just in writings, but with our own eyes we have seen and have touched, as if with the hands of our minds, God's gifts and all the great virtues in the blessed one, preserved inviolate as if in a divine treasury. And they did not remain forever fruitless, for no wind could buffet, no frost destroy them, but they always offered countless flowers and fruit unto the Lord Christ, the Gatherer of fruit. Of this there is trustworthy evidence. In him was the hypostatic Wisdom, together with His eternal Father and All-Holy Ghost, dwelling in the most pure abode of his soul, and from Him there flowed through his lips a melifluous spring of divine teaching which gladdened and healed the souls, and withered the passions, of others. In him was divine reason, whereby he rightly understood and stoutly defended Orthodox doctrines, the rulings of the holy ecumenical councils, the traditions of the Church, and the teachings of the church doctors, our pious fathers, and he kept these from harm as the apple of his eye. In him was counsel, which he rightly and in accordance with the teaching of the holy fathers gave to those who required it of him, and those who received it with faith were preserved unscathed from the snares of the enemy and progressed in the keeping of God's commandments. In him was the fear of God, whereby he safeguarded God's commandments as the apple of his eye: he would lay down his life for the least of them, and so he taught us to do. In which virtues was the blessed one inferior to our holy fathers of old? If we consider this with equanimity, we shall see that he in no way fell short of the saints of old. In him was fiery love, wherewith he had loved God with all his soul from his youth, and he excelled in his fervor to extend himself equally to all, loving all, comforting all, giving instruction to all, commiserating in everything and embracing his spiritual children with his soul. He never turned away anyone who came to him seeking spiritual or bodily mercy, but would take pains for him. He was always at peace with everyone, nor did he ever bear enmity or bring another to grief, even though he might have suffered from him; and he instructed us in this always. Forbearance and meekness were coupled together in him as if innate qualities, nor was insolence ever to be seen, but only tranquillity and piety. He chastised with love, showed mercy with tranquillity, and always forebore in the expectation of amendment. His humility was so great as to be difficult to describe, and there was a childlike goodness and simplicity about him, though his understanding was divine and not at all childlike. His temperance in everything came to him naturally from his youth: he ate very little, and never by special dispensation for illness or weakness or extraordinary labor when the monastic rule did not normally permit certain foods. Nor did he ever in his life partake of intoxicating drink. When he began to live with brethren on the Holy Mountain, important monks and confessors there advised him to drink a little wine for his health's sake, the air there being exceedingly noxious, for they felt great sympathy for him, lest he should come to harm and they should lose the great benefit which he afforded them. But he scarcely heeded them, using only a very little wine, for he had made a resolution not to partake of intoxicating drink as long as he lived.

Recalling Paisij's early experiences

When the blessed one left the world, he and his friends had resolved to seek out a spiritual father who lived in solitude, in attention to himself, and to give themselves body and soul in obedience to him, to live with him in solitude and to obtain the necessities of their livelihood by the work of their own hands. After the first loss of his friend and countryman Dmytro, who remained in the world, he then lost another, Aleksij, who when he became a monk broke his promise to the blessed one by giving himself in obedience to a certain elder without taking counsel with the blessed one. Because of his meekness and lack of boldness he could not bring himself to remind his friend of the promise he had broken, but forebore in silence, protecting the other by his humility and reproving himself as unworthy to live in the other's company. He was unable to give himself over to a spiritual father of that sort, fearing lest he should be forced against his will to accept the great dignity of the priesthood, concerning which the other fathers had warned him and from which he ran with fear and trembling, not wishing to receive it ever in his life. Though he was pure and undefiled in soul and body from his mother's womb, he reflected inwardly as follows: "If I give myself in obedience to one of these venerable fathers, sooner or later I shall surely be forced to accept the priesthood, of which I am afraid, and I shall fail in my intention to follow the Royal Path in the wilderness in obedience to a spiritual father." Thus he went thence to the Holy Mountain, desiring to fulfil his purpose there, for God did not want him to be hidden away in the solitude of the wilderness, like a lamp under a bushel; rather, He made ready to place him upon a lampstand[164] on a high mountain, that he might illuminate many lands through his blameless way of life and correct teachings. Nor did He want him to be instructed by men, but the Holy Ghost Himself was his guide and instructor from youth: He Himself taught him all that was necessary and set him before all the world as an image drawn not by man, but by God, in order that all who desired salvation might copy in themselves good behavior and a virtuous life from his image, and from his teaching might learn to keep the commandments of God and the true monastic way of life. Thus the Holy Ghost was well pleased that he should first dwell in solitude, until by His divine providence He brought to him as disciples a great community of those who desired salvation, to serve Him in the monastic state, in order that he who learned from Him mysteriously might teach all of them manifestly all things necessary to their salvation.

After a short time, then, He brought to him one brother as a companion, and the blessed one was comforted and thanked Him for His mercy. He thought that his desire had been fulfilled, to follow the Royal Path in unanimity with a brother, sharing all the necessities of life: each renounced his own will before the other, and they became participants in holy obedience. But they had not lived there long

[164] Cf. Matt. 5:15.

before others began coming to him, begging him to receive them as disciples. He refused, unwilling to receive even one of them. But it was impossible not to receive those who were brought by God and, albeit unwillingly, he received them and revealed to them the path of salvation and the mystery of holy obedience. They received his instruction with joy and performed their obedience with fervor, renouncing their own will and disregarding their own discernment. Seeing their great fervor for the word of God, the blessed one rejoiced in his soul and glorified God with tears. Trusting in the almighty providence of God for their spiritual and bodily nourishment, he continued to receive them; and soon twelve brethren had gathered, and they made a beginning of a common life upon the Royal Path, that is, living with one or two others in solitude. Then the Lord removed him to the Hermitage of Elijah the Prophet, from the sea below to the mountain above,[165] that others sleeping in the darkness of ignorance might also see the the light of reason. Now he shone yet more brightly and illumined all the Holy Mountain through his renewal of the cenobitic monastic life and his institution in it of the chiefest virtue, thrice-blessed obedience. All of the monks of the Holy Mountain were amazed by the brightness of this great light. Those whose spiritual sight had been damaged covered their eyes in envy, lest they should be exposed for having strayed from the right path: they chose to follow their own will rather than to be exposed. Others despised and reproved themselves, and came to him to hear his teaching. They confessed their infirmities and received healing and direction in order to safeguard themselves in the future, and they went off rejoicing and glorifying God because of him. Yet others, as if risen from the dead, shook off the darkness of ignorance and came to the light with nimble feet, praising and glorifying God who had shown them His great servant and guide to salvation. Coming to him they fell at his feet, begging to be received in obedience, giving their souls into his keeping as into the hands of God.

After the brethren had multiplied at the Hermitage of Elijah the Prophet and there was no longer enough room for them, the Lord took the blessed one from thence and brought him to this Orthodox land of Moldavia, as He had taken our pious father Antonij to Rus', in order

---

[165] The Hermitage of St. Elijah stands on a height overlooking the Monastery of the Pantocrator, near which the brethren had lived earlier, and the sea beyond.

that he might more perfectly confirm the cenobitic life and illuminate those who abode here in the darkness of ignorance of the true monastic life, and might shine from hence also to other countries with the light of his blameless way of life and correct teaching of the Gospel. How many were the labors performed by the blessed one in this holy endeavor, especially in these wretched and terrible times when monasticism had degenerated to the last and was visible only in its outward form. They did not know what monasticism was, or the mystery of obedience, or how great a profit it brought to the novice in his progress toward understanding; nor did they know what action was, or vision, or the mental prayer of the heart, performed by the mind in the heart.[166] He taught them all these things. He himself had been taught by God and by the teaching of the holy fathers through the reading and translation of their books. The holy fathers of old had had models which shone in many countries with the light of their God-pleasing way of life and correct teachings. They also had had instructors from whom they learned and, abiding with them from an early age and looking upon their blameless lives and teaching as upon animate pillars, they themselves were animated and were turned into pillars by succession, and became lights and pillars and teachers of the cenobitic way of life. Our blessed father, however, had no such instructor: he sought but could not find one. Enlightened by God's grace he toiled by himself. He dug with humility and tears, and he found in his heart a spring of the water of life, from which he himself drank in abundance and unstintingly gave others to drink as well: the more that was drawn off, the more abundantly it flowed. The monastic life was renewed by him. And what of the books of the fathers? Just as iron eaten away and covered by rust loses its brilliance, so had they lost the brilliance of their meaning: it had either been confused by an inept ancient translator, or else very greatly obscured by unlearned copyists who were ignorant of the rules of grammatical orthography.[167] Seeing that there was great obscurity in them, the blessed one toiled in search of their sources, the Greek books from which they were derived. At first he began by correcting and striking out certain parts, but then he realized that this effort was useless and translated them anew. In this way the beauty of grammatical skill and the clarity of meaning in

[166] See above, n. 95.
[167] See above, n. 163.

them shone forth; and he also translated many which had not existed in our language and set them forth for the benefit of present and future generations.[168]

Comparing Paisij to St. Antonij of the Kievan Caves Monastery

This blessed man our father Paisij, whom we hold in everlasting remembrance, was similar to our father Antonij of the Caves Monastery: he was his true descendant, even though he flourished many centuries later, for it was the same Ukraine[169] which produced them both. The other was sent from the Holy Mountain to Rus' in order to illuminate it and to establish there the true monastic life. He gathered monks together and gave them instruction; he shone forth to all the corners of Rus' and became the father superior of all the monks of Rus'. And it was at this very same Holy Mountain that our own holy father first shone forth, renewing the cenobitic monastic life which had fallen into decay and establishing in it the tree of life, thrice-blessed obedience, in order that by this very thing, whereby our forefather Adam was driven from the paradise of the senses, his descendants who followed the right path might enter the heavenly paradise, wherein entered the Lord, the Father Superior of all obedience. When divine Providence had gathered together a community of more than fifty brethren, It brought him and all of them to this Orthodox and hospitable land of Moldavia, where by Christ's grace the community was established in the monastery of Dragomirna. More than one hundred brethren from the Rus' lands gathered around the holy Antonij, and more than five hundred brethren from nine countries, speaking divers languages, gathered around our own blessed father. The pious Antonij attended the sick brethren; our holy father attended the sick and the healthy, and he cooked food, baked loaves for the eucharistic oblation and did handiwork when the community was still small. But when God increased the number of brethren, he no longer had any respite, day or night, from his responsibilities. Nor did he prefer his own solitude to his neighbor's welfare. However, after he had

---

[168] For a discussion of Paisij's literary activity, see Tachiaos, ῾Ο Παΐσιος Βελιτσκοφσκι; and Hieromonk Leonid [Poljakov], "Literaturnaja dejatel'nost' sxiarximandrita Paisija Veličkovskogo," *Messager de l'Exarchat du Patriarche russe en Europe occidentale* 21 (1973):69–104, 203–37.

[169] *Malorossia.*

finished conducting the common affairs, he would shut himself up in his cell and so rigorously practice solitude that he could not even hear his servant when he required an answer from him concerning some needful matter, as was noted above.

Paisij similar to Athenian philosophers

In his teaching, his maintenence of a community, his spiritual struggles, his labors beyond human endurance, his wisdom and divine understanding, his counsel, his discernment, and his other gifts from God, our blessed father was in every way like the pious fathers of old and all those who have come after them. He was adorned with all virtues, external and internal, even as the holy fathers of old. His face was radiant like that of an angel of God, his appearance gentle, his speech humble and without boldness. He greeted all with love; he answered with piety; he was filled with goodness; he was always inclined to mercy; he attracted all to himself even as a magnet attracts iron. His humility and meekness were profound. He was forbearing in all things. In every way was this great man godly and full of grace. His mind was always united with God in love, to which his tears bore witness. Whenever he spoke of theology, his heart was flooded with love, his face shone with gladness, and tears poured forth from his eyes in confirmation of the truth. Whenever we stood before him our eyes never tired of the sight of him: we desired insatiably to look upon him; nor were our ears ever stopped with displeasure or tedium at his speech, for as I have already said, in the joy of our hearts we forgot ourselves. When we looked upon his face, we kept our ears always near his mouth, even as the Athenian philosophers of old did. For whenever they saw someone who excelled in wisdom, they desired to talk with him, and the eyes and ears of all were fixed upon him in their desire to hear some new bit of wisdom. How much more were our eyes fixed upon our blessed philosopher! For from his mouth we always heard new things concerning spiritual mysteries or the moral precepts of the God-bearing fathers.

Witness of mystic experiences

This short history written by me in my witlessness will only obscure, rather than elucidate, the blessed one's virtues. It ought to have been written by a very wise man, though I think that even such a one would grow weary in an attempt to touch on everything, and would also be unsuccessful on account of the loftiness of the blessed one's life. Now, anyone with an envious eye reading this about the elder will accuse me of exceeding the bounds in my praise of him, and I therefore beg such a reader to forbear just a little longer, in order that, once he has heard these words, free from any falsehood (for all falsehood comes from the devil[170]), he himself will not hesitate to praise this holy man, who is beyond all human praise, and will proclaim, "God is wonderful in His saints,"[171] and also, "Blessed are your eyes which have seen him and your ears which have heard words from his mouth."[172] For on three occasions I was terrified upon looking at the face of the blessed one. Once in Dragomirna I went to him after vespers. I was about to knock at the door and announce myself to the brother in attendance, in order to learn whether the blessed one would receive me. But seeing the door open, I entered, and uttering a prayer,[173] I went in to him. Seeing that he was lying down, I prostrated myself and said, "Bless me, Father." He answered nothing, as was his custom. Standing there I looked upon him, and his face was as if ablaze. I waited a little while, in amazement, and again in a louder voice I uttered a prayer; but he made no answer. I was amazed by the sight of him, for I had never seen his face thus. By nature he was pale of face, and I realized that the love of the fervent prayer in his heart had also filled his face with grace. I stood there for a while and then withdrew, telling no one of this. Many years later I twice saw his face shining as he conversed with us: he spoke with ineffable love, smiling in his spiritual joy, drawing forth spiritual words out of himself and, as it were, instilling joy into our souls. I stood in amazement as I looked upon him, and I conversed with him in the fear of God. I asked none of the other brethren who had been there about this, nor did I tell anyone else, fearing lest the blessed one should hear of it afterwards and be grieved. For he was very humble and avoided praise like so much stench. He reproved himself always and laid the blame for all that occurred in the community upon himself, saying, "This has happened because of my sins." And if it was something

170   Cf. John 8:44.
171   Cf. Ps. 67(68):35.
172   Cf. Matt. 13:16; Luke 10:23–24.
173   See above, n. 55.

good, he attributed it to the prayers of the community. The more he avoided glory, loathing it as stench, the more God glorified him in all lands. His name was, and is, venerable to all, and talk of him is cause for the glory of God: all praised and still praise God for manifesting in these wretched and terrible times His true servant and faithful teacher, who enlightened and renewed the cenobitic monastic life. It is not inappropriate to apply to him the words of Isaac the Syrian: "Glory flees from him that pursues it"; and elsewhere he says, "A man who can suffer honor is scarcely to be found, if he is to be found at all;" to which, for ease of understanding, one might add: "not even if he be equal to the angels in morals."[174] But our pillar of humility suffered glory with ease: he had it and bore it without harm, for from youth he had fled from it when it might have overcome him in the world, when he saw many important personages clapping their hands in expectation of him becoming their pastor and teacher, as the successor in his father's church. But he spat in the face of the deceitful Belial, and rejecting glory in all its stench he ran from it. Throughout his life he remained unharmed by it, considering himself dust and ashes beneath the feet of all and indebted for everything to the brethren. Not once did he dream of his own loftiness, but put his hope for salvation in the prayers of the brethren. Wherefore God extolled him, glorifying him in this life; and we believe without doubt that He will glorify him with the pious fathers in the life to come.

He did not lack the gift of foreknowledge, and whatever he predicted came to pass. He predicted a terrible death for a certain important personage, and so it happened. Concerning another he sighed and wept and made admonitions, and on the third day that person drowned. Admonishing another, whilst I too was in his cell, he said at last, "Do you not see, brother, the place whither you are soon to go?" In a week the other was dead, and the blessed one wept bitterly for him. And what are we to say about this? That although the blessed one remained in his cell, never going anywhere except to church, he knew the state of mind of all the brethren, even those whom he never saw. I was once in his cell during a conversation, and one of the foremost of the confessors came in and said something to the blessed one. Said the latter, "How can you not know the brethren's state of mind, when they come to you every day to confess

---

[174] See *Svjatago otca našego Isaaka Sirina slova*, Discourse 1, 1–2.

their thoughts? I, who remain in my cell, know this, but you do not." How could you have known, holy Father, unless the Holy Ghost dwelt in your heart and revealed this to you? There were many other instances, but I omit them for the sake of brevity.

There is no need to write about miracles and healings, for it is not by miracles that the holiness of truly holy men, their holiness before God, is recognized, but by true Orthodox faith and doctrines, the keeping of God's commandments, and a pure and blameless way of life. For many heretics have worked miracles. Of these the Lord has said, "Many will say to me in that day, 'Lord, have we not been baptized in Thy name? And in Thy name done many wonderful works?'" And the Judge said to them, "Verily I say unto you, for I know you not; depart from me, ye that work iniquity."[175] And to the rich man who asked of the Lord, "How may I have eternal life?" He said, "Keep the commandments."[176] And again, "A new commandment I give unto you, that ye love one another as I have loved you. By this shall all men know that ye are my disciples, if ye have love one to another."[177] The holy John Chrysostom teaches that it is not right for an Orthodox man to prove his holiness by signs and prophecies, but by the goodness of his life, even as the Lord has said, "By their fruits ye shall know them."[178] The Apostle described the fruits of a truly spiritual man when he said, "The fruit of the Spirit is love, joy, peace, long-suffering, goodness, faith, meekness, self-control; against such there is no law."[179] If a man attains such fruit, whether he performs signs or does not, it is clear nevertheless that he is holy and a friend of God. Our blessed father also worked many miracles, but in as much as he was unwilling even to hear about this, ascribing everything to the most pure Mother of God and the prayers of the community of brethren, I shall leave off, lest I oppose his wishes, though I know of many miracles which occurred before and after his death.

---

[175] See Matt. 7:22–23; 25:12.
[176] Cf. Matt. 19:16–17.
[177] John 13:34–35.
[178] Cf. *Homily* XLVI on Matthew, PG, 58, 480b; Matt. 7:20.
[179] Gal. 5:22–23.

Cenobitic life

Our blessed father Paisij had in his community brethren of different grades of accomplishment. I write of this on the basis of a letter in his own hand to his first friend, the hieromonk Dmytro of Poltava, written in Dragomirna in the year 1767. The latter had asked him to send a description of all the grades in the monastic life and of his way of life with the brethren. The blessed one most graciously and fittingly described the grade of eremitical solitude and all that it entailed, and also the grade of cenobitic life, the Royal Path, expounding very clearly the teaching of our pious fathers. To this he added information about himself and about the community of brethren: in what state of mind the brethren then were, and what progress they had made in Dragomirna. He wrote thus, "Not all in our community are in the same grade, nor would this be possible. For some, a very great number, have already mortified their own will completely: they heed the brethren in everything and perform their obedience for them as if for the Lord Himself, with fear of God and great humility, enduring dishonor, abuse, reproof, and every sort of trial; and they do this willingly, with the greatest of joy, as if they were thus deemed worthy of God's grace. Without ceasing they reprove themselves before God in the secrecy of their hearts, considering themselves beneath everyone, the last of all. Then there are others, not a few of them, who fall and rise up, sinning and repenting, enduring reproof and trials, albeit with difficulty. These same strive with all their souls to become like the others, beseeching God for this with tears. Still others, not very many, are weak and feeble, like infants still unable to partake of solid food, that is, to endure reproofs and trials, and they must still be fed with the milk of mercy, benevolence, and indulgence for their weakness, until they reach the spiritual age of patience, when they will be able to satisfy their needs solely through a good disposition and constant self-reproach. Often these brethren strive beyond their strength to endure dishonor and to abandon their own will to the point of shedding blood, that is, to pour out before God great effort, as blood, in this labor, beseeching God with tears for help. Such ones, though they be very weak, are reckoned before God among those who take the heavenly kingdom by violence.[180] But even if all of the brethren are not in the

---

[180] Cf. Matt. 11:12.

same grade, as has been said, still, they all strive in common to keep the commandments of God and of the holy fathers, united with one another by the indissoluble bond of God's love; and for the sake of their love of God and their salvation they endure constant bodily privation with magnanimity and constant thanksgiving to God: even as they trust in God for their salvation, so also for the provision of necessities for the sustenance of their lives.''

Paisij's life drawing to a close

Our present life is as far removed from that one in Dragomirna of old as the Old Testament is from the New. Behold, O beloved brethren, you who have not seen the angelic face of our holy father, I have fulfilled the promise I made to you in the preface, to write an account of his holy life: his flight from the world, his travels, his poverty, his life with the brethren, and his labors and struggles beyond human endurance. Of his spiritual struggles no one can give a description, nor could anyone have seen the outpourings of divine grace and enlightenment upon him which proceeded from his heart even to his face, and which in his love he poured out for us, like a drink of spiritual joy: these only God and he himself saw within himself, for he concealed them from others with his most profound humility as with a curtain.

I come now to his blessed end. As our divine father continued in his toils and struggles day and night, the ineluctable debt of the separation of the soul from the body drew near. I think he had been given knowledge of his death from the Lord many days beforehand, for he had ceased translating books. I asked him one day, ''Father, what are you translating?'' and he said, ''I am not translating anything. I am reading through books and making the necessary corrections.'' He bade me perform a certain obedience, and when I had done it, I brought the finished work to him on the twenty-fifth day of October. There happened to be no one else there at the time. I remained in conversation with the blessed one for an hour and a half or even two hours, for I saw that he was exceptionally joyful, and at last I was able to pose four lofty questions of theology, requesting solutions from him. For a long time I had sought an occasion to do this, but never until then had I found one. Rejoicing, he gladly and most graciously gave me solutions and explanations of all that I had asked him. I glorified God, who had deemed me worthy to attain what

I had sought, and I thanked the blessed one, not wishing to trouble him further. I said to him, "Give me a blessing to retire, Father;" and uttering a prayer, I prostrated myself on the floor before him, saying, "Forgive me, Father, and bless me." He stretched out his holy right hand, his fingers bent, to give me his priestly blessing and said, "May God bless you and forgive you." I kissed his holy right hand and his feet and went out rejoicing and glorifying God. It was then Wednesday, and after my departure the brother in attendance locked the door and let no one else go in to him that day. The next day he fell ill. Thereafter the attendant let no one disturb him further, lest the blessed one's illness should worsen. Three days later, on Sunday, his health was improved, and desiring to hear the divine liturgy, he went into the church and sat down. When it was over, he could scarcely return to his cell, even with his attendant's assistance and support. From that time he grew more and more ill, and they admitted no one to see him, for the blessed one desired to pass away in solitude. If they had allowed the brethren to go in to him, they would have brought upon him an untimely death with their tears and importuning. As the end approached, he partook of the divine Mysteries and, summoning two confessors, he gave his blessing and peace to all the brethren through them. He died as if falling asleep, committing himself into the hands of God, having left it to the community to choose collectively whomever they would as elder and pastor. O humble and meek soul! O man full of divine discernment! O spiritual philosopher excelling all the wisest men of this world! Even as you wisely did throughout your life, considering yourself beneath all men, the servant of the brethren, their debtor, one inept and lacking in boldness, so also did you do before your death, not making bold to decide anything. Rather, as if having fulfilled your debt of service, you departed to the Lord in peace, leaving it to His divine providence to make choices and decisions. When word went out of the blessed one's decease, a multitude of monks and priests and simple people gathered, and the lamentation was common, ours and theirs; and we buried him in the church.

This praise is offered to you, our most holy Father and teacher, by your unworthy servant and disciple, the schemamonk Mytrofan, though you by no means require it, for you have been glorified by God before the angels. I offer this to you as a duty imposed upon me by the community: receive it as a loving father. Forgive my ignorance, and cease not to pray for your children, that by your prayers the good Lord may deem us all worthy to find mercy at His judgement seat and to become heirs of His Kingdom. To Him belong all glory, honor, and worship, with His eternal Father, and good and life-giving and All-Holy Ghost, now and forever and unto the ages of ages. Amen.

Our blessed father departed this life in the year 1794, on the 15th of November.

SELECT BIBLIOGRAPHY

Amand de Mendieta, E. *Mount Athos*. Berlin, 1972.

Amvrosij, Archimandrite. *Moldavskij starec Paisij Veličkovskij 1722–1794. Kratkij bibliografičeskij očerk s priloženiem učenija starca Paisija ob umnoj molitve*. Počajiv, 1902.

Anghelescu, Antim. *Scrisorile unor monahi. Scrisoarea stareţului Atanasie către stareţul Paisie. Răspunsul stareţului Paisie către stareţul Atanasie*. Buzău, 1947.

Askočenskij, Victor. *Kiev s ego drevnejšim učiliščem Akademieju*. 2 vols. Kiev, 1856.

Balş, Stefan, and Nicolescu, Corina. *Mănăstirea Neamţ*. Bucharest, 1958.

Behr-Siegel, Elisabeth. *Prière et sainteté dans l'église russe, suivi d'un essai sur le rôle du monachisme dans la vie spirituelle du peuple russe*. Paris, 1950.

Bianu, Ioan, Hodoş, Nerva, and Simonescu, N. *Bibliografia românească veche*. Vols. 2 and 3. 1936. Reprint. Nendlen, 1968.

Bloom, André. ''Contemplation et ascèse: contribution orthodoxe.'' In *Technique et contemplation*. Études carmélitaines, 28. Bruges, 1949, 49–67.

Bois, J. ''Grégoire le Sinaïte et l'hésychasme à l'Athos au XIVe siècle.'' *Échos d'orient* 5 (1901–1902):65–73.

Bolshakoff, Sergio. *I mistici russi*. Turin, 1962.

Borovkova-Majkova, M. S. ''Nil Sorskij i Paisij Veličkovskij.'' In *Sergeju Fedoroviču Platonovu učeniki, druzja i počitateli*. St. Petersburg, 1911, 27–33.

Četverikov, Sergej. *Optina Pustyn'. Istoričeskij očerk i ličnye vospominanija*. Paris, 1926

————. ''Put' umnogo delanija i duxovnogo trezvenija. Starčestvovanie Arximandrita Paisija Veličkovskogo na Afone i v Moldovlaxii.'' *Put'*, 1926, no. 3:65–83.

————. *Moldavskij starec Paisij Veličkovskij, ego žizn', učenie i vlijanie na pravoslavnoe monašestvo.* 1938. Reprint. Paris, 1976.

_____. *Paisie stareţul mănăstirii Neamţului din Moldova. Viaţa, învăţătura şi influenţa lui asupra Bisericii ortodoxe.* Trans. Patriarch Nikodim. 2nd ed. Neamţ, 1940.

_____. *Starets Paisii Velichkovskii. His Life, Teachings, and Influence on Orthodox Monasticism.* Trans. Vasily Lickwar and Alexander I. Lisenko. Belmont, Mass., 1980.

David, P. I. "Cuviosul Paisie cel Mare (Velicicovski), un desăvârşit Român! Noi cercetări şi ipoteze." *Biserica Ortodoxă Română* 93 (1975):162–93.

Fedotov, George. *The Russian Religious Mind.* 2 vols. Cambridge, Mass., 1966.

_____. *A Treasury of Russian Spirituality.* Gloucester, Mass., 1967.

Florovsky, Georges. *Puti russkogo bogoslovija.* Paris, 1937.

Furtună, D. *Ucenicii Stereţului Paisie în mănăstirile Cernică şi Căldăruşani. Cu un scurt istoric asupra acestor mănăstiri.* Bucharest, 1928.

Hainsworth, Cuthbert. *Staretz Paisy Velichkovsky (1722-1794). Doctrine of Spiritual Guidance.* Rome, 1976.

Hasluck, Frederick. *Athos and Its Monasteries.* London, 1924.

Hausherr, Irenée. *La Méthode d'oraison hésychaste.* Orientalia Christiana Analecta, 36. Rome, 1927.

_____. *Direction spirituelle en Orient autrefois.* Orientalia Christiana Analecta, 144. Rome, 1955.

Heppell, Muriel. "Slavonic Translations of Early Byzantine Ascetical Literature." *Journal of Ecclesiastical History* 5 (1954):86–100.

Horbač [Horbatsch], Olexa. *Rukopysna cerkovnoslov''jans'ka "Ritorika" z 2-oji polovyny 18 v. monastyrs'koji biblioteky v Njamc u Rumuniji.* Rome, 1972 (=Extractum e *Bohoslovija* 35 [1971]).

Ilarion, Metropolitan [Ohijenko, Ivan]. *Starec' Paisij Velyčkovs'kyj. Joho žyttja, pracja ta nauka. Istoryčna literaturno-bohoslovs'ka monohrafija.* Winnipeg, 1975.

Iorga, Nicolae. *Roumains et Grecs au cours des siècles*. Bucharest, 1921.

_____. *Istoria Bisericii Româneşti şi a vieţii religioase a românilor*. 2nd ed. 2 vols. Bucharest, 1928–1932.

_____. *Mănăstirea Neamţului*. Neamţ, 1925.

_____. "La Vie monastique chez les Roumains." *Revue historique du sud-est européen* 8 (1931):113–19.

[Jacymyrs'kyj, Oleksander] Jacimirskij, Alexandr. *Slavjanskie i russkie rukopisi rumynskix bibliotek*. St. Petersburg, 1905. (=*Sbornik otdelenija russkogo jazyka i slovesnosti IAN* 79).

_____. "Vozroždenie vizantijsko-bolgarskogo misticizma i slavjano-asketičeskoj literatury v XVIII veke." In *Počest'. Sbornik statej posvjaščennyx Prof. M. S. Drinovu*. Xarkiv, 1905.

_____. *Autobiografia stareţului Paisie Velicikovskii*. Trans. Stefan Berečhet. Iaşi, 1918.

Joantă, Romul. *Roumanie. Tradition et culture hésychastes*. Spiritualité Orientale, 46. Bégrolles-en-Mauges, 1987.

Kadlubovsky, E., and Palmer, G. E. H., trans. *Writings from the Philocalia on the Prayer of the Heart*. London, 1951.

Kologrivov, Ivan. *Essai sur la saintité en Russie*, Bruges, 1953.

_____. *Santi Russi*. Brescia, 1977.

Leonid, Hieromonk [Poljakov]. "Sxiarximandrit Paisij Veličkovskij." *Žurnal Moskovskoj Patriarxii*, 1954, no. 10:53–59.

_____. "Starec Paisij Veličkovskij kak učitel' asketiki (1722–1794 gg.)." *Žurnal Moskovskoj Patriarxii*, 1956, no. 10:44–55.

_____. "Literaturnoe nasledstvo Paisija Veličkovskogo." *Žurnal Moskovskoj Patriarxii*, 1957, no. 4:57–61.

_____. "Afon i russkoe monašestvo." *Žurnal Moskovskoj Patriarxii*, 1958, no. 8:60–65.

_____. "Literaturnaja dejatel'nost' sxiarximandrita Paisija Veličkovskogo (21/XII 1722–15/II 1792 g.)." *Messager de l'Exarchat du Patriarche russe en Europe occidentale* 21 (1973):69–104, 203–37.

Lilienfeld, Fairy von. *Hierarchen und Starzen der russischen ortho-doxen Kirche*. Berlin, 1966.

Lossky, Vladimir, and Arseniev, Nicolas. *La Paternité spirituelle en Russie aux XVIIIème et XIXème siècles*. Spiritualité Orientale, 21. Bégrolles-en-Mauges, 1977.

Meester, Placide de. *De monachico statu iuxta disciplinam byzantinam*. Vatican City, 1942.

Metrophanes [Mytrofan], Schema Monk. *Blessed Paisius Velichkovsky. The Life and Ascetic Labors of our Father, Elder Paisius, Archimandrite of the Holy Moldavian Monasteries of Niamets and Sekoul. Optina Version*. Trans. St. Herman of Alaska Brotherhood. Vol. 1. Platina, Calif., 1976.

Mihail, Paul. "Două manuscrise necunoscute din secolul al XVIII-lea." *Romanoslavica* 10 (1964):457–64.

———. "Manuscrise românești din Biblioteca Mitropoliei Moldovei." *Mitropolia Moldovei și Sucevei* 50 (1974):432–60; 51 (1975):133–64.

———. "Traduceri patristice de starețul Paisie." *Mitropolia Olteniei* 24(1977):217-23.

———. "Schitul Poiana Mărului, un centru ortodox cărturăresc." In *Spiritualitate și istorie la întorsura Carpaților*. Vol. 1. Buzău, 1983, 355–84.

Moine de l'Eglise d'Orient. "La Prière de Jésus: sa genèse et son développement dans la tradition religieuse byzantino-slave." *Irénikon* 20 (1947):249–73, 381–421.

Năsturel, Petre S. "Aperçu critique des rapports de la Valachie et du Mont Athos dès origines au début du XVIe siècle." *Revue des études sud-est européennes* 2 (1964):93–126.

Nikodim, Archimandrite. *Starcy: Otec Paisij Veličkovskij i otec Makarij Optinskij i ix literaturno-asketičeskaja dejatel'nost'*. Moscow, 1909.

Păcurariu, Mircea. *Istoria Bisericii Ortodoxe Române*. Vols. 2 and 3. Bucharest, 1981.

Papoulidis, Constantin. "El starets Paissij Velitchkovskij

(1722–1794).'' *Unidad cristiana-Oriente cristiano*, 1949, no. 4:429–35.

————. ''Le Starets Paissij Velitchkovskij (1722-1794).'' Θεολογία, 39 (1968):231–40.

————. ''Portée œcuménique du renouveau monastique au XVIIIe siècle dans l'Église Orthodoxe.'' *Balkan Studies* 10 (1969):35–57.

Pirard, Marcel. ''Le Starec Paisij Veličkovskij (1722–1794). La tradition philologico-ascétique en Russie et en Europe orientale.'' *Messager de l'Exarchat du Patriarche russe en Europe occidentale* 21 (1973):35–57.

Platon, Schemamonk. *Žitie blažennejšago otca našego Starca Paisija. Sobranoe ot mnogix pisatelej, i sočinenno....* Neamţ, 1836. Reprint. Anthony-Emil N. Tachiaos. *The Revival of Byzantine Monasticism among Slavs and Romanians in the XVIIIth Century. Texts Relating to the Life and Activity of Paisy Velichkovsky (1722–1794).* Thessalonica, 1986, 151–225.

Pomjalovskij, Ivan. *Žitie iže vo svjatyx otca našego Grigorija Sinaita.* St. Petersburg, 1894. (= *Zapiski Istoriko-filologičeskogo fakul'teta Imperatorskogo Sanktpeterburgskogo universiteta* 35).

Raccanello, Dario. *La Preghiera di Gesù negli scritti di Basilio di Poiana Mărului.* Alessandria, 1986.

————. ''La Figure de Basile de Poïana Mărului et son enseignement sur la prière de Jésus.'' *Irénikon* 61 (1988):41–66.

Racoveanu, Gheorghe. *Viaţa şi nevoinţele Fericitului Paisie stareţul sfintelor mănăstiri Neamţul şi Secul.* Râmnieul-Vâlcia, 1935.

Rouet de Journel, Marie Joseph. *Monachisme et monastères russes.* Paris, 1952.

————. ''La direction spirituelle dans la Russie ancienne.'' *Revue des études slaves* 38 (1961):173–79.

Ruffini, Mario. ''Gli inizi del monachismo in Valacchia.'' *Oikoumenikon* 7, vol. 1 (1967):141–58.

————. ''Le origini della vita monastica in Moldavia.'' *Oikoumenikon* 7, vol. 1 (1967):303–24.

————. "La Cultura monastica in Romania sino alla metà del secolo XVI." *Oikoumenikon* 7, vol. 1 (1967):411–20, 507–26; vol. 2:12–42.

————. *Aspetti della cultura religiosa ortodossa romena medievale (secoli XIV–XVIII)*. Rome, 1980.

Russkij obščežitel'nyj skit Svjatogo Proroka Ilii na Svjatoj Afonskoj Gore. 4th ed. Odessa, 1913.

Schwartz, M. "Un réformateur du monachisme orthodoxe du 18ème s.: Paisios Veličkovskij." *Irénikon* 11 (1934):561–72.

Scrima, André. "Les Roumains et le Mont Athos." In *Le Millénaire du Mont Athos 963–1963*. Vol. 2. Chevetogne, 1964, 145–52.

Smirnov, Sergej. *Duxovnyj otec v drevnej Vostočnoj Cerkvi: istorija duxovenstva na vostoke*. Sergiev Posad, 1906.

Smolitsch, Igor. *Leben und Lehre des Starzen*. Cologne and Olten, 1952.

————. *Russisches Mönchtum. Enstehung, Entwicklung und Wesen. 988–1917*. Würzburg, 1953.

————. *Santità e preghiera. Vita e insegnamenti degli "starets" della santa Russia*. Torino, 1984.

Špidlik, Tomaš. *La Spiritualité de l'orient chrétien. Manuel systématique*. Orientalia Christiana Analecta, 206. Rome, 1978.

Suttner, Ernst. "Paisy Veličkovskij im Spiegel des geistlichen Testatments seines Schülers Gheorghe de la Cernica." *Ostkirchliche Studien*, 22 (1973):184–89.

————. "Klöster Neamţ als Vermittler byzantinischer Literatur an der Wende von 18. zum 19. Jahrhundert." *Ostkirchliche Studien* 23 (1974):311–17.

————. *Beiträge zur Kirchengeschichte der Rumänen*. Vienna and Munich, 1978.

Tachiaos, Anthony-Emil N. Ὁ Παΐσιος Βελιτσκόφσκι *(1722–1794)* καὶ ἡ ἀσκητικοφιλολογικὴ σχολή του. Publications of the Institute for Balkan Studies, 73. Thessalonica, 1964.

————. "Σύμμεικτα περὶ τῆς σχολῆς τοῦ Παϊσίου Βελιτσκόφσκι." Ἀριστοτέλειον Πανεπιστήμιον

Θεσσαλονίκης. Ἐπιστημονικὴ Ἐπετηρὶς τῆς Θεολογικῆς Σχολῆς 10 (1965):673–83.

————. "Mount Athos and the Slavic Literatures." *Cyrillomethodianum* 4 (1977):30–34.

————. "De la Philokalia au Dobrotoljubie: la création d'un 'Sbornik.'" *Cyrillomethodianum* 5 (1981):208–13.

————. *The Revival of Byzantine Mysticism among Slavs and Romanians in the XVIIIth Century: Texts Relating to the Life and Activity of Paisy Velichkovsky (1722-1794)*. Thessalonica, 1986.

Tarnanidis, I. "Les Derniers créateures de 'Sborniki.'" *Cyrillomethodianum* 5 (1981):214–17.

Turdeanu, Émil. *La Littérature bulgare du XIV siècle et sa diffusion dans les pays Roumains*. Travaux publiés par l'Institut des études slaves, 22. Paris, 1947.

Velyčkovs'kyj, Paisij, trans. *Svjatago otca našego Isaaka Sirina episkopa byvšago ninevijskago, slova duxovno-podvižničeskija perevedennyja s grečeskago….* Moscow, 1854.

————. trans. *Dobrotoljubie*. 5 vols. Moscow, 1884–1905.

————. *Ob umnoj ili vnutrennej molitve. Sočinenija blažennogo starca, sximonaxa i arximandrita….* Moscow, 1902.

————. *Autobiografia di uno Starets*. Trans. Fratelli Contemplativi di Gesù. Abbazia di Praglia, 1988.

Višnevskij, Dimitrij. *Kievskaja Akademija v pervoj polovine 18 v.* Kiev, 1903.

Ware, Kallistos [Timothy]. *The Power of the Name: The Jesus Prayer in Orthodox Spirituality*. Oxford, 1981.

[Xarlampovyč, Kostjantyn] Xarlampovič, Konstantin. *Malorossijskoe vlijanie na velikorusskuju cerkovnuju žizn'.* 1914. Reprint. The Hague, 1968.

Zaharia, Ciprian. "Païsij Veličkovskij et le rôle œcuménique de l'Église orthodoxe roumaine." *Irénikon* 58 (1985):61–73.

Žitie i pisanija Moldavskogo Starca Paisija Veličkovskogo. S prisovokupleniem predislovij na knigi Sv. Grigorija Sinaita, Filofeja Sinajskogo, Isixija Presvitera i Nila Sorskogo, sočinennyx drugom i spostnikom, Starcem Vasiliem Poljanomerul'skim, ob umnom trezvenii i molitve. Moscow, 1847. 3rd. ed. Moscow, 1892.

INDEX OF BIBLICAL REFERENCES

INDEX